Guy Be

D0427663

From Paris to Berkeley

Memoir

Les Editions de Montrose
Berkeley, California

Guy Benveniste
©2010

All Rights Reserved

ISBN 14: 5362-6751
EAN-13: 9781453626757

Contents

—

Acknowledgments

I wish to thank Karen Nelson, our children, grand children and their descendants without whom and for whom this book was intended in the first place. My friend Hank Massie got me started on this project, Ivar Nelson and Bill Glick provided editorial and publishing advice. Fernando and Eliana Kusnetzoff led me into finding my way into the self publishing world of Booksurge.

Readers of early drafts convinced me it was an interesting tale and strongly suggested I proceed. I cannot mention and remember everyone but among many, I recall: Bridget Connelly, Lauren Blanchard, Sandra Elman, Maresi Nerad, Abby Tolin, Kristina Lim, Jane and Stanley Brandes, Marc Blanchard, Avrum Gratch, Greg Loew, Monique Loew, Ellen Davies, Beverly Cheney, Marilyn Farrar, Gerald Wasserman, Steve Brown, Marilyn McGregor, Raquel Scheer and of course, Karen Nelson who read, corrected and encouraged me to persist. My cousins, Colette Piault and Renee Scialom provided much historical background. My extended family in Europe and in the Americas also encouraged me. Marjorie Lovejoy, Bill Chatman and Corey Hickey provided necessary technical assistance. The Spanish photographer Cristina Garcia Rodero provided my back cover photograph. Stanley Brandes made it available.

Three doctors kept me in good health during this time: Edward Kersh, Peter Carroll and Patrick Swift. Finally, many friends, the lovely California weather, the ocean beaches at Carmel, the birds in the Berkeley patio and a faithful Dell computer combined with the alchemy of the foods in the markets, all together made it possible to undertake this publication.

—

I

PARIS, ESCAPE FROM THE WAR

Paris and Berkeley, two university towns, frame this tale. First difference: I was born in Paris, I left, and I returned and I left again. Since I was far away most of the time, I often wore a T shirt of the University of Paris with the emblem "Fluctuat Nec Mergitur" Tossed by the waves, it does not sink. In contrast, later, when I became a member of the faculty at Berkeley, I never wore a University of California Berkeley T shirt. Second difference: Paris is not close to a sea or ocean but Berkeley is. Why do I mention the sea? My ancestors lived close to the sea for centuries. Maybe they lived in Barcelona before 1492. They may have traveled to Venice. They certainly lived for several hundred years in Salonika, a port city of the Ottoman Empire. My story is strangely influenced by history and geography. I left France during the war, spent many years attempting to return to Paris. Yet it ends in Berkeley overlooking the Bay Area, the ports of Oakland and San Francisco. Barcelona, Salonika and Berkeley are roughly at the same latitude. Salonika is on the Bay of Thermaikos. Is this sign of an atavistic memory of ports, of boats, of endless travels?

—

This is a personal account. A good friend told me after reading a draft: "Guy, this is a very personal account". She meant the emphasis to be on the word very. I do cover many aspects of my life. I describe my family background, my childhood, World War II and my 1942 departure from Europe on the SS Serpa Pinto. I cover my experiences in Mexico where I discover the American School. I describe the problems of young men who begin to discover their own sexuality. I go on to college, to Harvard and then to the University of Pennsylvania. You will be told how some young men were initiated into sex in the society I lived in. The story covers my immigration to the United States; life in California, and a move to Washington D.C. I describe how I repeatedly attempted to return to Paris, how I obtained a PhD at Stanford and became a Professor. I will tell you about the women I loved and married. I will report on my work, my various careers, my accomplishments, mistakes, and conflicts. I will tell you as much as I can while still in good taste.

My story takes us from the Roman Empire and the Middle East, to Spain, then to the Ottoman Empire, to France where I am born, on to Mexico, the United States, back to Mexico, back to the United States, back to France and finally as the oscillation finally ceases, the ball comes to rest and remains in Berkeley. I see my "modern" migrations as symptomatic of current trends. Yes, I was an immigrant like many others, but my migrations took place in an informed society, in an age of global communication. Migration allowed me to become well educated. I began to travel when young, in ways that have become more common today. I immigrated twice and lived my teens in three different cultures, speaking three different languages. Many young people have similar experiences nowadays. They travel, they study abroad and they learn to appreciate the foods and manners of distant lands. Since I may have

—

started a bit earlier, propelled by World War II into leaving Europe, my experience may inform, and at times amuse some.

This migration takes place in a definite period of history. My father provided my first years with experiences imbued by a traditional culture that had survived close to four hundred and fifty years in what was once the Ottoman Empire and had been transferred to Paris in the early 1920s'. My mother's New York youth provided me with a vision more attuned to understanding the changing world of the 30's and 40's. My own experiences would slowly allow me to move into todays time frame.

As my friend noted, this is a personal account. In this age of mass communications, this age of endless networking, the personal is too often hidden. Yet our choices and the life turns we take also depend on personal, even intimate experiences. In my own case, the personal is not dominated by religious fervor or a deep philosophical inquiry as to the meaning of life. My main personal concern is my relationships with others, especially my intimate relationships. Love as well as family mattered as much if not more than Work. I have tried to be truthful because I think it is useful to understand that we are affected in ways we not always recognize at the time they happen. My first migration was due to war but as the story unfolds, love, family, chance, and opportunity comes to create "a geography" of its own.

This tale is framed by the events preceding and following World War II, and the Nazi attempt to exterminate the Jews. I was fortunate to migrate to Mexico when Mexico City was still small and smogless. I graduated from Harvard and flunked from the University of Pennsylvania. I had a brief career as a construction

—

engineer in Mexico and became an economist. I moved to California and became a policy analyst when policy analysis was in its infancy. I worked in a research institute and in government. I managed to go back and forth between the USA and France by working for international organizations. Thus I traveled, including a one month trip to Afghanistan in 1962. My personal life obliged me, in 1965 to leave Paris and return to California. I took a late PhD at Stanford, learned what sociologists have to say about organizations and, à la fin, became a Professor at Berkeley where I wrote books about planning and bureaucracy. During those years I became an amateur painter, I had shows, sold paintings and continued to do so after I retired.

Thus the story begins in Paris, or better still, it begins in Barcelona, Venice and Salonika. It ends in Berkeley, on a hill overlooking the San Francisco Bay and the Golden Gate.

Salonika With Some Early History

I was born on Sunday, February 27, 1927 at 7 A.M. in a birthing clinic situated at 12, rue Boileau in the XVIeme arrondissement of Paris. This, for those of you who know, is the fanciest arrondissement of Paris but my parents lived in the more bourgeois VIIeme, close to the present location of the main UNESCO buildings, at 6, rue Léon Vaudoyer. There is a weekly market on the Avenue de Saxe, the kind where they install stalls made of tubing and canvas which are taken away once the market is closed in the early afternoon. It is one block from 6, rue Léon Vaudoyer to the Avenue de Saxe which is wide and has a large middle trottoir where I played during a good part of my early youth. My father Raphaël Maïr Benveniste had moved into an apartment on the 3rd floor in the early 1920's and when

—

he married my mother Lucy Léa de Botton on Friday, March 26, 1926, she moved in with him. I should add that the religious ceremony of their marriage took place in the Jewish Portuguese Temple on the rue Buffault two days later, on Sunday, March 28, 1926. This was the Temple that Jews from Salonika frequented; my father was born in Salonika while my mother was born in New York City. I should, by tradition, have been named Maïr Raphaël. The oldest son of the oldest son had been reversing those two names for several generations. But my mother insisted on a more western name, a family compromise was reached. I was called Guy Maïr.

Let me digress for a while to explain about the Benvenistes and the de Bottons.

These, are Jewish families who left Spain in and around 1492 when Queen Isabella and King Ferdinand decided to ask the Jews in Spain to either convert or leave their kingdom. There were Jewish settlements in Spain ever since the Roman conquest of the Iberian Peninsula. Jewish tribes from Palestine settled in many parts of the Roman Empire including what are now Spain and the south of France. They were persecuted under the Visigoths in the 600's; they flourished during the Moslem invasion in the 700's, and were again persecuted by the Christian kings. For example the Jewish settlement at Tarragona south of Barcelona was established at the time of the Romans. For a while under Moslem rule, Tarragona was mostly Jewish.

I have not done any extensive research on the history of my family. In the literature on Spanish Jews, the name Benveniste appears fairly frequently. The name de Botton is less frequent. Luis Suarez Fernandez, *Judios Españoles en la Edad Media* Madrid 1980 mentions a Benveniste, who grew vines in Montjuich, now part of

—

Barcelona, in 963 more than a thousand years ago. There were Benveniste's in Toledo in 1200, in Castilla in 1300's, in Saragossa in 1380. The *Jewish Archives of Navarra* includes documents with the name Benveniste for the period 1339-1357. Luis Marcós, in *Jueus als Països Catalans Segles X-XV* lists a Doctor Avubraim Aben-Venist, who was given the right to be a doctor by King Alphonso I in 1180. I have no such information about the de Bottons, but I assume that without much trouble, one can find them also, living in Spain before the signing of the decree of expulsion on March 31, 1492.

The spelling of the name varies. Sometimes Benveniste is the given name like in the case of Bienveniste de Porta who lived in Barcelona in 1260 or Bienveniste de la Cavalleria who was in Saragossa in 1380. Some authors like Suarez Fernandez interpret the given name as "well arrived" and spell it Bienveniste, a Spanish form for the Hebrew "blessed be the one who has arrived." Other authors look for the Moorish form of "son of" and the usual aben — the son of — as in the case of Avubraim Aben-Venist mentioned above. I opt for the "well arrived" version of the name. One argument I make is that it is rare to find original documents with the A from the Aben-Venist. Yet, just to give an example, the Jewish archives of Navarra have Benveniste in the index with the A. For my choice I obviously prefer to be "well arrived".

In any case, there were Benvenistes in Spain before 1492 and the most recognized or most cited was Abraham Benveniste who in May, 1432 managed to renegotiate with the Spanish crown the statutes of the Jewish communities of Spain. It gave them the right to raise their own taxes on meat, wine, marriages, circumcisions and burials; the rights to establish their own schools and have their own judges. There were other famous Benvenistes close to the Royal

—

Court and it is also said they had a magnificent library they took with them when they left Spain to go to the Ottoman Empire. They were invited to settle there by rulers who wanted to have a "docile and laborious" population occupy empty lands and towns.

How did the Benvenistes I am related to relate to these distant ancestors? I do not know. How did my branch of the Benvenistes travel to Salonika? I am not sure. We do know that the Jews of Spain were invited to go to the Ottoman Empire and that Salonika was part of the Ottoman Empire in 1492. In fact Salonika was supposed to have been founded by Alexander's brother-in-law named Cassander who gave it the name of his wife, the sister of Alexander, Thessaloniki. During the Roman Empire, Salonika was linked to Rome by the Via Egnazia. It became part of the Byzantine Empire, then the Goths, the Huns, and the Normans of Sicily invaded it and sacked it until 1430 when the Turks finally took it over. The town was quite run down by then and when the Spanish Crown decided to rid Spain of its Jews, the Ottoman Empire was quite happy to have them settle in its new occupied lands. Thus, in addition to Salonika, many Spanish Jews went to Bulgaria, Macedonia, Asia Minor, and even Sarajevo—all parts of the Ottoman Empire of the 15th and 16th century. Others went elsewhere, for example to Amsterdam, or to France. But, at first many Spanish Jews went to Portugal where, very soon, they were obliged to convert or were kicked out. From there, some went to Venice and to other Italian towns.

The Benvenistes, I am related to, lived in Salonika in the 19th century but they were members of the Jewish-Italian synagogue in Salonika which suggests they may have traveled to Salonika via Venice. It turns out that there are many Benvenistis in Venice (in the meat business I was told) so it is not impossible my family went that way. In 1571 there was a very important naval battle where western powers defeated the Ottoman Empire's navy. This is the battle of Lepanto after which the spread of the Ottoman Empire was halted. This is also where Miguel de Cervantes was wounded and maimed his left hand . After 1571 the fortunes of Venice rose, at least for a while. Venice had considerable trade with the Ottoman Empire and this trade was channeled through the Port of Salonika. There was therefore considerable traffic between Salonika and Venice. There exists extensive documentation that indicates that Benvenistes were in Venice in the 1500's together with Doña Gracia Nasi, a well known Renaissance Jewish leader. They would have mingled well since Benveniste in Venetian dialect translates again as welcome. Did my Benvenistes come via Venice? Or did the current Benvenistis of Venice come via Salonika? I am afraid we will not know, but it is fun to think that we went from Barcelona to Venice to Salonika, ports on the sea, just like San Francisco (or even Berkeley). It is a guess, but not impossible and probably not too different from what really happened.

In 1492 some 20,000 Sephardi, namely Jews from Spain, arrived in Salonika. According to some authors, the population of Salonika was, from the end of the 1400 hundreds to about 1917 half or more Jewish, 20% Turk, 20% Greek, 5% Bulgarian and small percentages including Armenians. The dominant Jewish population included Jews who had been there prior to 1492, called Romaniotes; Sephardi Jews from Spain, Jews who had come from Provence in the South of France, Jews from Italy and later, Jews who came from Russia and Poland. So, in many ways, Salonika was mostly Jewish during some 450 years . In 1912 the total population of Salonika was 170,000 with some 85,000 to 90,000 Jews. After 1943 when the Nazis eliminated the Jews of Salonika, the Jewish population was never very significant. In the early 1990's it amounted to some 1200 individuals.

By 1523, the Jews of Salonika had obtained a charter from the Ottoman Empire similar to the statutes Abraham Benveniste had negotiated with the Crown of Spain in 1432. They were ruled by a council of Rabbis, they raised their own taxes and paid a portion directly to the Ottoman Empire, keeping the rest for running their own schools (Talmud Torah) and having their own system of justice (Beth Din). By 1515 the Jews of Salonika had their own printing press. The Turks were not to have their own until much later.

In 1891 when my father Raphaël was born, the Jewish community of Salonika was flourishing. The Jews lived all over the town; they engaged in all commercial activities, they had their own schools. In addition, the Alliance Israélite Universelle created in Paris in 1860, had, starting in 1873, established a set of schools (at first for boys) in the Ottoman Empire including one in Salonika. Very soon girls were admitted and by 1912 the Alliance had 52 such schools in the European part of the Ottoman Empire and more in Asia Minor. French was taught in the Alliance schools and this is how my father learned French. Gradually, the Jewish community of Salonika was influenced by modernizing influences of Western Europe. The photographs I have of my family taken in Salonika toward the end of the 1800's show men and women wearing the traditional costumes they had adopted over the centuries. But by the beginning of the 1900's they began to dress in western clothes, sharp suits and boater hats for the men, long dresses, western hats and parasols for the women. The spread of western, mostly French culture into Salonika transformed the Jewish elite. By 1880 the Jewish

—

Talmud Torah schools affiliated to the various synagogues, had changed their curricula. In addition to teaching the old Spanish, that is Ladino or Djidio, that the Sefarad community had kept alive through the centuries, they too began to teach French and Italian.

At the beginning of the 20ᵗʰ Century, Salonika was one of the more enlightened towns of the Ottoman Empire. But that Empire had been disintegrating for a while. Therefore it was also a town where considerable political, religious, and artistic ferment took place. Among the Turks, there was also a transformation taking place, an awakening under western influences. By 1908 the revolt of the Young Turks that was to transform and modernize Turkey had begun, and it had begun in Salonika. Mustafa Kermal, the great Turkish leader who was known as Ataturk and who transformed Turkey, was born in Salonika, and the city of Salonika has kept his house, it is in fact now owned by the Turkish Consulate in Salonika.

The Young Turk Revolt of 1908 weakened the hold of the Ottoman Empire on its European possessions. In 1910 the Ottoman Empire covered Macedonia including Salonika, all the north of what is now Greece, portions of Montenegro, Bulgaria, Serbia, and all of Albania. It also included vast portions of North Africa, including Libya. In 1911 Italy went to war against Turkey to conquer Libya, and in 1912 the Balkan wars began. The Greeks, Serbs, and Bulgarians also attacked the Turks and this is when Salonika was taken over by the Greeks. The Balkan wars brought with them much uncertainty and trouble. Vast areas that were controlled by the Turks were now controlled by other ethnic groups, and as we have seen more recently, a lot of bad feelings across ethnic groups surfaced. The Greeks tried to push Turks out of areas they controlled and as a result, the Turks began to push Greeks

—

out of areas, particularly in Asia Minor, where they had been allowed to live for centuries under the benign control of the Ottoman Sultanate.

In 1914, the Archduke François Ferdinand of Austria was murdered in Sarajevo, and as a result, the Balkan wars of 1912 spread to become the first Great World War involving most of the western powers with France and England on one side, and Germany on the other. Keep in mind that the Archduke and his wife, both were murdered actually, were in line to become the rulers of the Austro-Hungarian Empire. They were murdered by a Serb who was disgruntled because the Austro-Hungarian Empire had recently taken over a portion of Bosnia, which this Serb thought should be part of a greater Serbia. The Austro-Hungarians put pressure on the Serbs for reparations, the Russians came to help their friends the Serbs, the Germans came to help their friends the Austrians, the French and English jumped in, and World War I started. Keep also in mind that the Austro-Hungarian Empire had contained the spread of the Ottoman Empire in the middle of Europe. Actually, the Hungarians had resisted the invasion, so I suppose that in this scheme of things, the Jews of Salonika were, at least in theory, against the Austro-Hungarians. In fact, they wanted to have nothing to do with the war.

At the beginning of World War I, the King of Greece who had annexed Salonika announced that Greece would remain neutral, but this neutrality did not last. The Bulgarians had been beating up the Serbs when in 1915 the French and English landed in Salonika. This expedition served to help the Serbs. At that point, the Prime Minister of Greece, whose name was Eleftherios Venizélos, broke rank with his King, and the Greeks joined the French, English, and Serbs in the war against Germany, Bulgaria,

—

and the Austro-Hungarian Empire.

Salonika was a turbulent city. I should also tell you that on August 5, 1917, Salonika suffered a major fire that burned vast sections of the city, including many Jewish homes, so that the Jewish community was further upset.

My father, Raphaël Maïr Benveniste, was born on April 5, 1891, the first son of Maïr Raphaël Benveniste who was the eldest son born on March 22, 1869 of Raphaël Maïr Benveniste, a Rabbi himself born in 1844. The Rabbi and his wife Myriam, had married my grandfather to Oro Simha (my grandmother) who was also the daughter of a Rabbi named Samuel Simha. So on both sides, there were Rabbis. My grandfather, Maïr did not become a Rabbi, but he was a member of the Communal Council of Jews of Salonika, which was the council that among other tasks ran the schools, the Jewish court system, and so on. In other words, he was in government, the local Jewish sub-government. His main contribution was to raise enough taxes and to schedule these taxes so that the Jewish community would be able to pay their teachers. After 1917 the main preoccupation of my grandfather was housing because so many families had lost their home in the fire. My impression is that my grandfather had not lost his home. In fact, when he died of pneumonia in Paris on 12 December 1937, he still owned one-half of a building situated at 6, rue Venizélos in Salonika.

The Rabbi, Raphaël Maïr and his wife Myriam, had six children. There were Maïr, Jacques, Reyna, Tamar, Marc, and Albert. Then Myriam died and Raphaël Maïr married Hannah, and there were again six children including Daniel, Haïm, Asher, Maurice, and Janine. As you can see, this can generate a lot of Benvenistes. The women married into other Jewish families with names like

—

Angel, Jossua, Asseo, Modiano, Alcaly, Ovadia, Tiano, and Carasso. Reyna, the sister of Maïr, married Marc Amon, had a son, Saby Amon, who then married his first cousin Marie, my father's sister born a year later in 1892. The Jewish community of Salonika was small and the families were linked in many traditional ways.

Grandfather, Maïr, married Oro Simha in October 1886. She was two years older than he. At the time of the marriage, she was 19 while he was 17. Therefore, he did not yet have much in his name and they waited four years before having children. Some form of birth control was obviously practiced at the time. Why did he marry so young? Because Oro was the daughter of a close colleague of Rabbi Raphaël, she was 19, it was time she married and if Maïr was young, they should wait n'est ce pas?

Maïr and Oro also had six children: Raphaël (1891), Marie (1892), Allegra (1894), Joseph (1899), Maurice (1901), and Nelly (1907). At the time Nelly was born, Oro was 40 years old. By the time I knew them, say when I was five or six, my grandparents Benveniste, were in their sixties. Maïr, erect and serious, Oro a heavy woman, silent and sad. Tradition still weighed on her. At large family dinners in Paris in the thirties, Oro and her daughters did not sit at the table with the men, we children and the few "modern" wives. They moved from the kitchen to the table, serving, attending and sat only briefly on chairs along the wall when Maïr would pray or talk to his family. Maïr and Oro were still in the traditions of 19th century Salonika. Theirs were a mixture of Jewish and Ottoman tradition patriarchal family. Surely their marriage had been arranged and his life determined by the wishes of parents. Why did Maïr not go into the rabbinate? Was he not talented? I doubt that, as he had a huge reputation when he died in Paris. He did serve his community, as I said, and

—

had a store in Salonika. Was it economic necessity, and the fact that he was marrying young? They married their eldest daughter Marie, with her cousin Saby Amon. This had to be an arranged marriage in a tradition influenced by Ottoman practice. The Turks kinship pattern called "general exchange" is based on the marriage of men to their mother's brother's daughter, a pattern that maintains the superiority of the male descent line.

Pictures taken in Salonika invariably show the older generation that of Maïr and Oro, dressed in the traditional costume of the "orient." The men are wearing long robes that cover their pants and a kind of short vest. The women are wearing a small hat and a long skirt. They are surrounded by Persian carpets and hangings.

The next generation was different. The pictures of my father as a young man in Salonika show him in western dress, very elegant with a tie and a bowler. My father only completed primary school, he claimed that he never liked school, and began working in his father's store. There, he learned how to make packages, and he learned how to buy and sell, how to make deals, and how to be in business. He had many friends, men friends, who went out together and had a good time. In 1917 he was 26 and unmarried. He had not followed in the footsteps of his father—no arranged marriage for him. But arranged marriages for the older daughters were possible. Marie must have married her cousin Saby Amon in 1914 or 1915. Their daughter Jenny was born in 1916. Allegra (later known as tante Andrée when the family became French and "Christian") was married to Ugo Modiano and had a son Ralph (Kiko) born in 1917.

Some time after 1917, Raphaël or Raffo as he was known, moved to Milan, Italy. I assume this was part of

—

the export-import business of his father. He lived in Milan for three years a happy bachelor. There were other young men from Salonika with him. They went to cafés, they went to the opera. He heard Caruso many times at La Scala of Milan. They would find young women here and there, and life seemed very pleasant for them.

World War I bypassed Raffo. The Jews of Salonika made every effort to stay out of the conflict. Those who came from wealthy families were able to obtain foreign passports for their travel. Foreign Consuls in Salonika gave passports to non Ottomans usually for commercial advantage, to facilitate trade between their country, Salonika and the Ottoman Empire. Thus, all the Benvenistes seem to have traveled out of Salonika with Spanish or Portuguese passports and as Spaniards or Portuguese, they also avoided the war. Those who went to France and did not naturalize French were protected by Spain or Portugal from the Nazi holocaust of World War II. Did they obtain Spanish or Portuguese passports because of the original agreement between Isabel La Catholica and the Sultanate? Presumably, the Jews of Spain had been allowed to come into the Ottoman Empire on the condition that they would remain an autonomous community, which would not be Turkish. They were to remain Spanish or Portuguese in the eyes of the Sultanate. The Turks were the warriors. They conquered and occupied but let each community run their affairs. If Spain wanted to populate a portion of the Empire and thus contribute to its economic well-being, that was fine. In their long stay in Salonika, the Spanish Jews had no role in matters of warfare. By 1924, my grand father and his family were facing constant upheavals in Salonika. There was considerable friction between the well to do Jewish community and large numbers of destitute Greeks kicked out of Asia Minor who replaced the Turks kicked out by the Greeks. Many other

—

families had already moved to various parts of the world, the United States, France and even Mexico. At that time my grandfather and his family immigrated to France and settled in Paris.

New York

I know much less about my mother's family. Moïse de Botton, who also lived in Salonika, married a woman named Grace or Graciela. They had eight children: Victor, Albert, Léon, Jacques, Isaac, Leila, Esther, and Sarah. My grandfather, Isaac, was born in 1863 six years before Maïr Benveniste. Isaac de Botton married outside Salonika, but like my paternal grandfather, he married a woman older than he. In fact, my grandmother Esther Asariah was already a widow from a previous marriage. She was living in Constantinople. She was born in 1861. I assume they were married around the end of the 1890's. She already had a daughter and married Isaac in her late thirties. As I say, I know little about Isaac because my mother knew very little. He died— a suicide, when my mother was five in 1908. There was an economic panic starting in 1907 and this may have been the cause of his despondency. After his death Esther destroyed every trace of his existence. He died at age 45. He had come to New York at the end of the century and was importing tobacco, most of which was sold to a Greek family, originating in Epirus, the Stephano Brothers, Constantine and Stefano Stephano, who fabricated cigarettes in down town Philadelphia since 1895. They produced the Stephana, Cascade, Marvels, Vogue, Ramses II, and other brands using mostly Turkish tobacco.

Isaac was naturalized a United States citizen on 25 November 1902. The document does not tell me if he also had a Spanish passport. Anyhow, Esther left Constantinople, leaving her first daughter with her mother

—

and moved to New York where they lived at 424 Central Park West, overlooking Central Park, certainly a good address. Presumably, Isaac made lots of money in the tobacco business, and also spent a lot. He took big risks—that much is clear. Did he die because of debts resulting from the crash? He and Esther had two daughters, both born in New York Grace the oldest, and Lucy born on October 7, 1903. These girls did not live in Salonika; they lived in New York and went to the Fieldston School of the Ethical Culture Society which was conveniently located close to their home on Central Park West. Later, Lucy attended and completed the College Entrance Diploma in Arts from Hunter College High School in June 1921. At the time it was an all girl school. The University of the State of New York issued her diploma. She then briefly attended Hunter College and also began taking dancing classes. Grace played the piano. Their early pictures show them in front of a large inside apartment door wearing Japanese costumes. At one point Lucy became such an accomplished dancer that her teacher offered to take her on tour as part of the troupe. But Madame de Botton would have nothing of it. For her the only central problem was the marriage of her daughters.

After the death of Isaac, Esther was able to make ends meet thanks to the constant help of the Stephano family as they continued to use Isaac's firm to import tobacco. My mother was always thankful for their help and I visited them when I attended the Wharton School in Philadelphia in the fall of 1948. As a result, the two young women were brought up in New York and in due time Esther wanted to marry them properly, that is into a similar Sefarad family. The problem was that there were very few Sefarad families in New York in the early twenties of similar wealth and background. Earlier in time, Esther had taken her daughters to Constantinople where her mother

—

still lived. That trip had been a failure. First, it turned out that at the time of the trip, there was a plague in that part of the world. Esther wanted to leave immediately but her mother had said not to worry, "after all we have blue blood in our veins and blue blood does not catch the plague." The more serious problem was that the Sefarad community of Constantinople was unchanged. The old traditions prevailed. Esther's first daughter Henriette was being married to Monsieur Aaron Mallah who was used to traditional life. The women served the men, stood behind their chairs at meals, and so on. Grace and Lucy did not fit this mold. A husband had to be found elsewhere. Wanted was a modern Sefarad man who would understand that his wife ate at the same table, at the same time. That she would be allowed to go out of the house on her own, that she would even do some shopping, go to tea houses, attend the opera or the theater, have servants, and nannies to take care of eventual children, in other words be "modern."

Paris

Raffo left Milan and came to Paris in the early twenties—my grandfather came in 1924, I do not know exactly when my father came, but not long before that date. He went into business on his account with his brother-in-law, Saby Amon. They created Benveniste & Amon, a wholesale and retail cloth merchandising firm. Shortly after that, his brothers Maurice and Joseph (nicknamed Momo and Péppo), came over from Salonika. They worked briefly with Benveniste & Amon and rapidly created their own firm, Joseph-Maurice on the Boulevard Poissonnière. In 1924, Maïr and Oro and the rest of the family moved out of Salonika and settled in Paris. Why Paris? First of all, there already was a large community of Jews from Salonika in Paris. As the Greeks, thrown out of Asia Minor, continued to settle in Salonika, tensions arose

—

further between these communities. Many more Jews left and since many spoke French, learned in the schools of the Alliance, it was natural to move to Paris. Others went to South America, a few to the United States, even Australia. But Paris attracted many. When Raphaël arrived, he found many friends and distant relatives and had little trouble settling in and opening his own store. As the entire family moved, the business of marriage resurfaced. In 1925 Raphaël was 34 years old. It was time to do something.

Meanwhile, Madame de Botton had taken her daughters to the continent. First, they went to Dresden where they stayed in a downtown hotel and enjoyed meeting potential suitors. In fact, Lucy met a young man named Sam Ovadia whom she liked very much but for one reason or another nothing came out of it. Madame de Botton decided to try Paris where, as we have seen, many Sefarad Jews from Salonika, Izmir or Constantinople had settled. Lucy met Raphaël and this meeting must have taken place in Paris sometime in 1925. They were married on March 26, 1926 and the religious ceremony took place on Sunday, March 28, 1926 at the Jewish Portuguese Sefarad Temple at 28, rue Buffault. Lucy then moved into Raphael's bachelor apartment at 6, rue Léon Vaudoyer in the seventh arrondissement. We are back where I started, at the beginning of this account. Close to the Avenue de Saxe where there is still a weekly market; close to the École Militaire, where in the early 30's one could see elegant officers ride on their horses all the way along the Champs de Mars past the Eiffel Tower to the river and back; and close to the Avenue de Breteuil and to the Invalides with Napoleon's tomb, and on the top floor, a series of miniature scaled recreations of French military towns from before the French Revolution which I spent hours examining when I was six or seven.

—

Marriages followed marriages. Péppo married Lily Ajiman and had a son Roland in 1930; Maurice married Alice Benrubi and had Gérard in 1929, Colette several years later in 1933; Nelly married Richard Benrubi (Alice's brother) and Roger was born in 1928. In addition, Marie and Saby Amon had a second child, a son, Marcel in 1924. Thus, the cousins born in France were either an only child or had one sibling. As a result we saw a lot of each other and the cousins substituted for non-existing brothers or sisters. Modern times had come to the Beneveniste family. Where Rabbi Raphaël had twelve and Maïr six, the new norm was one or two at most. The new "modern" wives Lily, Lucy, and Alice were quick to infiltrate the younger members of the more staid Benvenistes. Nurses were hired to take care of the children. I had an English nurse at first, a Miss "Papat" who smoked Lucky Strikes in green packages. The cousins had theirs from Switzerland or elsewhere. We often went to the Champs de Mars, the park by the Eiffel tower. Roger who lived at 46, Avenue de la Bourdonnais, close to the Champs de Mars was often there and our nurses would keep us there and we played in the sand pile, rode on wooden horses and attended a guignol. Later, I would walk back the longer distance, along the Avenue de Sufren past the long wall of the École Militaire, back to rue Léon Vaudoyer.

Grandfather Maïr lived at 6, Avenue du Général Détrie, very close to the Champs de Mars. He had invested in the two businesses of Benveniste & Amon, and Joseph-Maurice, and had more or less retired. He was nevertheless a leading member of the Association Culturelle Sephardite de Paris, was important in the Amicale Salonicienne and in the Union des Israélites Saloniciens de France. Maïr kept close to Salonika and the old ways. But the next generation was something else. They went out, they danced, they went to the opera, they spent a fair amount of time in cafés,

—

took many vacations. I think that they did not suffer very much in the 20's or 30's even if they were not rich. Each year my father took his own separate vacation lasting some three weeks when he would go with his friends from his bachelor days and settle in a spa like Évian-les-Bains or Vichy and as far as I know enjoyed the kind of freedom a married man looses and presumably misses. As far as I know they were careful and never caught venereal diseases, at least not to my knowledge. Obviously, the men also worked a lot. Joseph Maurice was more successful than Benveniste & Amon and both my uncle Maurice and my uncle Péppo were able to buy residences in Paris while we remained in rented apartments. Maurice bought a villa with a garden in Neuilly s/seine—on the outskirts of Paris. Péppo bought a villa in Auteuil in one of the rare Paris neighborhoods with independent houses with gardens.

Their success depended on their contacts. Raffo kept in touch with a large number of Sefarad Jews from Salonika and elsewhere who were their trading partners. Money was borrowed and repaid to wealthier Sefarad Jews. Imports were obtained from friends and relations settled elsewhere in Europe or France. Their own courts settled conflicts among them. In other words, while Raffo had all the advantages of western living and liberties, he also relied exclusively on the network of Sefarad Jews and their institutions to compete in the business world. There was no need for banks or lawyers and more importantly, there was trust. You could borrow or lend money knowing that Monsieur Gategno or Monsieur Assaël would come through. If there was a conflict, the Sefarad communities had their own courts and would resolve the dispute. They had a set of flexible working institutions well suited to international trade and commerce.

Thus, my parents in the early thirties had a car, a

maid, a nurse for me until I was five, and when I was six they had a delightful young girl from Alsace (she must have been 17 or 18) whom I liked a lot even if I had no idea as yet about young nubile girls. Anyhow, Lucy did not like her and she was fired within a year. And they took trips. For example, in 1926 after their marriage, Raffo and Lucy had gone to Monte Carlo, later that summer they went to Deauville and after that, they went to Chamonix. On many trips they went with friends or found friends where they went.

A large portion of the Salonika Benveniste family had moved to France. Jacques (Maïr's brother, son of Myriam), Haïm (son of Hannah), Ascher (also son of Hannah) had also come. Hilda Benveniste a daughter of Haïm had married a Henry Benveniste and they still lived in Paris in the 90's. My cousin Colette saw them and their son Yves, who plays in Jazz bands. After the war, uncle Ascher was known as uncle Achille, and uncle Hector substituted for uncle Haïm. The Salonika colony in Paris was very large and my father knew most of them. He would often say to Lucy: "Patico" (he called her little duck, a common form of endearment in Ladino), "tu te rapelle? Do you remember the little Ovadia, the one that married Sam?", and she would not remember—not the Ovadia and Modiano, no the other one..", and so on. There were innumerable acquaintances, friends, and relations.

All of them were "de los muestros" (as contrasted to nuestros in modern Spanish) they were of ours, namely Sefarad Jews from what they called "the Orient". Raffo would say he was "oriental", namely from Salonika, or Smyrna, or Izmir, or Rhodes, or wherever the Sefarad had been since leaving Spain, in the orient as contrasted to the west, namely France. They kept their Mediterranean

—

customs, Raffo loved to go to cafés and sit with men friends: please, no women or children. They would talk and read the newspaper, including the newspaper of the Salonika colony in Paris. The shops (Benveniste & Amon, Joseph Maurice, and even a little store called Chiquita that Raffo had in 1926, and where Lucy worked briefly before my birth) were situated with many other Sefarad stores in the 2eme arrondissement, in an area of Paris called Le Sentier (there is a métro station with that name). Thus, contacts took place all day as one could go from store to store to see uncles or friends. There is a book in French by Annie Benveniste (not a direct relation) titled: Du Bosphore à la Roquette, that describes a similar settlement of stores held by Paris Sefarad Jews in a less affluent area called La Roquette.

Madame Esther de Botton had also moved to Paris. She had married her elder daughter, Grace to Jacques Scialom who was in the import-export business and who lived briefly in Constantinople where my cousin Renée was born on the very day Lucy married Raffo (therefore we know Grace was not there). Jacques then moved to Prague, and Grace, Renée, and later her brother Claude would come to Paris to visit my grandmother and join Lucy and me on vacations. At first, Esther lived in the Hôtel de la Bourdonnais, not far from my Aunt Nelly; later, probably in 1935 or 6 she took an apartment at 5, rue Pérignon, just one block from 6, rue Léon Vaudoyer. Actually, I should not say "one block" since the streets of that part of Paris go in every direction. It was one turn and a few steps away from us. My aunt Marie and uncle Saby had also moved into a rented flat in the same building. Thus, I would often see my cousin Marcel who was three years older and with whom Roger and I would play. Jenny, their older daughter was eleven years older than I, and therefore more of a babysitter, although there was no need for family

—

babysitters in Paris where there were maids and nurses.

Our playgrounds were by and large the empty corridors of these apartments which consisted usually of a reception room, always closed and with the furniture covered with sheets so that it would not suffer dust or light, a dining room, a kitchen giving on the back on an interior court without much light, and then a long corridor leading to the bedrooms also in the back on the interior court. One could only see the street from the dining room since the "salon" was closed. The salon did have glass doors, so you could see the ghosts of furniture waiting there with their sheets. Very rarely, when guests came, the salon was opened, the sheets were removed but the children were sent away. The other playground was outside, starting with rue Léon Vaudoyer where once every morning the Voirie, the street cleaning, made a little river run all along the length of the street and little boats could be made out of leaves or pieces of wood. Later, I played on the Avenue de Saxe, and when the nurses were around, I went dutifully to the Champs de Mars.

Objects were rarer then. The furniture had its sheets because it was supposed to last a lifetime or maybe more. I had toys but not many, mostly lead or aluminum soldiers, and a few cars. We also played monopoly but on a set manufactured by Uncle Richard, Roger's father. It had been copied on a large cardboard and colored by hand, same for the cards, the money and so on. I had roller skates and a trotinette, namely a two-wheel plus pedal pusher. Sometimes I would join a soccer game on the Avenue de Saxe, but since I was on the small, weak side, I usually had a minor role. Sometime in 1934 when I was seven, Kiko, Tante Allegra's son who was seventeen then, started me on a stamp collection, a French stamp collection. He bought the album, a few stamps, got me the book on French stamps

—

and showed me how to identify them, find their number, paste them and write the number below. From then on my main function in life was that of collectioneur: Que fais-tu? Je collectione. What do you do? I am a collector.

Lucy organized lavish parties for my birthdays, cousins and friends were invited. There were hot drinks such as chocolate, pastries, and one year there was a big cardboard boat she had made in the middle of the table with favors for each child hidden in portholes which could be obtained by pulling on a little string in front of each plate. I think we made a lot of noise and certainly had a good time.

The best fun of course was the holidays. Lucy and my aunts would plan and rent one or more villas in a resort for a month or more. In 1928 it was St. Lunaire in Britany near Dinard and St. Malo at the Rance river, in 1929 and 1930, again in St. Lunaire, in 1931 Perros Guirec deeper in Britany, in 1932 Royan on the Atlantic, in 1933 we went to Switzerland to Chesières (in the summer), in 1934 Le Touquet- Paris-Plage way in the north, in 1935 back to St. Lunaire. While mothers and children, plus nurses went to the beach, the men continued to work and then escaped on their own vacation in Vichy or Évian-les-bains (to do the waters ?) and would rejoin later.

The family gathering at the beach often included my cousins, Marcel, Roger, Gérard, Roland, Colette, then there might be Grace with Renée and Claude and Robert, the son of Lucy's half sister Henriette with his brother and sister. There would be others—cousins of my cousins like Claude Ezrati, who much later under President Mitterrand became well known in the French Socialist party under the name of Claude Estier or Raoul Coenca who was a bit older. Kiko and Jenny, our elders, were sometimes around. The nurses organized the children, and the women often played cards

—

or went to the beach. A cabin was rented on the beach so that we could change after the cold swim—well not swim —bath immersion at best. I did not know how to swim until later when I went to MacJannet camp on Lac d'Annecy. The husbands would appear over the weekend or stay for a while. They spent most of their time playing bridge. Raffo might visit on the beach but never went into the water. He never learned to swim, and anyhow in the north the water was considered cold. He usually would sit in a folding chair in white pants, white shoes, shirt, and tie. That was the correct attire for the beach. Lucy would be in a bathing suit, after all she was l'américaine—she knew how to swim the crawl. The older youths (11 +) were in awe.

My second cousin Raoul Coenca told me much later how he had been naked in the changing cabin with my mother. Since the water was considered "very cold" it was of utmost importance to rush to the cabin after bathing and remove the heavy woolen wet bathing suits. He arrived running at the single cabin at the same time as my mother, both dripping wet. She looked at him, he looked at her. He was in his early teens. She told him to come in with her since there was no time to lose less one caught cold. She told him to face one wall, she would face the other. He told me much later: "there I was with a naked woman behind me, it was marvelous".

In 1933 we went to Chesières in Switzerland, but the 1930 Talbot died on the steep road. The Talbot was a French- British car with not much horse power. You may remember, a square car with huge fenders, a spare wheel on the left side, and running boards to step in. The road leaves Ollon and it is a steep climb. Around Les Combes the motor overheated. Mother and child were picked up by a passing motorist. Raffo stayed with the Talbot until he

—

could coax it to destination. Uncle Maurice had wanted to go to Chesières, but Raffo did not really like the mountains. He preferred the sea or lakes. In any case, whether at the mountains, at the lake, or at the seashore, his activities did not vary: eat, play bridge, go to a café if there is one, and play bridge in the evening. Basically, he never exercised except at work when he had to move heavy rolls of cloth.

In 1935, the vacation schedule shifted. First, there was slightly more money. Second, Lucy had had enough fights with my uncles or aunts to reduce the desire to co-habit again in a villa. Maurice had once told her that if there was only one glass of water left, and my feet happened to be slightly dirty, she would use that last glass of drinking water for washing my feet; this had left a lasting impression on her. Third, I had scarlet fever during the summer of 1935, so we went nowhere. Lucy became a full time nurse and did not leave me.

By fall Lucy decided I needed to recuperate and we spent several weeks with Grace, Renée, and Claude in a sanitarium in Baden bie Wien, in Austria. Doctors in white robes came every day to select a menu and a set of activities. There must have been nurses, but at age eight I was completely unaware of gender differences. After that we stayed in Vienna briefly. In 1936, we went south to Juin-les-Pins, near Nice. Marcel and Jenny were there. In fact, I saw more of my cousin Jenny as a vacation babysitter in those years. Already in 1933 (when we also went to Chesières) I had also been sent alone with Jenny, age seventeen, to spend one or two weeks at the English beach in Eastbourne; why, is not clear to me, except that Lucy always hoped I might learn English. Michelle Sarde, (Jenny's daughter), recalls that her parents were attempting to wean her from a young man she had just met in Switzerland where she had had great fun. At Eastbourne the

—

beach around the pier had breakers advancing into the water. I was six and I was throwing stones into the deeper water at the side of one of the breakers. I managed to nearly drown by throwing a heavy one and going with it, falling from the side into water deep enough for me to go under. Now then, why was I sent alone to Eastbourne with Jenny? Did Lucy or Raffo have other plans? But poor Jenny got far more scared than I. I only remember a lot of white bubbles as I was fished out by some obliging English man who jumped after me, and was left with wet pants and shoes in the process.

Vacations were big in France, then and now. As the family became more affluent, they began to take a second one week vacation at Easter time. Starting in 1936 and in 1937, the aunts went to a hotel with a large enclosed park near Tours on the Vouvray side of the Loire River. "La Moisanderie" was wonderful. There were large groups of children, the mothers would spend the day on the terrace playing bridge and since the hotel park was completely enclosed by a tall wall, the children were left on their own. Somewhere, hidden in the park, was an old 17th century tower with an inside tunnel. By then we had bicycles which we rode with wooden swords. We had encampments —girls and boys had separate camps, we had ceremonies, gatherings and visits from camp to camp. The children were back in the middle ages. The mothers played bridge on the terrace. In 1936 my parents and I also spent the summer, first with Grace and the children at Menthon St. Bernard at what was then the Grand Hôtel de Menthon St. Bernard on Lac d'Annecy. The hotel is now the headquarters of a large corporation. At the time, it had all the facilities my father might need, namely bridge games and plenty of space for me to play. The hotel was on one side of the Roc de Chère, there was a precarious path around it. I would explore it with another boy staying at the

—

hotel. Much later, at Harvard I would find him again. His name was Francis Cahn.

That same summer, after a few weeks at Menthon, my parents left after depositing me together with Renée at Camp MacJannet, an American camp in France at Angon, near Talloires on the same lake. Talloires is on the other side of the Roc de Chère. The MacJannet's were running the American School called The Elms, I was going to one day a week, just outside Paris in St.Cloud. They also had this summer camp which was well attended as there were few such facilities in Europe. And they also took children on skiing vacations in winter. In 1937 and 1938 I went to the same camp and also went skiing with them at Caux in 1937 and at Font Romeu in 1938. As I said earlier, Talloires on Lac d'Annecy is where I learned to swim. I had taken swimming classes in a pool in Paris. They had a harness tied to the ceiling that moved the length of the pool. There was a "maître-nageur" who moved my arms while I was held by the harness. That meant that without "maître-nageur" or harness I sank (memories of Eastbourne, bubbles of white, etc.). At the camp they got bored. They threw me in, and since by then, I knew what to do, I swam.

Of course, I went to school. I attended only one school in Paris, the Lycée Buffon on Boulevard Pasteur in the 15ᵗʰ arrondissement, walking distance from rue Léon Vaudoyer. I started in the douzième (first grade, the grades go backwards in France) really the equivalent of kindergarten. I remember standing in line to enter class in the onzième (the next grade) at the beginning of the semester and telling a child who had missed the first week that the onziéme was so much harder, so much more difficult. Lycée Buffon was built like a big square with classrooms all around a recreation area. The recreation area was filled with little sharp stones designed to cut your

—

knees if you fell. There were girls in the classes until the
septième (fifth grade) and only boys after that. We took all
the subjects at the same time and I cannot say I enjoyed
school very much. There was a little antisemitism; I was
called "sale juif" by a few bullies, got in a few fights here
and there. In any case I was a very mediocre student or felt
to be so by teachers who had little interest in me. Our gym
teacher was a very fat man who could not get up from his
chair but gave us instructions on how to climb ropes while
he sat there, reclining. Our art teacher would have us copy
endless apples and make heavy corrections when he came
to look at our work. We also took history, mathematics,
English, later German also, French literature, and grammar.
I never learned to spell in any language. They gave us our
homework papers or our test results back in order of
accomplishment. The instructors would read the names and
grades aloud and hand the papers back. Sometimes an
instructor might even sneer while handing back the worse
ones. So it would go: Brissac 18, (the highest grade was
20), Auric 16, somebody else 15, many other good French
names 14, 13, 10, 8, 7, and then not quite at the end but
close, Benveniste 6 or 5 or 4. I was not a good student.
There was much lamenting at home. "Your cousin Roger
does so well in school. Why do you not try to do as well?"
I was "étourdi," in a cloud, not able to concentrate. I did
like to draw; in fact one of Lucy's friends collected my
early drawings. But even in the art class I was not doing
well, as for English I could not keep up with the class even
if I had had an English nurse, gone to McJannet camp and
had an American mother. Thursday was our day off in the
French school. As mentioned above, I was sent on
Thursdays to the McJannet American School in St. Cloud,
just outside Paris where I assume I must have taught some
French to other children, but never really learned much
English.

In 1937 my parents moved from rue Léon Vaudoyer to a better apartment in the same building as Maïr and Oro at 6, Avenue du Général Détrie close to the Champs de Mars. I was 10 then and could easily walk the longer distance to the Lycée. I would often stop at my aunt Marie on rue Pérignon and get a bite to eat before continuing my longer march home.

There was more money, I suppose, and Lucy was able to do some remodeling. Instead of the more rigid arrangement at Léon Vaudoyer (the closed salon), she opened doors and the wall between the salon and the dinning room at Général Détrie so as to obtain a very large room overlooking the Avenue de Sufren. We must have been at the 4ème étage because we were above the trees on the Avenue and those rooms had plenty of light. A piano à queue appeared, maybe it had been in storage and belonged to the New York era, and it dominated the living room. There were some comfortable chairs, and Lucy and Raffo had an elegant cocktail table they had received as a wedding gift from their friends the Akchotés, who had an antique store specializing in Asian art on the rue de Rivoli, a Japanese screen that had been converted into a cocktail table. Then there was a sofa. Gone were the more rigid chairs standing in a circle, this was really "modern" and in addition, no more sheets, this was an open room, a free room. Such liberty was beyond comprehension!

I was promptly given piano lessons so that the piano would be put to good use, and I did use it to store a collection of paper airplanes, which we cousins had become addicted to. We would fold them, decorate them and "fly" them out from the windows over the trees, then would rush out to salvage those that had made it over all these obstacles and had still managed to land safely on the trottoir. Some, unfortunately, would land on the avenue

—

and would be decapitated by the traffic.

While we were in the same building as Maïr and Oro, we did not visit them often. By now Maïr was 71, and Oro, 73. We ate at their place at Passover. My aunts (Marie, Allegra, and Nelly) who were still in tradition, served us. They went back and forth and prepared most of the meal. Maïr and Oro lived above us at a higher floor, but on the other side of the building giving on the Ave. du Général Détrie. 1937 was the year of the World Fair in Paris that took place on the Champs de Mars, under the Eiffel Tower across the river all the way to a new Trocadéro building. The Fair was rather convenient to our apartment and while I visited several times, we were not yet that rich that we could afford too many entrance tickets. In any case, it made a big impression seeing all these different pavilions from many countries, tasting strange foods in stands, and the world seemed then to be so magnificent, the boats, the flags, and the many foreigners visiting.

Most of the social life I saw during my first ten years took place at home, or sometimes on weekend outings. My parents had close friends such as the Akchoté's who would go on trips with them and I was taken along. They would often go to the Pré Catelan, a restaurant just outside Paris in the Bois de Boulogne. It had good food and a large garden. I would play in a field and then eat with them. I know that I went to Veulettes-sur-Mer in April of 1932 with my parents and the Akchotés, Veulettes is due north of Paris on the Manche. There are high cliffs and the beach below where one finds the bones of dogs and sheep that failed to see the end of the cliff. I went back to Veulettes in the sixties when I lived in Paris and it was as wild as I remembered. On the other hand, when I saw St. Lunaire again in the sixties it seemed tiny.

—

The beach I remembered as huge was very small indeed. I have had occasions to return to the sites of my childhood, to Annecy to Font Romeu and I again lived in my neighborhood by the Champs de Mars. In addition, my camp at Lake d'Annecy is in a movie by Eric Rohmer called "Claire's Knee." The movie takes place next door to the camp and one can clearly see the site, the surrounding mountains and the lake. Oddly enough Rohmer made another movie in 1996 which takes place in St. Malo and St. Lunaire. You can see the small beach of St Lunaire in his other film titled "A Summer Tale".

The family social life centered on meals of Salonika food which Raffo preferred above anything else. The aunts had taught Lucy these Salonika recipes, which resemble Greek or Middle Eastern cooking. They were Huevos Enhaminados, eggs cooked for 3 or 4 hours in water with oil, onion skins, and coffee grounds. These were eaten as aperitif with the traditional Raki (although Raffo could not drink much alcohol—he was allergic and his nose would turn deep red). Raki is an anise spirit which was well liked in the Ottoman Empire There would be Borekas, little pastry like cakes of spinach, cheese or meat sometime made with filo dough although that was not traditional and instead, they might use pâte brisée. For the Incussa, a large cake of eggs and various cheeses, they always reverted to the pâte brisée. Then there was Swongato. You took eggplants that had to be slightly burned on the open flame, then peeled and beaten with a wooden spoon (it had to be wooden)—you added eggs, various cheeses and once again baked all this in pâte brisée in the oven. The piece de resistance for Raffo was Fijones: a white bean and meat "navarin" which includes slightly burned onions, veal meat balls (kifkes) small sausages, bone marrow and a few chunks of beef. For desert, the French influence dominated. Chocolate Mousse made with eggs, cream and chocolate was the preferred end to the banquet. Food was very important and French food was served, but within the family Salonika still dominated, if only because it was not available elsewhere. Oil, eggs cheese, and meat dominated the traditional menus. The French influence added cream and butter. Pâte brisée according to Julia Child should be tender, crunchy and buttery. Yes, there were plenty of beans and vegetables, but notwithstanding the current popularity of the Mediterranean diet, it was not the best heart or cancer foods in the world.

My uncle Ugo Modiano, the husband of Allegra was my best friend among the elders. This, for two reasons: he painted and had a genuine interest in my drawings and second, I was his most successful "medium." Ugo had extra sensory powers. He would leave the room, people would decide a task: "have him go to the window and open it." Ugo would come in, then I would hold a finger up and he would touch it with his. I would then concentrate hard and think silently: "go to the window, go to the window." After a while he would do so. Then I would think: "open it, open it, open it." He would open it. I was very impressed by this power and by my role in it. It seemed very mysterious, suggesting a much more complex real world we knew nothing about. After that, the bridge game was started and the children would play in the corridor only to be obliged to remove fortifications or armies when someone had to go to the bathroom.

World War II

Hitler came to power in Germany in 1933. The next year, on February 6th there were right wing riots in Paris. I remember being in the kitchen at rue Léon Vaudoyer with the maid who was worried because neither Lucy nor Raffo had returned home, and she had heard

—

about the riots on the radio. But they did return soon enough. In 1936 the civil war of Spain began. I was 9 then and old enough to follow the news. I knew there was fighting going on and in the family we always paid attention to Spain. Both Raffo and Lucy had become naturalized French citizens on 27 November 1932, but Maurice had kept his Spanish citizenship, and in 1932 Maurice was only 31 years old which meant that he paid attention to what was going on in Spain or France regarding possible military service. On April 26, 1937, at about the time we were moving from Vaudoyer to Détrie, there was the destruction of the little town of Guernica by the Falangists. Tension with Germany was rising and the family was certainly preoccupied, not so much about what might happen to Jews—we had no information at that time on Hitler's plans of extermination—but on the prospects for a war between France and Germany that would inevitably affect us. Several aunts or uncles understood German and I remember that on more than one occasion we would all be around a radio listening to Hitler's speech. The one who understood German kept saying: "il dit que..." he says that, "il dit que..., il dit que..." and I could hear the shouting man and the shouting crowd: "Heil, Heil, Heil...."

My grandfather who was in good health suddenly caught pneumonia in December 1937. At first the family doctor, Doctor Cazès, a Salonicien, took care of him, but when he got worse the family called on Doctor Guy Laroche, a prominent French doctor. He died on December 26. There were no antibiotics in 1937. His sudden death was a big blow to my father, and I think to the rest of the older generation. Maïr had represented Salonika and all the traditions implicit in the concept of Salonika. His own death had been in the tradition: he was purged, went to bed, said goodbye to sons, daughters, and their husbands and wives, and died. He was until the end in charge of his own

—

death. As far as I remember, I did not go upstairs, or if I did I have blocked the memory. The building was then covered in black around the front door on Général Détrie with the initials MB in gold. There was a one night vigil with his body in the apartment. The next day the embalmer came, the casket prepared, and Maïr was taken in a convoy to the Cimetière de Pantin where he had already purchased a plot for the family. Again, I have no memory of going to Pantin. I went to Pantin when my father died, but not in 1937. The mourning in Salonika took place at the home of Daniel Benveniste, the oldest of Hannah's children who had stayed there.

Thus, the end of 1937 and beginning of 1938 was a turning point for the family. From 1926 to 1937 Raffo had established himself—he had prospered. The move to Détric in '37 was full of hope, the new furniture, and the new rooms. There were chintz curtains on many windows. But on 14 March 1938 the Nazis took over Austria and there was a lot of tension about the possibilities of war. I think that in France, there were a lot of contradictory currents at the time and I kept hearing "Benveniste c'est quoi ce nom là?"—Not so much anti-Semitism, but an anti-foreigner attitude. What is that name Benveniste? In 1937 France had many fewer foreign names in evidence than now. My classmates had French names and I did not— why? Luckily it did not sound German.

During the summer of 1938 I went to MacJannet camp and right after my return, on September 29, it was Munich. The Prime Ministers of England and France had met with Hitler in Munich and essentially allowed Germany to move into the Sudetenland, a German speaking part of Czechoslovakia, and peace had been "saved." Since we were at peace, I went skiing with the MacJannets at Font Romeu. The Spanish civil war had ended earlier that

—

year, Madrid had fallen on March 28, 1938, so I suppose it was okay to go to Font Romeu to ski—Font Romeu is very close to the Spanish border in the Pyrenées. Meanwhile the President of Czechoslovakia, Edvard Beněs, resigned and left his abandoned country.

In the summer of 1939, I believe I went again to MacJannet Camp, although I have no photographs or memory of what I did then. The talk of war was back as Hitler had invaded Bohemia and the rest of Czechoslovakia in March and was proposing to invade Poland. Raffo and Lucy were certainly concerned, and were worried about possible aerial bombardment of Paris. The French had built the Maginot Line, a set of fortifications all along the French-German border which was, presumably, impregnable. So the worry was air strikes. 6, Ave. du Général Détrie could turn into rubble and the way to avoid this was to go out of Paris. Therefore in late August 1939, Lucy and I went to stay on a farm in Gisors, a small village north of Paris. A farm was desirable, because the German planes would not waste a bomb on a farm, would they?

As the war was beginning to become reality, worse and persuasive news had also reached us. Aunt Grace and Uncle Jacques Scialom had arrived in Paris coming from Prague with their chauffeur, children, some belongings, and their Tatra car. They had arrived in 1938, before Munich. Renée had gone to camp with me. The Tatra had created a big sensation in Paris because it was one of the first cars that allowed the hood to be opened in one single upward move. Other motor cars had hoods that opened on each side of the motor whereas the entire Tatra hood went up. So we were in the street, I think in front of 5, rue Pérignon and the chauffeur was demonstrating to the assembled Parisians this marvel of invention, up went the entire hood —aah! said the Parisians. But Aunt Grace had news about

—

what the Germans were doing to their Jews and that did not sound good. In 1938 they had settled in a furnished apartment at 24, Avenue Charles Floquet near the Champs de Mars. I saw much more of Renée and Claude, although they went to the American School in St. Cloud, while I was at the Lycée. When we were both at home sick we would play naval battle by telephone.

The farm at Gisors fascinated me, there were boys my age who slept in a shed and I was greatly impressed by their freedom. They rose when they wanted, worked, but seemed so free of restrictions. They often went bare-foot and did not seem to have to worry about school or about how to sit on a chair or what clothes to wear and certainly not to worry about dirt. This was a huge revelation. Everyone did not live the way we lived. Everyone did not aspire to do well in school as I was told everyday. Dirt was not enemy number one. I do not think that Lucy enjoyed Gisors and anyhow the Germans were not bombing Paris, so why not return. We went to Paris on September 1, 1939, the same day the Germans invaded Poland. War was declared on September 3, 1939. Again, there was no question about Lucy and me staying in Paris. Grace and family had left for Pau in the south of France. A town located as far as possible from the Germans next to Spain but not near the coast. But Pau was too far for easy travel for Raffo who was staying to run the business, so Vichy was chosen since Raffo used to spend some of his summer vacation there, and Lucy rented a flat. Raffo would come down, go to Lyon where he had cloth suppliers for his store and return to Paris.

Fall of 1939 was the "drôle de guerre" the strange war. Nothing much was happening. We were all issued gas masks that were carried along. The gas masks were made of rubber with a place for the eyes and some kind of

—

primitive canister to filter the air. One looked sinister with the mask on. The mask went into a metal canister and you had this to carry on your back, what with your school books in a "cartable" (a school boy brief case), it was a mess. In Paris, when we visited briefly, there had been a few alerts. The sirens would sound and everyone had to go in the cellar of 6, Avenue du Général Détrie. Not a big cellar, it was a bit humid and Raffo and Lucy would get bored with the whole episode and sometimes stay in bed. There were also alerts in Vichy, but fewer. Mme. Akchoté and her daughter Josette were with us in Vichy and I only remember that we lived on a hill, that my bicycle brakes failed and that I crashed coming down—but nothing else really. By mid-December, Mme. Akchoté and Lucy were bored with Vichy and it was decided to go briefly back to Paris and for Lucy and me, to rejoin Grace, Mme. Esther de Botton, Jacques, Renée, and Claude in Pau. The distance was greater from Paris to Pau, but Grace continued to be worried and her fears were affecting Lucy. In addition, Grace had found a lovely apartment right on the Boulevard des Pyrénées with a wonderful view of the mountains and she had found a marvelous cook and there was an empty apartment in the same building to rent for us. We should come, and so we did.

Pau And French Defeat

In Pau, I went to the Lycée Louis Barthou while Renée and Claude were at the American School; there was one outside of Pau strangely enough. I joined the cub scouts; I rode my bicycle and learned how to fish. The cook did marvels. Pau, for me, was the revelation of gourmet cooking. Her tarts, I never again tasted better tarts, and the stews, yes, there was a war on, but we ate very well indeed.

—

In early May 1940, Lucy decided we might as well go back for a vacation in Paris. We had hardly arrived there, that the drôle de guerre was no longer drôle. The German Panzer divisions bypassed the Maginot Line and invaded Holland and Belgium, the French and English troops then moved forward into Belgium. My cousin Kiko, who had gone to the military school at Saumur (cavalry) and was now in charge of a platoon of lightly armed carriers wrote that they were moving north into Belgium. Lucy and I immediately departed back to Pau when it became clear that the Germans were moving rapidly south while the bulk of the French and English were still going north, but closer to the sea. In no time, the Germans had looped around the French and English and encircled them at Dunkirk. By then we were back in Pau. Kiko was killed at some point in these battles, but we did not hear of it until weeks later when my father had rejoined us in Pau.

Late May to mid June was the "débacle." French troops retreated. Many were captured in Dunkirk while some managed to escape with the English across the channel. Refugees poured into the roads going south, in cars loaded with a mattress on the roof to protect (?) against German planes. At the train station in Pau, refugees were coming in daily. Lucy and I volunteered. We helped people walk from the trains to buses taking them to provisional housing. By June 14 the German army was parading in Paris. Raffo had left and arrived safely, the German army had occupied half of France and gone along the coast all the way to the Spanish border. On June 22 1940, Maréchal Pétain, a hero of World War I, signed an armistice with the Germans. France was divided into two areas. One in the north and the Atlantic coast was controlled directly by the Germans. The second, including Pau, Lyon, Marseilles, and Nice was non-occupied France controlled under German supervision by the Vichy

—

government headed by Maréchal Pétain.

The Germans were only several miles from Pau. Grace, her mother, Jacques and the two children immediately left for the Americas. Grace was convinced the Germans would kill the Jews. They left via Barcelona. We remained in Pau for several more weeks. In Barcelona, Claude, Renée's brother was killed accidentally by a doctor when he was given a shot to which he was allergic. We received a telegram from Jacques that started: "Fou de Douleur...". But my father was not convinced we should leave France. In the family, no one thought that the Jews would be persecuted. In general, the Jews in France were convinced that what might have happened, or seemed to happen elsewhere in Germany or Poland would somehow not happen in France. Let us not panic was Raffo's view; let us see what the Germans do next. The tragedy of Claude's death in Barcelona indicated the dangers of travel. But since Pau was so close to the German lines, neither of them wanted to stay there. Raffo came up with the idea of going to Nice. Nice was close to the Italian border, the Italians were not the Germans, and in any case Raffo spoke Italian well, one would always be able to manage with the Italians. Therefore, let us go to Nice.

Nice

We must have left Pau in August of 1940. Raffo had driven from Paris, before the worst of the débacle and we therefore still had a car. Some gasoline was obtained, my bicycle was strapped in front of the car and all our possessions jammed inside. We rode on fairly empty roads as far as just north of Marseilles, when gasoline ran out and in addition, Raffo got lost at night because he could not see the road as my bicycle obscured the headlights. We somehow made it to Marseilles where gasoline was no

—

longer available. We stayed in a hotel on the old port for several days while train passage was obtained, the car was sold or given away and our goods packed in cases. We arrived in Nice and were helped at the station by friends of Raffo, other Saloniciens who had already taken refuge on that side of the coast. An apartment was rapidly found in a new building at 48, rue Rossini. We lived there from August or September 1940 to May 1942. After our departure in 1942, friends of my parents, Binio and Vicky Ventura, kept the lease and Binio hid there for a while. The building stood relatively alone, surrounded by vacant lots planted with vegetables. It was near the Bld. Gambetta and not far from the Lycée du Parc Imperial where I was immediately enrolled. We visited 48, rue Rossini with Karen in the 1990's, the building was no longer new and all the vegetable lots were built upon. I went back to school where I continued to be a mediocre student. One of my best friends then was Sylvain Lourié, a refugee from Paris like me who lived on Bld. Gambetta, very close to our place. We rode bicycles together, built little boats out of balsa wood and went camping together. I was to find Sylvain again many years later when I worked for UNESCO. He and his family also left in 1942 but they went to the United States. Later in the sixties I met, at a diner, Stanley Hoffman, a well known Harvard professor. We discovered we had been together in that class at the Lycée. He remembered our teachers. I finally remembered him as the " good student". He remained in France until the end of the war hidden outside of Nice.

Food shortages rapidly became a major preoccupation. We did not have much money so that a good deal of our ravitaillement was done by barter. Raffo was able to go to Lyon on several occasions to buy cloth from producers who knew him, and this cloth was then exchanged for legs of lamb, rabbits (or were these cats?) or

—

eggs. We accumulated a hoard of tuna tins, olive oil (very precious) and rice. These would later also prove useful to the Venturas. I would go on my bicycle just outside of Nice and obtain eggs from farms and bring them back hidden in a basket.

The Sefarad community in Nice kept obtaining dire news about what had happened to the Jews. Monsieur Akchoté appeared one day, he had been mobilized, being French and younger than Raffo, who in 1940 was over the age to be a soldier, had been taken prisoner and finally had been released by the Germans after the Armistice. He related that he had hidden the fact he was Jewish and thus escaped. His worse souvenir of captivity was that in their barrack (some 40 men) there was only one glass to share for all. If you wanted to drink there was that one glass only. One of the prisoners had false teeth and at night he kept them in the glass. So, if you or he was thirsty at night, you had to take the teeth out and get fresh water. That story did it. Lucy said we had to leave. We could not stay any longer.

Daisy Saurel, Lucy's cousin, the mother of my second cousin Sylvette, Daisy, who was a very amusing woman, who designed for Henri à La Pensée, a famous Paris couture house, came with her new husband, Benoit Jehiel. They had heard the worst also. It was imperative not to appear to be Jewish. Since Daisy's father was Jacques de Botton (brother of Isaac) we would all say that the de Botton were good Catholics. The de Botton name sounded French and was not a well known Jewish name. As for Lucy's mother, Esther Asariah, let us say her name was really Asarian or Azarian and that she was Armenian, the point was first, to convince ourselves, and then others , that we were not Jewish under the Nazi's definition. Under their rule you had to have at least three grandparents who were not Jewish, not to be considered Jewish. With two Catholic de Botton and one Armenian Asarian, Lucy was under Nazi definition non Jewish. This left Raffo and me. As initial precaution we would be baptized. Lucy was convinced we should leave but these alternative plans were elaborated just in case. This long conversation took place on the beach at Nice, Raffo was in his usual white pants and shirt, but Benoit, who was quite skinny, was in a tiny slip.

Henriette, her husband, Aaron Mallah, their son Robert, who was my age, and his older brother and sister also came down, they settled in Juin-les-Pins. We would take the gazogène bus from Nice to visit them (the gazogène bus burnt some kind of waste instead of gasoline which by then was very difficult to obtain). Uncle Maurice who had remained in Paris, had no trouble crossing in non-occupied France because he had not been naturalized French and had kept his Spanish passport. He would visit us from time to time when he crossed the border into Vichy France to buy cloth in Lyon. We would eat in restaurants on those occasions, once we went with my aunt Lolo, Maurice, and Gérard to Juin-les-Pins and had quite a banquet. Maurice and his brother Péppo did not seem to feel the need to leave France. Péppo, who had naturalized French, was just 40 in 1939. He had been mobilized but he had served in the rear. They were convinced nothing would happen to Jews in France. Lucy did go back to Paris in 1941 to see if she could recover some of our belongings from the apartment at Ave.du Général Détrie which the Germans had taken over. She did not recover anything but managed to go to the storage company where Mme Esther Asariah's de Botton (veuve de Botton as the French would have her sign) goods were stored since her departure from Pau. She changed the name from Asariah to Asarian and told the company that she was Armenian. This move saved

—

a set of furniture, dishes, and other goods. Robert, Henriettes' son, would be the only one from that family to survive the Vichy and German attempted obliteration of the Jews. He recuperated much of that furniture later after the war.

Lucy was adamant that we should leave. She went to the American Consulate in Nice (there was one in Nice) and the Consul assured her she would obtain an American passport in no time that a visa would then be obtained for Raffo and me. But a few days later the Consul had bad news. Lucy had married in 1926 and not returned to the United States. She had become a French citizen in 1932 when Raffo had been naturalized. Under U. S. law of the time, an American woman who married a foreigner abroad, who did not return to the United States and acquired the nationality of her husband, automatically lost her U. S. citizenship even if she was a U. S. citizen at birth. We would have to apply for visas, but the Consul who was very friendly, was sure this would be no problem. Unfortunately, it turned out that one of the references Lucy gave in the visa application, a woman from her Hunter High School days she had since seen in Paris, turned out to be a well known Nazi sympathizer who stopped in Paris with her husband on their way to Berlin. The visas were denied.

At this point Lucy, who was not Jewish since she somehow had convinced herself that she had two Catholic and one Armenian non-Jewish grandparents and was as non-Jewish as Daisy was non-Jewish, if you follow the logic, had Raffo and me baptized into the Eglise Reformée de France. This was a Protestant church in Nice with few decorations; more along the lines of the Ethical Society Lucy had attended in New York. Raffo was not happy about it but did it and I was sent to attend Sunday school.

—

By now we were Catholic, Protestant, Armenian non Jewish, and a tiny bit Jewish.

Since Lucy was determined to leave, Raffo came up with Mexico. He knew of several Saloniciens who had gone to Mexico. He wrote to a friend of his, Saul Carasso who had once borrowed money from him and was now very wealthy and apparently still owing Raffo a big favor. Letters and phone calls began with Mexico. There was a Mexican consulate in Marseilles. Applications were made. Saul Carasso paid the necessary "mordida" in Mexico City. The paper work was rapid. The phone calls took place in the lobby of the apartment building where there was a public phone cabin right next to the elevator. In 1941, to call Mexico City from Nice was a major enterprise. The connection was at best chancy. Raffo had to shout in the phone, but the visas came, the Consul of Mexico in Marseilles stamped Lucy's passport in which I was included and Raffo's. An exit permit had to be obtained from the Vichy authority, and this was done in January while I was still 14. We applied for permission to leave France only for a brief vacation in Barcelona presumably to visit the tomb of my cousin Claude who had died there in 1940. It was obtained. Passage on a boat was negotiated with a Jewish relief agency helping Jews leave Europe and first class passage was paid in advance. Lucy sold some jewelry.

We left Nice the second week of May 1942. Before our departure, all Jews in Nice were informed by the press and radio that they should register, as such, at police headquarters. Raffo, who either feared illegality, or did not like being baptized , or both, went and registered.

Allied forces landed in North Africa in November 1942 and the Germans occupied all of France, doing away

—

with the Vichy regime. But Nice was occupied by the Italians as Raffo had correctly predicted. What he had not predicted was that the Vichy government picked up all the Jews of Nice in October, 1942, and sent most of those they arrested to camps in France, and then to the gas chambers in Germany. My cousin Robert's family was all caught and Robert only escaped because he was hidden away at the time. He remained hidden until the end of the war. My uncle Péppo and his wife were caught shortly before the Normandy landings. The rest of the family escaped. Maurice was protected by Spain, the rest hid. My cousins Roger, Gérard, Roland and Colette were hidden in a village with protestant clerics who saved their lives. This village is called Chambon-sur-Lignon and a film was made about it, titled "The Weapon of the Spirit". Colette (daughter of Maurice) tells me she appears in it briefly. I have not been able to recognize her when I watch it.

She told me that toward the end of the war, the Germans decided to house soldiers wounded on the Russian front in Chambon-sur-Lignon. One of the German recuperating centers was just across the street from her building. From a terrace where they hanged their bedding she could observe all the goings and comings. In time, both she and her roommate began talking from terrace to terrace with some of those wounded soldiers who were busy every morning shining their boots. The Germans would wave to them, say hello, nice weather or things like that and they would respond in kind. At liberation time, months later, the Germans were gone, Colette and her roommate were to leave but before doing so they witnessed French women, who had been with Germans, being paraded in town with their heads all shaven clean. Colette was 12 then. When they asked what the women had done, they were simply told the women had "talked" to Germans. Both children were devastated. They had also talked to German soldiers;

they feared they too would have their hair shaven off.

The Benvenistes who had remained in Salonika did much less well. The Nazis invaded Greece in 1941 and on 11 July 1942 gathered all the Jews of Salonika for deportation. Few escaped. The Jewish colony of Salonika went from 60 – 80,000 pre-World War II to about 1200 in the 1990's. Had we stayed in Nice we would have been deported in October since my father had dutifully registered as Jewish.

We left Nice separately. Raffo traveled on his own, and Lucy and I did the same. The idea was not to give the impression of a family leaving. My parents had arranged with Binio and Vicky Ventura to keep the lease on the apartment in case we did not make it at the border. Later, when the Jews were being rounded up, Binio Ventura would use the apartment to hide keeping all the shutters closed as if it was empty. They survived and, with their daughter Lily, would eventually go to Buenos Aires. Lucy and I took the train from Nice and changed at Avignon for the train to Spain. Raffo went through Marseilles. While we waited on the quay at Avignon, two French gendarmes moving a prisoner waited with us. The man was evidently badly beaten up. The gendarmes were propping him up. We were much shaken.

In Port-Bou at the border, we found Raffo. He went in with the passports and exit permits. We waited. I had reached 15 on February 27, 1942, and men 15 and older were not allowed to leave France since they might be needed for the war effort against the Soviet Union. Raffo was too old, but I was prime for service. Luckily my exit permit had been issued before my 15th birthday. The border guard realized we had bought the train tickets in good faith. Raffo assured them we would return very soon.

—

We were only going to Barcelona to visit the tomb of his nephew. We were allowed to proceed. This was a very long half-hour.

We walked to the Spanish train while porters helped with suitcases. Spanish trains were on a narrower gage, so one had to change train. We entered through the last car, and there: miracle— there were bananas and oranges on a table! We had not seen bananas and oranges since 1940. It was a very emotional moment, eating that banana, knowing we were in Spain, not in France, knowing we were going to Mexico, knowing that we were escaping something dangerous—we still had no idea how bad it was to be, we just knew that bananas and oranges had come back, that we were leaving the war behind.

Spain And Portugal

We went to Barcelona where Raffo had friends, and where we visited the crematorium where the ashes of my cousin Claude had been left by my aunt Grace and my uncle Jacques.

I was never told much about our financial situation. We stayed in a small hotel not far from a Gaudi house on the Paseo (or Passeig in Catalan) de Grácia. My sense of the family finances was that my parents spent roughly what the business brought in and that they had saved something for emergencies. Lucy had some jewelry also, and most of it was sold. But by and large, from May 1940 onward, Raffo had not been able to do very much, although he did go to Lyon on several occasions. I believe that he had been able to buy and sell some lots of merchandise (cloth) with the help of his brother Maurice whose Spanish passport allowed far more freedom. I tend to remember that when Benveniste & Amon was closed, Maurice helped sell the

—

stock of merchandise at hand. This stock must have been the main source of resources to finance our stay in Nice, the trip to Spain, Portugal, Mexico, and as you will see, our extended stay in Portugal. Tickets on a Portuguese ship going from Lisbon to Veracruz had been obtained through a Jewish philanthropic organization that was helping Jews escape from Europe. But since my parents had enough money to pay for it, they had paid the full first class fare and we were not subsidized by the organization whose name I do not think I knew.

We stayed 4 or 5 days in Barcelona, doing what we could to catch up on eating. None of us were at anything like a starvation level, but as I said before, food was tightly rationed in France. A barter of cloth for food had helped, for example. Raffo had obtained quantities of green, not roasted coffee in exchange for some meters of silk. The coffee had been roasted in the apartment, but we were scared of being denounced by a neighbor who would surely smell the roasting aroma. So every crevice and window had been sealed while the coffee roasted in the oven. As I recall, you could smell it in the middle of the street, coffee aroma is wonderful that way, no little towel at the door or masking tape is to stop it. Luckily, the neighbors were not bad sorts, and, anyhow, I think a little distribution was made. But by and large we were on the thin side and quite fit since we all had had to ride bicycles to go anywhere within Nice, or even to the outskirts. My father, who had never exercised before, had now lost most of his "embonpoint" his girth. Standing up straight he could again see his feet. Food had become an overriding preoccupation for those two years, and when we reached Spain we were suddenly aware to what extent we had been deprived.

Barcelona, in May of 1942, was certainly not the Barcelona of the Olympics, or what it is today. The

—

Spanish civil war was still ever present everywhere. There was a lot of poverty, and compared to France, one saw more than the usual share of amputees or clearly wounded people on the street. But there was much more food to be had in stores, in restaurants, everywhere. My father who loved fish could not stop looking into the fish mongers stalls or the displays of the better restaurants.

From Barcelona, we went by train to Madrid where we did not stay—except overnight near the station, and the next day we left by train for Lisbon. The Spanish train, like other European trains of the time was divided in compartments sitting six, plus the corridor running the length of the train on one side. We were slightly shocked when we discovered a German officer in uniform already in our compartment where we had 3 reserved seats. As the train left the station, we also realized that while other compartments were full, ours was not, and the 4 of us were the only ones in that one. The German officer was polite and Raffo who could speak a little German exchanged a few words. But by and large we traveled in a subdued way, never too sure why we had this companion. The German officer read a book most of the time. When we neared the Portuguese border he closed the book, searched his baggage, took out a camera and waited. We waited also, increasingly tense. The custom people came through, we showed our passports and our transit visas, and he showed some document and sat down again. As soon as the train left the border post, he suddenly got up, went to the window with his camera, took several pictures, closed the camera, sat down and went back to reading. In Lisbon he said goodbye pleasantly, helped with some of our suitcases and went his way. We were met on the quay by a delegation of friends and families, including the Assaëls, the Amons (related to my uncle Saby) and among the Amon's, there was Mounet, a close friend of my father and

—

his daughter Nicole who, much later, became a Professor of French and taught for 34 years at San Jose City College just down the peninsula from Berkeley and then part time at San Jose State and Santa Clara University in the south bay of San Francisco.

We were not to stay in Lisbon very long, as we were to leave within a week on the boat for which we had purchased first class tickets. We went to a small hotel in town and the next day Lucy went to inspect the boat to determine what cabin we might obtain. One look at the boat and she said she would not leave on it. Apparently, it was much too small and Lucy feared going across the Atlantic on a small boat. In retrospect one might argue that a small boat would be safer, it would be less visible, or be less important so that a German U Boat—a submarine would not sink it accidentally. But—it was not a matter of submarines here. Lucy felt that we had paid the full first class fare and nevertheless the Jewish philanthropic organization that had arranged the passage had somehow placed us on a class less boat with no first class. Since we had paid full fare, she felt we had the right to a big boat with more amenities than what was being proposed. She went, with Raffo and me in tow, to the Office of the Jewish Philanthropy and told the man in charge that it was a scandal, that she was not taking the proposed small boat and that she would wait in Lisbon until something "convenable" was proposed. The Jewish Philanthropy pointed out, that they did not know exactly, when and if the next bigger liner would ever leave, but Lucy was not to be taken by what appeared as a mere ruse. We would wait, and we waited.

Since we were to stay in Portugal for some time , Lucy found a school where I could be enrolled. This was an English school, called The St. Julian's' School in

—

Carcavelos, next to Estoril and Cascais, all resort towns
west of Lisbon. The school was located at the site where
the telegraph cables to America originate. The site was
well protected and since it was at the end of a little cape, it
was surrounded by the ocean. I was suddenly an English
child boarding at school. Well not quite, and quite frankly,
I do not remember this period too well. I went to class, ate
in the dining hall, and managed to hold a cricket bat and hit
a ball without upsetting the wicket. Schools must have
been more flexible in those days, so that a French child
who had just left the Troisième of a French Lycée (where
he was told he might have to repeat the grade) could be
incorporated for one month in an English school without
any dramatic problem. As it turned out my cousin Nicole
Amon attended that school for seven years, as they
remained in Portugal until the end of the war.

I had a tendency to small time illegalities which
surfaced again. Already in Nice, I had once bought a sheet
of stamps—this was a stamp that had been printed first on
sheets without perforation (old stamps had to be cut with
scissors). This issue was a pale color and worth much more
than the second issue that had been printed on perforated
paper (like stamps that you tear along the perforation) and
was darker. I had found a perforated sheet that might have
been in sunlight for a long time, so that it was more like the
color of the non-perforated issue. I had cut the stamps out
carefully, avoiding the holes of the perforation, leaving as
much margin as possible. On Sundays there was a stamp
market in Nice, and I had sold a few of my concoctions.
Encouraged by the apparent eagerness of my buyers, I had
offered some of my stamps at philatelic stores in town.
There I was found out. A store owner had lectured me. It
was not difficult to see that my stamps had small margins,
that I had too many and the color was not quite right when
placed next to the real item. The experience had impressed

—

me deeply, the store owner had done a very good job of showing me the lack of elegance in fakes—it was not so much that I felt guilty, but that I realized, I did not really want to be associated with a set of stamps that were nothing at all, since they no longer even had the original perforations. I destroyed my stock there and then.

At the English school there were Boy Scouts, English scouts. I had been with the Éclaireurs de France in Nice so I attended some of the meetings. I had my scout uniform with me including badges—4 or 5 badges I had passed in France. In France 2nd class scouts could pass badges, but in England only 1st class scouts could do so. When they saw my badges they said I was 1st class and I did not say—no, in France 2nd class scouts can pass some badges, I kept silent on the subject, so when they gave me a complimentary English boy scout card, they wrote 1st class. From then on, as far as I could see, I was a 1st class scout. It seemed the patriotic thing to do—at least that was the way to explain it to myself. It simply said that what was only 2nd class in France, was 1st class elsewhere.

The school closed in mid-June, and I returned to Lisbon. There was still no sign of a larger liner leaving for Veracruz. Lucy had brought some dresses made in France with cloth from Raffo on recent well known couturier patterns that Daisy had obtained since she had connections with the big couture houses of Paris. Since it was difficult to obtain these patterns in Lisbon, Lucy had been able to lend the dresses to a shop that had had them copied. She had made a little money that way.

It was getting warm, Lucy and Raffo decided to move to Estoril, a near by beach resort west of Lisbon. Estoril, in 1942, had lots of nice little villas and few big hotels. In Portugal, in 1942, men could not expose their torso on the beach. In France, we wore small slips, but in Portugal one needed an old fashioned wooly costume without sleeves, but mid-thigh length, covering the upper torso. On the other hand, these wooly beach costumes were tight around one's private parts, so that it tended to accentuate their presence. Worse still, the wool tended to rub when one walked so that I kept discovering to my surprise, that I was getting an erection, which made visibility that much worse.

Until then, my experience with any aspect of sex was totally nil. I knew absolutely nothing about the subject. Way back, I had been told that children were brought by the stork. The stork and Papa Noël came at the same time. Papa Noël disappeared to my great chagrin. When I was told in answer to my repeated questioning that no, he did not exist, that parents place presents by the chimney, I had been quite saddened. As a consequence, I had not pursued the stork story. I knew at 15 that storks had no role, but did not inquire any further. Mothers suffered when one was born, I knew that, since my mother and all the aunts had often said how much they had suffered at the birth of their children, but the role of the father was quite unclear to me. Fathers were reported to be very happy at the birth of their children, and it seemed to me that the mothers, at some time or other, say when they were ready, or stoic enough to suffer, had children and the role of the man, who somehow received this gift, was to work hard and make money for his family. It is true that people often said "oh he has the eyes of his mother and the nose of his father" but I did not pay too much attention, first it did not seem factual to me, and second, I saw it as people trying to please my parents. As for erections and wet dreams, I had encountered this before, I think in Nice if not before and I had approached my father on the subject but he had dismissed it—saying it was normal but nothing more.

But now in Portugal, I was having more erections and more wet dreams. In Lisbon, I would often walk long distances on my own, walking the avenues and the main city park while having fantasies where I would fantasize that I walked barefoot, that I would meet interesting people who were also barefoot. Then I would begin to have an erection, and since I was wearing short pants (we French children wore short pants most of the time—certainly when it was warm and we wore golf pants (not knickers) in winter). Anyhow, an erection with short pants in the middle of the austere Portugal of Dictator Salazar was troublesome. You had to send a hand casually through the pocket and try to contain or redirect the trouble to reduce external visibility, but then you had real trouble walking and the friction generated by the new positioning made matters even worse.

In France, I had had hardly any contact with girls. In the family, Colette was much too young, Jenny too old. Girls more my age such as Sylvette, the daughter of Daisy, Josette, the daughter of Madame Akchoté, or Nicole Amon, I had not had much occasion to see since 1940. The Lycée after the sixième was boys only. There were Lycées de Filles for girls. At the Parc Imperial, we gathered every morning in the courtyard wearing a kind of physical exercise costume (short shorts, tank top, espadrilles) and we did some movements together and sang the Vichy hymn: "Maréchal, nous voilà, tu nous as donné l'espérance, Maréchal…."(Marshall, we are here, you gave us hope …) But the gym was boys only and while I could see their bodies, no ideas came to my mind, and probably none came to my cohorts as we never talked about a subject we did not know existed. I had male friends in Nice, Sylvain Lourié, Maurice Bellone, and somebody named Porcinet because

—

he was plump. We played, we ran, I once cut myself severely being pursued by Porcinet in the rue Rossini apartment by trying to shove open a glass door with my hand, and the glass cut deeply—but all this had no sexual awareness. With the boy scouts, we did a fair amount of camping and the atmosphere of the French Boy Scout movement under Pétain was devotion to traditional values, land, work, purity of thought. I did hear a dirty joke , I still remember (Mommy, what is that you have there? A brush my son. Oh that's why daddy washes his teeth with the maid's brush) but I do not think I understood it beyond the absurdity of the daddy doing something so stupid. It did not seem so funny to me, but if older kids found it funny, then I had learned to laugh with them. I really knew nothing about sex, and next to nothing about the differences between boys and girls. I had no idea what it was about. Erections seemed to be a difficulty boys had to live with, an unpractical aspect of the urinary track.

In Estoril, it was late June then, vacation time. I met on the beach a group of girls and boys—mostly English—and by then I could manage that language sufficiently so that I joined their group. We would play and swim. Later, we would all get together in a villa and they taught me to play poker so that we could play strip poker together. Now for reasons quite unclear to me, I found strip poker great fun. This business of having either boys or girls, or even myself having to remove clothes seemed a genial idea. Why? I do not think I knew why, but it was fun. We did not go beyond outer garments, but we managed to spend endless hours playing this game through July and August. Mind you, there was no kissing, at least I never saw any and never thought of it. Strip poker was a bit of my early fantasies of walking barefoot a bit of exhibitionism without any touching.

—

Relative to American children of that time, Western European adolescents were far less aware of sex. It is also my sense that the disruptions of the war had further retarded the process of discovery. The fears and the separations caused by the war had taken children away from their friends and potential explorers. I had had no young girl close by in Nice or in Portugal that I knew sufficiently well to do anything with. Our collective strip poker had its rules and sharp limitations. But it was a beginning.

The SS Serpa Pinto

In late August we returned to Lisbon. The SS Serpa Pinto, the flagship of the Compañia Colonial de Navigação was leaving Lisbon early in September to sail to Casablanca, Bermuda, La Habana, Veracruz, and would end in Miami, U. S. A. We would leave the ship in Veracruz. The Carassos would meet us there and take us to Mexico City.

Lucy had made so much trouble with the Jewish Philanthropy that we had a good cabin below deck in the first class section. Before leaving Lisbon, I walked with Lucy around the park where I had walked alone earlier when we had first arrived. Lucy was nervous, we were all getting worried about the crossing. Portugal was a neutral country and the ship should be allowed to proceed without difficulty, but errors were always possible and the big fear was the stray torpedo. Also, since these ships were known to be taking large numbers of Jews, would a Nazi submarine just sink it to deter further trips? By now Lucy was half sorry we had not left on the small ship, since we knew that one had arrived safely. She was quite pensive and she told me that "life was very strange, here we were on this earth and we did not really know why we were here

—

and what for."

The SS Serpa Pinto left in early September. Since most of the war traffic between the United States and England went north, we went due south toward Africa. At the time we left, Lucy was only 38 years old, Raffo, 51, and I was 15 .We were immigrating, me for the first time, my parents for the second.

There were two classes on the ship. We were on first with access to all of the main deck and the upper deck. Our cabins were at the next level down while the second class was crammed on the lower deck at the tail of the boat with their cabins below ours. In contrast, first class passengers had much space and I could always escape to the upper deck where I would spend time with the telegraph operator as I knew the Morse code and could even help him a bit.

The trip was to take about a month as we were taking a very long route south to Casablanca then back to Bermuda, then south to La Habana and finally west to Veracruz. We never had any contact with the second class passengers except in Bermuda when we visited the home of the governor. In first class most of the passengers were Jewish, but a few were not. Carlos Aruza who was a well known Mexican matador, was returning home after a series of bullfights in Spain (Aruza was nearly as well known as Manolete who was at that time the biggest name in fighting bulls). There were Jews from France, and Jews from the rest of Europe, but since many of the Jews from Poland, Hungary, Germany, and Austria had no money by the time they reached Portugal, most were in second class—those who had money had already left. In first class we had a large group of French speaking Jews, a few Sefarads—but most were French Jews. It also seemed that there were

—

many young couples, couples in their thirties, many younger still and without children. Madame Renée Müeller who remained a good friend of Lucy until her death, was a beautiful woman in her early 30's, traveling with her husband. There was a very young Sefarad couple, the Castros, she was very dark and vivacious, the Moutals were French, her name was Elise, and the Azouvi's were in machine tools, lived in Paris and had a son, Jean about my age. He now lives in Paris and my cousin Colette sees him from time to time. Everyone was young, very happy, slightly scared and therefore quite ready for a good time. There was a small orchestra on the first class section of the boat which played mournful music at lunch and tea time, but cheered up after dinner when there was dancing every night. The boat had a huge Portuguese flag painted on both sides of the ship—practically half the length of the ship and at night, the ship had all lights on plus illumination of the painted flags. The orchestra played at night and so fervently, I am sure they thought the noise they made would clearly tell the captain of any German U-Boat that this was a neutral ship.

For the first time, I realized these friends of my parents, I mean the women, particularly Mme Müeller, who was a large blonde and the small Madame Castro who always had a long smile when she looked at me; I realized that these women were pleasant to look at. I had had this experience briefly in Valberg where in the winter of 1941, Lucy and I had gone skiing. Valberg is just above Nice. Two young French women who had come alone had become friends with Lucy. They had met two men on the slopes and they had gone with them, only to return and tell Lucy about their adventures. They were probably in their early twenties, and wore the tight ski pants of the time. I realized I had liked them very much and had been sad to leave them, but neither at Valberg nor on the Serpa Pinto

—

was I aware why I liked them. Madame Castro would smile at me and I was embarrassed. This probably explains why I spent so much time in the telegraph office, or playing around the safety boats on the upper deck. At night I watched the dancing, but at the time, I did not know how to dance. Lucy would have me make a few steps, Madame Castro would smile. The wonderful, large Madame Müeller would dominate the floor and I would go to bed.

We went to Casablanca where we stopped while some stores were taken in. No one was allowed to leave the ship and no one had any desire to leave since Casablanca was under the control of the Vichy government (see the 1942 movie with Humphrey Bogart and Ingrid Bergman). There were some French police guarding our gangplank. I went to one who had boarded the ship and guarded at the top. I asked if he would mind terribly if I simply walked down, put both my feet on the ground and came right back up. That way, I explained, I would always be able to say that I had been to Casablanca or better still that I had been to Africa. In two or three minutes, I would add an entire continent to my travel repertoire—would he mind? No, he would not mind. He shouted to his colleague below that I was going down to set foot in Africa and coming right up… and this I did.

From Casablanca, we took a long southern route west to Bermuda, where we arrived toward the end of September, 1942. By the time we neared Bermuda, fears of torpedoes were dissipating. We were far enough from Europe that it seemed improbable that a German submarine that far from base would waste a torpedo on a noisy ship filled with happy Jews. We were to remain one week in Bermuda while the British searched the ship and reviewed our passports and visas. We were to be interviewed. Since the boat was going to Mexico and then to Miami, there was

—

fear that it might be used to transport spies pretending to be Jewish refugees.

When the British Navy boarded the ship, there was massive rejoicing. These were the first undefeated allied troops we had seen. As I remember, Madame Castro kissed some young sailors, we certainly were thanking them, there were a lot of effusive, spontaneous demonstrations of happiness at having crossed the lines of the war. We had left France occupied by the Germans; we had left the Spain of Generalissimo Franco, the Portugal of Salazar. We were in English waters, we were looking at English flags. We were with the allies again. We had to remain on ship during that week except one afternoon when all the children on board were invited to visit at the home of the Governor of Bermuda. This way I was able to add Bermuda to my list of places I visited. Buses took us to a garden party where we ate cake and had lemonade, spoke to kind English ladies and returned to the Serpa Pinto.

From Bermuda we sailed due west to the American coast, and then in full view of U. S. Naval forces, we sailed south, so that we could clearly see the American coast. In time, we were sighting Miami in the distance. By then it was the beginning of October. Mexico was coming closer and all the refugees who were going to Mexico, most of the first class passengers seemed to be bound for that final destination, were beginning to exchange stories about what they had heard. Rumors began to build up, how wild the country was, the Mexican revolution was still unfinished, rebel generals would come in small towns and force everyone to pay them money, how it was unsafe to drink any water anywhere, how doing business in Mexico was difficult because you had to pay up every government employee, how revolutionaries or communists were hidden in forests and would stop your car on the roads. Fear of

—

Nazi U-boats was replaced with fear of wild Mexicans with machetes.

We sailed south, and it became very warm—in fact, hot. We arrived in La Habana in Cuba. Here we did not even attempt to reach a pier. A few passengers were taken off in a small boat and a few Cubans boarded to go to Vera Cruz. It was dark when we arrived but we could see the port and the old tower. It was very hot during the night so we stayed up late waiting for the few Cubans to board. They came and we were amazed. We had never seen anything quite like it. They wore strange white shirts that hanged outside their pants. Every European man on board wore his shirt or tank top tucked in his pants. One wore pajamas that way, but not a shirt—and these shirts had little decorations, little buttons, also they were cut straight at the bottom. The men were dark, the women also seemed very flashy, they all spoke loudly. We were quite taken aback. As a group, the refugees, had very little experience of diversity, we were all very provincial in our European framework. Wearing a shirt outside one's pants seemed totally incongruous—we felt very uncomfortable.

Our ship left La Habana in the early morning and the next day, again in the early morning there was a cry from the upper deck: land, we see land. Indeed, many hours before we arrived in Vera Cruz, we could see the peak of the Orizaba mountain sticking out of the ocean. The sea was calm. The heat had abated, although it was still warm. The Orizaba stood a solitary distant guard in the flat middle of the ocean. That same evening on the fifth of October of 1942, we landed in the port of Vera Cruz. We had to wait until the next day to be able to go through the customs and immigration services. It was October 6. One day later it was Lucy's birthday. Awaiting us at the pier with a large Buick, a chauffeur and his wife stood Saul Carasso, the

—

man from Salonika who had made it possible for us to come. Lucy took one look at the pier, at the crowd waiting and said, "My, it is dirty." But we were happy—at least I was happy. We were in America. I had left Europe, gone to Africa, and now I was in America. This was America—I was looking at America. I thought it looked marvelous.

—

II

MEXICO IN THE 40'S

The American car looked immense, although it was a conventional four-door sedan that easily sat six people. It had an extra set of jump seats facing backwards. Lucy and I shared these, Raffo and Madame Carasso sat in the back seat and Monsieur Carasso went in front with the chauffeur. Saul Carasso had come to Mexico City at about the time Raffo had gone to Paris; he was also from Salonika and was several years older than Raffo. His wife was subdued in fact appeared to me to be just dull. Raffo had once lent him money in a tight pinch. Saul was repaying the favor with lots of interest. He had arranged to obtain our immigrant visas, and had come to fetch us in Vera Cruz, he would soon propose a business venture to Raffo that would solve our financial problems. He was a kind "Salonicien," the couple had no children, they had made their fortune in Mexico in the 20's and 30's, they owned an immense villa in Mexico City, he could talk business, a bit of politics, she did not talk. As immigrants to Mexico, they had retained many of the characteristics of the older generations of "Saloniciens," they reminded me of my grandfather and grandmother. He was serious, business like, but kind. The women were heavy, tired, ready for a little small talk and sleep. At least that was my impression. There was a huge cultural gap between these older generations and the Paris friends of my parents, Madame Akchoté, who was

—

vivacious and amusing, Madame Arpinée Pouljian, an American woman, who had married an Armenian, a very rich Armenian. She was very distinguished, dressed in haute-couture. She was the one who collected my early drawings (these were lost during the war) she was well-read, traveled a lot and represented for me the standard of elegance one should aspire to. Daisy Saurel, who became Daisy Jehiel, was a professional woman, a designer and was such a dynamic and inventive person. Again, these friends—more of my mother than my father—were living in totally different worlds than my grandparents or the Carassos. They had adapted and adopted French or American culture. Maïr and Oro, my grandparents, or Saul and his wife had not moved out of Salonika.

I felt French. We spoke French since Raffo knew no English. I did not identify with Salonika at all. First, because Raffo did not talk much about it, there was never any expressed desire to return, to see Salonika again. In fact, as far as I know, Raffo never went back to Salonika. He was naturalized to become French in 1932 because he wanted to be French. The Vichy government , after we left in 1942, canceled the naturalization of many Jews who had immigrated to France and acquired French citizenship after 1934 which explains in part why many more foreign born Jews were sent to gas chambers from France. Two-thirds of French Jews were saved, many hidden by French families. Raffo's only strong cultural tie to Salonika was food, the cooking he loved. But he also loved French food and a good many of the dishes we ate—say leg-of-lamb with lots of garlic, was more Provencal than Salonika. I therefore, arrived in Mexico with a strong French identity. I had with me very few objects, but I had a large white and black photograph of the Cathedral at Rheims—a picture taken of the façade with large gray clouds behind the towers which I would pin on a wall whenever I could

—

during the trip. Rheims was the Cathedral where Joan of Arc had come to crown the king of France. My last activity with the Éclaireurs de France (the French boy scouts) on May 1, 1942, had been to participate in Nice in a formal parade down the Avenue Jean Jaurès, to the Place Masséna in honor of that French Saint, since Jeanne's day in France is celebrated on May 1.

The Carasso's spoke French and Ladino, the old archaic Spanish the Sefarad Jews had brought to Salonika, but they obviously also spoke current Spanish since they had lived in Mexico for so long. Raffo spoke Ladino but had no trouble understanding Spanish. His intonation and pronunciation was off—there were many more "k" sounds in Ladino—some words he knew were really Turkish—but by and large he could manage. Neither Lucy nor I spoke Spanish.

Since the Carasso's had just come from Mexico City, they suggested we stay two or three days in Vera Cruz before climbing back to the high plateau. Lucy did not like Vera Cruz, nor did she like the hotel where we were to be housed. "If this was Mexico," she kept saying, "then this country was not much really." In 1942, Vera Cruz was a port city with low buildings spreading from the main square facing the ocean. The town is in the tierra caliente, the hot country, there was no air conditioning at the time, rooms in the hotel had large fans and the windows were screened. They tended to be dark, to be cooler and the general atmosphere was somewhat depressing. We did go one night to watch the "natives" dance in an open area where young couples, novios and novias were having a great time dancing to a band playing music from Veracruz. It was very spirited and colorful. Lucy admitted they danced well, but for the moment she was reserving about Mexico. I had the distinct feeling, that if she did not like

—

Mexico City when we got there, it would be the boat episode again except this time it would have to be another country—and it was not clear which one.

We left for Mexico City in the large black Buick, with the chauffeur, Monsieur Carasso in front, and the four of us behind. Some of our luggage was in the car, and the bigger cases were sent by train. They were sealed with wires to avoid pilfering. As soon as we began to climb, it became cooler and we had to buy wool socks on the road as our winter gear was in the cases on the train.

In Mexico City, the Carassos had reserved rooms at a pleasant hotel right on the Avenida Reforma. That did it. The avenue looked splendid, in 1942 the traffic was plausible and we were not too far from the statue of the "Angel." Lucy liked what she saw, Mexico City seemed to have elegant avenues, the rooms were large and gave on the Avenue. Okay, we would stay. Where could we have gone?

It took a few days to adjust to the altitude, since Mexico City is at 7,350 ft. In 1942 the population was nearly 2 million, but the number of cars was still small so that there was no air pollution to speak of. The views were splendid. One could easily see the snow capped Ixtaccihuatl (the white woman) and Popocatepetl (smoking mountain). While the hotel was pleasant it was also expensive. We would rent a furnished flat, while my parents looked for more permanent housing.

Saul Carasso had been approached to invest in a new business that would manufacture bathing suits and sweaters. At the time, Mexico was providing protective tariffs to new industries. This new firm had obtained the right to produce the "Catalina" designs for the Mexican and

Central American market. The new company would be called "Novelty Sales"S.A. It was given an American sounding name for the Mexican market. Mr. Carasso was proposing to invest in 33% of the business, he would lend half of his investment to Raffo so that he would have a 16 1/2% share, and the rest would be provided by a Mexican, Mr. Horacio Jacobs. He was a member of the Church of Christian Scientists, a man familiar with the United States. His mother was American; she was the one who had brought up her son in the Christian Science Church. The point of all this is that Raffo with Carasso's money would be on to something interesting.

Meanwhile Carasso also urged my parents to look and buy a house. The rental market was not too developed, and he would also lend the money for that. Raffo would be paid a salary while the business got started, when the business began to make money Raffo would gradually repay. It was their expectation that the business would do very well, since tariffs would be imposed on foreign competition, and the Mexican market would be theirs, or at least they would easily capture a large share of it. The plan was to repay the loan in five years if not before.

Within a few weeks, we had left the hotel on Reforma and moved to a rented flat in a two-story house on Avenida de los Insurgentes, between Avenida Coahuila and the Rio de la Piedad. This rio or river was active only during the rainy season and dry the rest of the year. It is now covered and has become a superhighway; the water is in pipes below. But in the early forties the rio was wide open. Insurgentes span it on a "puente", a wide bridge; wide enough to even have a bus stop. The rented flat had two bedrooms and a nondescript living room, it was in a modern construction in a neighborhood still filled with private houses with gardens. We had not been there more

—

than a week when late in the evening after we had finished dinner, we suddenly sensed something was wrong, the lamp hanging from the ceiling was starting to swing, there was a rumble, the house shook, dishes fell from shelves. I had no idea what was going on and Raffo said "earthquake" the shaking was already subsiding, and I was even pleasantly surprised. Lucy was slightly scared but it seemed over and we relaxed; now we knew that some force was able to shake the world, and one could be part of it. There was considerable noise outside. Every dog in the area was barking and we could hear people running in the street. After a while, the noise calmed down and we all went to bed. The next day we were to find out that a larger apartment house of the same vintage and general appearance as ours had collapsed several blocks from our new home. Apparently, several people had been in it and there had been casualties. We were in the land of volcanoes and, yes, earthquakes and violent death.

Since I did not know Spanish, I had two choices: The Lycée Franco-Mexicain de Mexico or the American School called The American School Foundation. My month at the Carcavellos School in Portugal had not been completely wasted, my English had improved, and the argument could be made that I had survived in an English school and might therefore survive in an American one. Lucy was in favor of the American School because she argued that I would then be able to go on and attend college in the United States. In 1942, it was not clear how long the war would last, and Lucy's argument was that I might not be able to continue my studies in France once I had completed the Lycée. Raffo did not see much point in these discussions, he thought that high school would be plenty. What mattered in his mind was acquiring the ability of doing business, and that was best acquired by experience—ergo, if I went to college or not, did not matter much to him. But he did emphasize, or at least recognize, the possible use of some professional training in the law or in engineering. Horacio Jacobs was talking of having his oldest son study textile engineering, and therefore one might study textile engineering and then invest and create some business manufacturing cloth. That seemed to him worthwhile. As for myself, I had no idea what all this implied. I simply assumed that I was a poor student and that once I completed high school, I would go to work, most probably with him. Meanwhile, I was not keen on returning to school. I had been doing very poorly that last year at the Lycée du Parc Imperial in Nice, I was fearful of having to transfer to an American school—what with language and cultural problems and I was also fearful of the Lycée Franco-Mexicain de Mexico given my performance in Nice.

Lucy took me to the American School to be interviewed by the superintendent, Henry L. Cain, and the principal, Paul V. Murray. The latter was a gregarious, jovial entrepreneur in education who seemed to like Lucy, decided with her that the son of an American woman who had gone to the Hunter College High School should also have a chance, and I was accepted. We never visited the French Lycée, Lucy was convinced I should go to the American School and that is where I went.

The American School was also located on Avenida de los Insurgentes, just below Avenida Coahuila, in Colonia Roma. It occupied an entire block, was fenced in with a high wall and gates and consisted of classroom buildings plus various sports fields. There was grass instead of the sharp little stones of the Lycée Buffon in Paris and this difference seemed to permeate every aspect of the school. First, it was a coed school. There were girls in classes, something I had not known in the French school since leaving the primary stream. But much more importantly, there were teachers who did not seem to be: 1) arrogant, 2) pleased to tell you how stupid you were, and 3) totally unavailable to help or talk to you. The French Lycée of the 1930's or 40's was dedicated to select the future elite's of France. It was highly competitive. Already a large proportion of the age cohort had been selected out and attended trade schools. Even in the Lycée the selection process continued. You either did well or sank. At the end of the last two years two terminal examinations, the first and second "Baccalauréat" or "Bachot" as they were commonly called, two difficult oral and written tests provided a final narrow passage into higher education. Therefore, the teachers seemed to operate on the premise that it was their duty to sink the riffraff. If you survived, then of course you had the right to claim access to higher education and to the prestigious positions in government. But a good proportion of the age cohort was expected to sink and thus find their way in the trades or in commerce or back to manual labor. In sharp contrast, the teachers at the American School seemed to think it was their duty to have you succeed. I had belonged to the riffraff in France, it was beyond my imagination that a teacher might take an interest in me, much less want to help me.

The American School had, in 1942, a very diverse student body. There were first of all the children of Americans living in Mexico City. These were by and large the children of American executives working for American subsidiaries in Mexico or the children of diplomats or of missionaries. Some of them had been in Mexico for years, others had just arrived from the States or from other countries. For example, Nancy Hatch, the daughter of a missionary who had worked in India had arrived in Mexico shortly before me. The next group included a variety of refugees, and Europeans who had come to Mexico before

–

the war or during the war and who for one reason or another were pursuing an American education. John von Mohr was the son of a Swiss doctor and had transferred to the American School—his parents had been in Mexico for a long time. Miroslava Stern, who was voted the prettiest girl of the class of 1943 was a refugee from Czechoslovakia, had beautiful blond hair, and was planning to go to college in the United States. Later she became a movie star. Ruth Zucker was Belgian and spoke five languages. Lastly, there was a group of Mexican students taking a special program combining a high school degree with the Mexican "segundaria" program, the Mexican high school leading to the "preparatoria" which leads to university admittance. Enrique Estrada, Gloria Padilla, Yolanda Esqueda were in this group, they tended to be the sons or daughters of wealthy Mexican families who wanted their children to complete a Mexican education while obtaining an American high school diploma to facilitate their continuing professional education in the United States.

In France, I had been a student with a foreign sounding name in a dominantly French classroom. Certainly in Paris and Pau, and in Nice I had been a "Parisian" in a classroom that was dominated by the "Niçois"—that is the kids from Nice who hated all foreigners including the refugees from Paris or elsewhere. In the American School in Mexico City, I was suddenly an equal member of a multicultural community where a "refugee from Europe" was someone "interesting". In 1942 both the United States and Mexico had joined the allies against Germany, Italy, and Japan, but the American or Mexican students at the American School were fortunate to be far from the war. So the European refugee contingent had a slight "aura" of having been in "danger." To be sure, this "aura" did not carry too much weight—say in comparison to playing football—but it was sufficient for

—

admission. The war seemed very distant from Mexico City and while we were aware of the importance of the American contribution, we, I mean the European students tended to be unaware of anything but the European and North African theater of war. In fact, my own awareness of the United States entry into the war had been filtered by the Vichy propaganda machine. We were still in Nice at the time of Pearl Harbor, and while we knew the United States had declared war, we knew not much more. But as soon as I started attending the American School in late October, I also became aware of the importance of the American involvement. In November 1942, the tide of World War II shifted with allied landings in North Africa. The Casablanca I had so recently "visited" was now no longer under Vichy control, and for the first time we realized that it might be possible to defeat Germany.

Lastly, I did better under the American curriculum because we followed fewer subjects at any one time. The French Lycée of the 30's and early 40's had us take all the subjects on a continuous basis. So we might have an hour of history, then some English, then algebra so that each week we went through all the subjects in the curriculum. In contrast, the American School had us take fewer subjects each semester, introducing new subjects or dropping others. The French system required a good memory and the ability to concentrate. My memory had always been my weak card, for example in recitation, I had huge trouble memorizing a poem or a portion of a Racine play, and in fact I do not think I ever managed, really. Today, I can only remember a few lines: "Oui c'est ton roi qui t'éveille"—or is it "Oui c'est Agamemnon, ton roi qui t'éveille"—anyhow two lines and nothing else. So I could never recall when asked to recall; that led me to the riffraff classification and the triage system came into action. In contrast, my cousins did well with their French education,

—

so I cannot generalize; all I can say is that I was "très étourdi" very distracted. I did much better where one could invent instead of relying on memory, and the American School was more accepting in this regard, than the Lycée.

As long as we were in the flat near Insurgentes, I could walk to the American School. But in December Lucy found and my parents bought a house in Colonia Navarte, a more recent development than Colonia Roma, at 27 Calle Oklahoma. This was also off the Avenida de los Insurgentes but further south, after the bridge over the Rio de la Piedad, and just after a small park. The house had a rose garden in front, a garage, and an inner tiny courtyard where the propane gas tanks sat. The house had two bedrooms upstairs, and the maid's room over the garage. At this point in time, Saul Carasso sold the first of a series of large black Buicks to Raffo. Saul Carasso bought himself the next one which he sold to Raffo several years later and thus, from 1942 to the late fifties, Raffo always drove large black Buicks that Saul Carasso sold at a low price.

A new life started. Lucy hired two maids (you needed two maids in a house because one did the more important work—some cooking and some cleaning. The other was the assistant and did such chores as waiting every morning at 7:00 at the corner of the street with all the other assistant maids of the immediate neighborhood for the "basura", the garbage collectors—the bassureros. Since the basureros were often late, the wait at the corner could take quite some time. Raffo drove the large black Buick into downtown Mexico City. At the beginning, Novelty Sales had their offices on the Avenida República de San Salvador about five long blocks from the Zocalo—the main square of Mexico City where the Cathedral faces the National Palace. He had a parking place on the street saved by a

—

"guardian" who also washed the car every day and made sure no one got close to the shining immense black Buick. At first he ate lunch near his work, but Raffo never even tried to like Mexican cooking. So as soon as the head maid had been trained to prepare dishes he liked, namely Salonika or French cooking plus pastas, he came home for lunch and went back in the afternoon, to return to dinner around 7:30 pm. At each return, the large black Buick would honk, the assistant maid would rush out to open the garden gate so the car could advance into the garden area. At night she would also open the garage door and the car would go into the garage. In the morning, Raffo left around 8:00 so that it mattered if the basureros were late, in which case the head maid would open and close the garage doors and garden gate. Now, you begin to sense why all middleclass Mexicans had the two maids. If my parents went out at night, the assistant maid stayed waiting until their return, running out when the honking Buick arrived.

I was given a black bicycle. In France I had had a beige Peugeot bicycle that was quite light—although I do not think ten speeds existed then—it had three speeds. The black bicycle was American and heavier. It had the brake in the pedals and you pushed backward to brake, something new to me. I did not like it nearly as much as my lovely Peugeot, but there was no alternative. I do not recall where it was obtained for it was not new. Saul Carasso did not ride bicycles, not did he have children, so it came from someone else. In 1942 or 1943 or 1944, there was no problem riding a bicycle down Avenida de los Insurgentes, up to the puente, down to the Glorieta of Insurgentes, and then a few more blocks to Avenida Coahuila and the American School. Cars were no problem, but dogs turned out to be. Sometime in 1943 as I was riding back from school, a dog ran after the bicycle barking. Usually I had no problems with dogs barking—they would run for a

—

while and soon enough give up. But this one was more aggressive, and he was trying to bite my leg, so I tried to kick the dog, which made the dog more determined to bite my leg, which he did, without much success—but enough to break skin. Unfortunately, I was not too sure which dog it was—I was very close to Oklahoma 27—but it was dusk. It could have been a neighbor's dog—and then, it might have been an unknown dog. As a result I had to get the injections against rabies. They took a very long time—I do not recall—but something like many injections over many weeks, and huge injections in the stomach area—anyhow, it was an ordeal. Luckily the Mexican Pasteur Institute that handled the rabies injections was—for a small compensation—willing to have the doctor come to Oklahoma 27 to perform.

If I did not ride the bicycle, I took buses. The buses tended to always be full and they did not always smell good inside—particularly when they were crowded. The smart thing to do was to hang outside the bus at the door, thus benefiting from fresh air and if the chap collecting fares was busy inside, I could sometimes manage to get all the way to the American School without paying. One would often have to catch the bus running because it was so full it did not stop at the bus stop. It would slow down enough to let traffic go by and to allow someone like me, to run along side, grab the handle and manage to join others with one foot on the step, the other in the air, hanging out of the door. The advantage of this position at the door was that if the ticket collector came close to the door when not too far from Ave. Coahuila, I could always jump out as the bus slowed sufficiently in the traffic. Luckily, Lucy knew nothing about these exercises.

One day on the bus, it was the middle of the day and this time I was inside sitting down because it was empty. This man was looking at me very intently and his expression was disturbing. Of course I had no idea what he wanted. He was sort of smiling at me and I did not like his smile, he made me uncomfortable. I must have been 16 then, and I do not think I knew anything about homosexuality. In fact, this will seem strange, but at that time I did not know—I still did not know what the sexual act consisted of. Therefore, it was way beyond my imagination to comprehend why an older man wearing a coat, a tie, and a hat would smile and look at me intently in a bus. As we reached the Puente of Insurgentes, I noticed a taxi waiting. The bus stopped, or slowed, and suddenly I got up, ran out, jumped, turned around and took the taxi. The taxi passed the bus, and I saw my man still sitting there looking annoyed.

My father rarely took the bus. But he did when the Buick was being repaired. This is the second story about the bridge of Avenida de los Insurgentes at the Rio de la Piedad. He was also sitting down on the bus; therefore it was a time when there was no rush. The seats on these buses are along the sides to give more room to people standing, so that more people can be packed in at rush hour. Windows were open and Raffo always wore a hat. So he sat with his back to the window. When the bus stopped at the bridge, someone outside jumped up, reached through the window, lifted the hat off his head and ran away with it. That was the only time my father or mother had anything stolen from them in the streets of Mexico. A few objects were lost or disappeared from the house. But by-and-large during the 25 or more years my parents lived in Mexico, they never suffered any robbery, mugging, or any of the problems that are so familiar today.

My parents quickly formed a group of friends. Some were from our month on the SS Serpa Pinto, for

—

example, the Azouvi's, the Moutal's, the Stossel's, or the Castro's. New friends tended to be other Jews already settled in Mexico. The Misrachis were from Salonika, had a book store and art gallery right in front of the Palacio de Bellas Artes, and they were representing the leading Mexican painters. Their son was making movies, and they had two daughters. One, Aline, was in my class and both were attending the American School. Léon Bejà and his wife Mathilde became very close friends, and through them, since Léon financed some Mexican movies, my parents and I became acquainted with the well-known Mexican movie star, Maria Félix at the time she was living with the song writer Agustin Lará. Leni Agostoni and her husband, Carlos were Italians, the Forcella's were French, Lulu Gutman was from Austria (?), the Henriquez were Jews from Portugal, Yvonne Legueux was French, Greta Ornstein was from Germany. It was an international, or at least a European group—mostly Jewish. Many good looking women, and men among them, all quite happy to get together, play bridge, enjoy an evening from time to time in a night club like the "Patio" where there would be dinner, a show, and the opportunity to dance. Since all of them had large houses with several servants, entertaining at home was frequent, consisting often of dinners followed by bridge tournaments and sometimes dancing with 78 rpm records, but this more rarely. They also would coordinate their vacations to be together, say in Acapulco or in Cuernavaca.

I first went to Acapulco in the winter of 1943, we stayed at the Hotel Las Hamacas on the Hornos Beach, my parents and a large group of friends were there. At one point there was a lot of excitement because dear Madame Castro came down without her husband. At the same time another man appeared and all the adults were talking about this "coincidence", but even if I gathered something was up, I did not know too well what was up. Another time, also at the Hotel Las Hamacas, in the afternoon there was a fairly severe earthquake, severe enough that I was running when it started and the shifting ground sent me tumbling in the grass in front of the Hotel. Luckily, there was no consequence on the ocean—no large wave to drown us all as the Hamacas was right at the beach. We did nothing. I recall my parents were playing bridge at the time. We did not know that earthquakes can sometime cause huge waves on the seashore.

The school term in Mexico followed or at least responded to the weather, namely that the best season for vacations at the beach is in the winter when Acapulco or Veracruz is less hot. Thus, the American School took a long vacation during the winter and a slightly shorter one during the summer that happens to be the rainy season in Mexico and is therefore less suited to travel out of the city. I therefore spent considerable time in Acapulco in those first years in Mexico, at a time when even nice hotels, such as the Hamacas were relatively inexpensive.

My parents did have a few Mexican friends, usually friends of friends, or friends of Horacio Jacobs, my father's partner. But by and large, they continued to live in Mexico as they had lived in France. My mother had a cabinet-maker who was conveniently located half a block from our house. She had him build studio arrangements in each bedroom in a style fashionable in France at the time—the bed slides into the built-in cabinet so that it can be a sofa during the day, built-in bookcases and cabinets surround the room. There were Chintz curtains for the windows. From our bedroom windows, we could see the two volcanoes covered with snow—the Popo and the Itza. Raphael, the cabinet-maker, also repaired cars, did plumbing, and electricity. The black Buicks went down the

—

street when they began to fail. The house was definitely European in terms of furnishing, nothing Mexican came in, well not quite. My parents went as far as purchasing a print of a Rivera painting from the Misrachi's—a print that shows a Mexican peasant woman with those large white flowers in a basket in front of her. There was almost never any Mexican food—Lucy and Raffo ate bolillos—a Spanish-style round bread, certainly no tortillas—the maids made and ate tortillas, we did not. Sometimes, maybe, we had a Mexican soup, but no refrito beans, my father had simply decided that Mexican food did not exist. Our sets of dishes were imported Bavarian-style. The foreign colony and the Mexican bourgeoisie seemed to prefer these ugly imports to the lovely Puebla Talavera ceramics. In short we lived in Mexico like true expatriates with very little if any contact with the very rich Mexican culture surrounding us. Of course, in due time, my parents did go to visit the pyramids at Teotihuacán, but I do not recall them ever visiting any other Mexican site. The visit at Teotihuacán was not their idea but was prompted by the visit of the Stewarts, the owners of the Catalina brand from Los Angeles, which Novelty Sales, S.A. was now manufacturing and selling in Mexico and Central America.

Bridge was the preferred activity of my father. He was a very good player and never did a week go by without at least one if not several games taking place either at our home or at friends. He went to Acapulco where, given the heat, he did more or less enter into the ocean, but did not swim. As soon as possible, he was back on a chaise lounge in the shade or better still, at a table near the beach with a bridge game in the cool shade. He was always in the shade as he could not stand direct exposure to the sun for any length of time.

The American School did not reveal Mexico to me,

—

but it did reveal the American culture of the time. My first task was to obtain long pants. On arrival in Mexico, I owned short pants which I wore in France during the warmer months, and golf pants which adolescents, not just children, wore in winter. Young boy children say to age 10 were in short pants winter and summer—but around 12, we went to golf length—namely a pant that attaches just below the knee, above the calf, and folds down to half way between the knee and the shoe. Well, they did not wear golf pants at the American School; neither did they wear short pants. I had to immediately obtain long pants. My next American experience took place right in front of the gate of the school where there was a small stand. I drank a Coca-cola and after that I drank a Pepsi-cola. I thought the drinks delightful, far more adventuresome than the benign "lemonade" I used to drink in France. Just looking at the shape of the Coca-cola bottle, I knew that it represented degrees of sophistication that my childhood in France had not prepared me for.

The greatest revelation was the girls. I was amazed by the demure, attractive way they moved. The girls I had vaguely known or seen in France—the girls my age were very much in the role of "girls that may still play with dolls and have little interest in boys." I mean they did not walk the way these American girls walked. In France, at least at the time I was there and within my age cohort, there had been no shifting of skirt from right to left and back, there was no hair flowing in the air, none of this "I know all" look. No painted lips, in short, they were girls, not young nubile women. French youth today is heavily influenced by American culture but this was not the case in 1942. My French girls or even the girls I had met on the beach at Estoril, were friends across a gender gap, they were not yet conscious of their potential role as woman versus man. But when Yvette de la Grave or Virginia Chaput came down

—

the hall wearing a skirt just above the knee, saddle shoes and bobby sock and their buttoned sweater and blouse, I was forced to stop and observe. I was further taken aback when I found that some girls and boys held hands while walking, and was told that they were going steady, all this was, as I said, evidence of the large advances of American culture over anything I had known in the old country.

In addition, I was immediately invited to parties. Given, as was the case for my parents, that most of the students at the high school lived in large houses with servants we also had parties every weekend, in fact often two, or even three. These parties were based on Coca-cola and 78 rpm dance music. They consisted in largish gatherings of boys and girls in a house where a parent might or might not be present but where the maids or the gardener had been strictly instructed to keep the liquor cabinet locked. There was no beer, nothing but soft drinks and food of one kind or another served around 10 pm. The living room would be cleared of furniture and we would dance from 8 to 11 more or less, when cars would begin to appear to repatriate every child home. The girls wore skirts, blouses, and sweaters, or dresses; the boys invariably wore jackets and ties. I learned to dance in a hurry. No classes were needed. There were no difficulties, girls were happy to show the new "Frenchy" how to move with the music, which I did holding the girl with one hand on her back and the other in hers. At the time, we jitter bugged, danced the fox trot and, since we were in Mexico, danced the rumba. I quickly discovered that if a boy and a girl liked each other, they might dance a slow fox trot cheek-to-cheek, head touching head, body pressed against body. Whoever was choosing the music to play often came back to slow fox trots—and as the hour advanced, the slow music dominated, as couples danced closer and closer. But that was the end of it. Rarely, one might catch a couple

—

known to be going steady kiss, or we might organize a game of spin the bottle where one had the right to kiss whoever the spinning bottle pointed to, but these kisses were mere brushing of the lips, a rapid contact quickly ended. The purpose of the parties—at least what I saw and experienced, was to dance, and we surely did dance during those years.

Not all the parties were that sedate. From time to time there was drinking. Either the liquor cabinet was poorly defended or beer was brought in, sometimes by older boys, brothers or sisters with dates. But I do not recall any drunkenness—some cigarettes might appear and a few puffs taken. The only serious trouble was conflicts with people crashing the party. Uninvited guests would surge suddenly in a large group, often coming from another party and forcing their way onto a crowded dance floor, asking our girls to dance with them and forcing us to defend them. Here, there were challenges, often with Mexican kids who would have heard of the party, come to crash it and were now inviting you to go outside "Para pelear" to fight. Some would claim, or might actually carry knives or even guns, but I never saw a knife come out or a gun pointed. It was more in the style: "Vamos afuera a pelear" lets' go outside to fight, and then the young man smiles arrogantly, opens his jacket and you may think you discern a gun handily tucked in his belt. Now he closes the jacket and repeats, "Vamos afuera," but meanwhile the gardener or the parents who came home, or the night guard who does the run of the streets at night, whistling every five minutes, has come to separate the combatants. The girl is liberated and we return to the slow fox for a few minutes more. Or the conflict would be "in house": one of the couples going steady is breaking up. She is dancing with someone else and he comes to reclaim her. He cuts in, that is, taps the other boy's shoulder and tells him to leave his

—

girl. The other boy pushes him away and this quickly results in a melee requiring several of the larger boys in the room. Football players served as police at these parties. They separate the fighters. Meanwhile, the girl has started dancing with a third boy.

Please do not get the impression that all our conflicts were with Mexican boys. Many of our classmates were Mexicans, they attended these parties and gave parties we attended. The conflicts were with other schools against which the American School played football. Those were the crashers, those were the source of a few difficult moments. A Mexican school with which we had played a game the previous Saturday was so incensed about an umpire's decision, that they came "en masse" the next Monday and tried to enter our school, luckily we had been tipped and the gates had been closed. There were hundreds of young men shouting in the street, throwing bottles at our windows. The bomberos (fire fighters) finally arrived and dispersed the attackers. But there were no guns, except possibly on the belt, in any case more a thought than actual, certainly very discreet.

My parents frequented some Mexicans, and as time passed, their friends became more varied. Many were French who by and large had many more ties with Mexicans than Americans or Jews tended to. French families, who had settled in Mexico some decades before, tended to inter-marry into Mexican families. There was an old and large French colony in Mexico, people mostly from the South of France, particularly the town of Barcelonette who had come in the 1890's and now owned all the department stores. We would go to the French Country Club for lunch on Sundays and I met several French boys and girls. One girl had a much younger brother who was clearly rather dark and I was told he was not the son of her

—

father but of the gardener at the French Country Club who was quite handsome. Apparently this was well known and somehow accepted.

At about that time in 1943, I was told that one of our classmates had done it with his girlfriend; or if not his girlfriend—with a woman. Done what?—I asked. We were just outside the main gate of the American School, across from the Coca-cola stand. Yes—done what? Well, he did it—you know…Well, I said I did not know. By then I was bored by all these allusions to something—what was the something? Well, the boy said, "you put your thing into her"—what? She has a hole—I was incredulous, it seemed patently absurd. The thought you would want to somehow place your private part into a woman who had some kind of additional cavity, made no sense at all. The only thought I had was that the nurse, a nurse, someone's nurse had told me, severely, eons of time ago, never to touch it—as it might fall if you did. So that was it? It was just too confusing and clearly uncalled for. Why might we be obliged to perform such a ridiculous act? And would it fall afterwards? And the boy said, as if he had penetrated many women, "it feels wonderful." I thought—how could it?

The next time we were in Acapulco, I joined French friends I had met at the Mexico City French Country Club. They had rented a villa, there was dancing every night. The girls were barefoot, they wore a sarong on their hips and a short sleeve blouse open and tied at the midriff. I danced well by then, and found many willing dancing partners. I danced cheek to cheek, I could feel the body of my partner, I could even feel my own surge of desire which obliged me to dance away from her as I was somehow ashamed. But I still could not see how one might do what I had been told one did. If my problem got too visible, I would go to the bathroom and wait until it calmed down. I knew of no other remedy for this unwanted display.

In school, I did well. I was not outstanding, but it was clear that I was learning English and doing better than average in other subjects. At first I had been placed in the sophomore class. The next year, toward the end of the first semester, Paul Murray, the principal, told me that I need not remain a junior, I would be allowed to graduate with the seniors; I would join the American School class of '44. For the first time in my life, I liked the teachers, particularly Gladys King, a young, rather good looking, bright, history and social science teacher. Wanda Johnson Montés, an American, married to a Mexican who also taught history, and Elizabeth Sheridan who taught English. I also had a good friend in Geneviève Duiret, the French teacher, although I did not take courses from her.

Lucy immediately went into a campaign to send me to college in the United States. She, herself, had gone to the United States earlier in that summer of 1943. She had no visa to go there since the visa had been denied by the U.S. Department of State in 1941 when we were still in Nice. Consequently, she traveled to New York and was able to enter the United States with her birth certificate. There she saw her sister Grace who had settled in New York after living for a while in Brazil. At first they lived at 115 Central Park West, later they moved into a large apartment at 88 Central Park West, essentially on the same side of the avenue where she and Lucy had lived as children. Renée was going or was going to go to college, therefore, Guy would go to college. After visiting her sister, Lucy went to Washington, D. C.; she went to the State Department and told whoever received her that she objected strongly to the denial of the visa, not to mention the loss of her American citizenship. She apparently gave

—

them a piece of her mind because when, many years later, I was cleared to work for the State Department, my clearance took some time and my boss Philip H. Coombs told me that it took time because my mother's file was so thick. In any case she was not arrested in 1943 although she took risks, and returned to Mexico City the same way she had left. American bureaucracy was more lenient in those days.

Which was the best college? Harvard. Therefore Guy would go to Harvard. Lucy had noticed that my American friends were taller than me. In France, I had tended to be of average height, but the American boys at the school were generally 3, even more inches taller. Lucy decided I should be taller. As if this was a requirement to be admitted to Harvard. This, of course, is easier said than done. Raffo was about 5'4", Lucy, probably 5'5". It looked like I would end in the same range. Dr. Becker, our physician, did not think much of Lucy's scheme, but he already understood my mother. He would recommend the best specialist on growth (glands and all that) in Mexico City, an American trained specialist with American diplomas on the wall, and see what happens. I dutifully went to the specialist who made a series of tests, took measurements, collected a large sum of money and informed Lucy and me that I was normal, and given the size of the parents, the child was doing as expected. It was too late for her to find a taller, more American husband.

Paul V. Murray, the principal, pointed out that Harvard did not automatically admit all the young geniuses that mothers discover among their only child. Well, he meant that, if he did not say it. As a precaution, he had us apply to four or five universities. Yale, Cornell, Princeton, I do not remember where else. He wrote the customary letters of recommendation. I do not think he thought I would be admitted to Harvard, but he was willing to try.

—

He was a good entrepreneur, and knew that the customer came first. Applications were sent.

Sometime in 1943, I attempted to go "steady" but this relationship rapidly deteriorated. In fact, we had only gone steady long enough to attend together the graduation prom dance of the class of '43. She was, I think, very shy and very unsure of herself. I was at my debut in human relations with someone my age. We had long moments of painful silence. I just did not know how to stand or sit. I would be suffering, wondering where my hands should be. It was painful for both of us, and she told me on our rare phone conversations that she thought it would be best if we did not continue to date. Our phone conversations were rare because in 1943 there were two phone companies in Mexico City: Erikson (Swedish), and Mexicana (American). She had Mexicana, and we had Erikson. To call her, I had to go to a public telephone stand. To arrange details of dates, or make last minute changes, we had to use another boy or girl blessed with a household with both phones.

After that, I had fallen head first (head over toe?), I mean I was "madly in love" with Fritzie Schiele, who was in the 8th grade when I first saw her, and whose older sister was already acting in movies. I had seen Fritzie in Acapulco with her sister, and I knew this was all one could desire: cars, boys and girls laughing, running here and there, dances, parties, the fast crowd of the time meaning also boats on which one could spend the day, out on Acapulco Bay, wearing bathing suits or shorts, drinking coca cola, rum… Fritzie knew vaguely that I existed. We never dated. It was just pain. She would appear on the steps of the school's staircase, and I would choke, my heart would beat madly. If only Fritzie would like me. But Fritzie and most of the dashing girls of the American

—

School liked the tall, strong, American, Nordic, football players. I was neither tall or blond, and worse still, I did not know where and when to move or place my hands when standing or sitting, and I suppose that Fritzie or Yvette, or Virginia, or Mariana Blago, and countless others could sense I had never properly kissed a girl, and probably would fumble.

So, early in 1944, I met Mercédes Lopez. Meche was dark, thin, and small. She went to a Mexican school for girls, she had a younger brother. She was my age—16. They lived in a small house in Colonia Roma, walking distance from the American School. Importantly, they had an Erikson telephone. We dated in the Mexican fashion of 1944. Nothing at night. We either walked together in the park with her brother in tow, or we went to the movies in the afternoon, paid her brother to sit far from us and held hands. Then we would go to her parent's house, I would be given chocolate to drink before dinner and go home. By the time I met her, I spoke enough Spanish to manage conversations. I think Meche spoke a little English. It was all very proper and decorous. Her parents were kind. I think her father had worked for the railroads or something, and had suffered an injury, so that he was on leave at home. Her brother was a pest. We must have dated once a week? I do not recall, except always paying her brother to sit downstairs while we held hands up in the balcony of the movie house. One day her parents invited me to join them the next Sunday. They were going outside Mexico City to a friend's house in the country, and we would have lunch there. So, the five of us went in their car, the still ailing father who drove, the mother, the brother, and Meche, and me. At the country house, it was decided to take a walk in the surrounding hillsides before lunch. Her parents, their friends, and the little brother led the way. Meche walked slower, and we trailed behind. We were climbing a hill,

—

and the parents and company had disappeared over the top. Meche was following the trail ahead of me. I had this urge to catch up with her. I walked by and passed her, turned around and took her in my arms, and tried to kiss her. But either Meche was scared, or she tripped on a root, in any case, she fell down, through my arms unto the ground and even rolled down the hill a bit. After that, we continued our path upward quite flustered. After that experience I began to think that kissing girls was indeed a very difficult task to accomplish. We continued dating, and holding hands after this failed attempt and while Meche continued to like me, I sensed I had broken the good image she had had of me, and she looked at me with sadness. Our dates continued but less frequently until I left for college in February 1945. I did see her again when I came to Mexico City for the summer vacation in 1946. After that, we lost touch. Much later in 1954 or 53, I saw her once in the street. By then I was married to Frances. She either did not see me, or did not want to see me.

On June 6, 1944 I was at the American School. I was in class. Suddenly, the French teacher, Geneviève Duiret, came running in and told me to leave the class and come with her. We went to her office. She had a radio. The allies were landing in Normandy. It was a Tuesday, and I joined her, several other European students and some teachers and we listened to preliminary reports in English telling us that the landings had started, that a narrow beachhead had been established. We were so overtaken, so exhilarated, some were crying. I can still see that room, the radio voice repeating the terse bulletin, everybody embracing. I think we had more emotion then, than when the English had boarded the SS Serpa Pinto. For the first time, it looked like the Nazis would lose the war.

Harvard and Cornell admitted me. I always said

—

that so few students were available—there was a war, remember. College students were drafted—that I made it because the pool of applicants was so small. "The Committee on Admissions is delighted to inform you…" With that letter we applied for a visa for me to enter the United States to begin my studies in the fall of 1944. The visa did not come, it was not denied, but it did not come. Washington was silent. I think I was relieved, Lucy was furious. Once again the American Government was misbehaving, it was too much. She called everyone she knew who might have influence somewhere. I am sure the American Consul in Mexico City prayed the visa would appear. Anyhow, Lucy contacted the legal firm that had advised her mother in the '20's, she wrote to Mr. Hoagland of Curtiss Mallet, et al, in New York City. They sent letters and became involved in the case. The visa was granted in the fall. By the time it arrived, Harvard's fall term was well underway. They suggested I begin in the spring of 1945 instead.

In the meantime, I was enrolled at Mexico City College, a new creation of Paul V. Murray. In fact it was a junior college and it had not yet been accredited. But there were college level classes and I took these with a number of other students. They were mostly graduates of the American School who for one reason or another had not gone, or not yet gone to study at Harvard or to whatever college they were applying or had applied to. Mexico City College was housed in the same building as the American School. I suppose there were no more than 20 or 30 students. I do recall taking a physics course with Jesse Vera, our high school professor. Either we did not study or Vera was a poor teacher (I recall he was a middle European with a terrible accent in English, I certainly had trouble understanding him). But the fact is that the entire class (maybe 8 or 9 of us?) was panicked when he announced

—

there would be a mid-term exam. We collectively decided we had to do something to avoid his flunking all of us. Vera had little sense of humor; he might even make it difficult for us to go to the Harvards, Cornells, etc. Two Mexican engineers were hired. Everyone paid a share of the fee. They were parked in a car just outside the school. It was possible to pass papers through a window in the men's lavatory. At the beginning of the exam, one of the students in the class left and passed the exam through the window to the consulting engineers. After half an hour someone else went to the lavatory and brought back the first answers, later another one until we had most of the answers to Vera's problems. These answers were then passed from desk to desk while Vera read the newspaper. We tried to miss one question each—and not the same one. All of us passed the course with success. Vera was beaming, we were good students after all.

I went out with a group of boys from the college, John von Mohr, the Swiss who had a house south of Cuernavaca on Lake Téquesquitengo. We did some hunting and swimming, his parents were doctors who had come to Mexico many years before. I killed my first duck, took it back to Mexico City, Lucy cooked it, and I ate it. It tasted wonderful. I was not a hunter but if wild ducks tasted so good I was not going to object to hunting from time to time. One day there were two girls with us on a little canoe. We killed what we thought was a duck but it was some other species that cannot be eaten. We were annoyed with this false duck and began tearing it apart throwing bloody parts, feathers, legs in every direction while screaming like wild North American Indians. I guess we were trying to impress the girls that we were fierce warriors. But it did not go farther. The girls were bored by our displays

In town we often went out together, 5 or 6 of us.

—

Someone would have a car and we would go dancing in the afternoon in dancing halls where there were "taxi girls". Women who worked at the club, danced with you as long as you paid their drinks which I assume were colored water. These women would dance real close and rub themselves against you. Much later in the evening, some members of the group would come back and pick up some of these women, but I did not participate in these debauches. One afternoon, we had gone just for one dance. One never stayed too long since the drinks were expensive. One of the women must have rubbed against one of our party just a bit too much, for he had had a "wet dream" while dancing. I remember being surprised: why would one have a dream dancing?

All my time was not spent in school or dancing. I had also joined the Scouts de México and was an active member. It is with the scouts that I met Mexican friends and was introduced to Mexican food and what little Mexican culture I absorbed. I learned to talk like a Mexican kid, slang and all except for a strong French accent. Once we drank "agua miel" the first fermentation before the production of Tequila. A sweeter taste, I recall. I went on several Mexican camping trips lasting a week or more, mostly in the mountains surrounding the Mexican plateau where Mexico City is located. What I remember of these experiences is cold, rain, mud, and very, very hot food in some little eating place on the closest highway to our camp site—where we retreated after our fire was drowned in torrential rain. I also went camping one summer with a Texan connected to the American School—camping is not right. First we stayed in a house in a village half way between Mexico City and Veracruz. It was terribly hot and we dragged painfully. The worst was that there were scorpions everywhere. We had to clear the rooms of their numerous incursions. But the scorpions returned before we went to sleep—there usually were ten or more per room. We did not find all of them, and more came in. They would climb the walls and proceed to traverse across the ceiling—somehow they did not do well once on the ceiling. The tail hanged down and if they took too big a step, the tail would vibrate; the scorpion would fall down to the floor —or on the bed. If you woke during the night, you immediately sent a flash of light to the ceiling to check on scorpion progress or lack of progress. We left the village and went instead to Alvarado, a small fishing village near Veracruz. There was not much activity in Alvarado at the time. We went to the beach, swam and ate fish soup, followed by fish, followed by more fish. But I have the memory of a sad little village, with empty streets with no colorful Mexican curios, but how good all that fish tasted. We loved Alvarado because there were no scorpions.

I had been corresponding with a "pen pal" in Hartford, Connecticut, and this correspondence had been going on for a year or so. When I was admitted to Harvard, the possibility of meeting my pen pal increased our rate of correspondence. She was, from a distance, an attractive person. I liked her letters and since Hartford was not too far from Cambridge, I felt reassured that I had this close contact where I was going. I was already making plans in my mind on how we might manage to go steady when we met.

I had tried to go steady. I wanted to accomplish this truly American relationship. I had understood that with Meche Lopez the relationship had been pre-novios. This should be contrasted to going steady, which in many cases ended after some months or years, although a few couples did seem to continue year after year, and even would ultimately marry. But, to be in the pre-novio stage, implied much more. It implied the expectation of becoming a

—

serious novio at which time, maybe kissing would seal the beginning of the courtship. Being a serious novio meant going to the movies maybe without her brother, announcing we were novios and waiting for that time when the boy would have finally acquired a beginning position in the world of work, sufficient to allow her family to negotiate the terms of a marriage agreement. Going steady seemed a better social arrangement to me. It implied the monogamy of dating. I thought that trying to make a date was just exhausting. You had to call her—assuming a connected phone was at hand—and then in as nonchalant voice as could be mustered—after a few inquiries about school work or recent trips—one asked, if by any chance, she thought of going to the so-and-so dance next weekend and would she want to go with me? Then, there was this silence, and finally the verdict would fall—no, sorry, I've already accepted to go with Peter, or John, or Fred. After which you had exhausted your first choice and you knew that every girl in school would know that you had called some one else first. When you did call someone else, she would seem resentful, and if it was an important dance, she would accept the white orchid with some kind of impatient movement, and as soon as you were on the dance floor, she would begin to look around and in due time, other boys would begin cutting in. All this was a lot of trouble. Going steady was an insurance scheme and girls who went steady only let very few close friends cut in (if at all) and in any case they always danced the last one with their steady, cheek-to-cheek, in a dreamy embrace. Two weeks later they could go steady with someone else, but for the time being the dating system had been simplified.

When I left for Cambridge, I had never successfully kissed a girl. But my father had finally decided to have a man-to-man chat with me. He realized that I would be far from home and Lucy must have prodded him to speak to

—

me. His lecture to me can be summarized as follows: Boys are attracted to girls that is natural. But, and this is the most important matter to consider, I must never, never do anything "personal" with a nice girl. The function of nice girls is to be nice. At some time in their life nice girls are married and they have children. He could not emphasize enough how important it was not to attempt anything "personal" with a nice girl. One might kiss a nice girl, but one had to stop right there. For the "personal" matters, there were many women around, he himself had enjoyed many of these other women (before his marriage—during?) but they were not nice girls. They were "artistes" or "des petites boniches" artists, small maids or waitresses in cafés, in other words, women of another social class who could be dispensed with. And heaven forbid if one did something with a nice girl, then there would be the terrible danger of getting her pregnant, and she would expect marriage. How could a freshman just entering Harvard marry since he, Raffo would be making all the sacrifices he could possibly make to send me to college? The negative consequences of doing something with a nice girl were so numerous that I had to understand that I never, never, was to do anything like it. Just do it, if you have to, but with a petite boniche or with an "artiste"—and even that can cause trouble because there is the danger of illness. He could say no more. I do not think he mentioned protective measures, much less explain the sex act. He had done his duty. It had not been easy.

This left me in the dark. Somehow I had an image: I was to go to the theater, watch the lovely actress, go to her changing room after the performance, give her the immense bouquet of flowers, sit in the chair with my spats, my cane, my top hat, and invite her to become my mistress, my "artist" mistress. And then what? You kissed, I knew that much.

—

In December 1944, Pierre Stassart, a Belgian
student who had graduated with me from the American
School, returned from college in the United States. We had
both applied to Harvard, but he had not gone there. I forgot
exactly why, in any case, he was back in town. His sister
Andrée, who was 3 or 4 years older had just finished
college, and was also in town. I must have seen them, and
they came one day to the house. Pierre was with his sister
and an American friend of hers from college who was
visiting Mexico for the first time. After a while, we put
some 78's on the turntable, and started dancing; Pierre with
the friend, and I with Andrée. Andrée was blond—a
Belgian blond. She was a very engaging young woman,
she danced well, wore a light dress, stockings, maybe she
was a bit taller. I had never met her before, and I was not
to meet her again. We talked while dancing, and the music
would stop, requiring new records. While talking, it
somehow came out that I had never kissed a girl. I
mentioned my hopes of going to Cambridge, my pen pal in
Hartford, and so on. It all must have been very pathetic to
the newly graduated college woman. In the next round
Andrée got closer to me, she had her hand on my neck
instead of my back, and I could tell that I was having my
usual "boy" problem. We danced slowly—Pierre and the
American girl, and Andrée and me. They were to leave
shortly. Andrée pressed herself closer to me, and as the
music ended, she took my face in her hands and began
kissing me, she pushed her tongue in my mouth, and
rotated her tongue against mine. Somewhere in the back of
my mind, something was telling me—this is a kiss, pay
attention, this is a kiss. Then Andrée moved back and said
thank you very much; laughing, she and her friend and her
brother, left. I had finally kissed, or been kissed. I could
leave for Cambridge. However fleeting the moment, I
realized, without knowing the words for it, that a rite de

—

passage had taken place. In fact, I did not know the word for the kiss either. Much later, I was told that this was a "French" kiss—how appropriate!

While I was dancing with taxi-girls, kissing my first woman, and copying answers during examinations, the allies reached Paris, and the French had liberated the city. Général de Gaulle had marched along the Champs Elysées on the 26th of August 1944, General Patton was moving toward Germany, the Russians were advancing on the Eastern Front, the allies had landed south of Rome, and letters were coming from France. We were again in touch with my uncle Maurice and we learned of deaths — my grandmother Benveniste had died (my grandmother, de Botton had also died in New York). My uncle Péppo and his wife Lilly had been arrested just before D-day, and deported to a concentration camp, Lucy's half sister Henriette, her husband and two children had been arrested in villages in the Jura where they were hiding and deported — Robert, her younger son was still alive. Should Lucy adopt him? He was a bit younger than me. We did not know exactly where he was. But Lucy had promised Henriette before leaving that if anything happened to them she would be responsible for her children. So many letters were written to find Robert and invite him to come to Mexico. Maurice wrote that Roland, son of Péppo and Lilly was alive and he was taking care of him. In those days we were not yet sure if any of those who were deported would not reappear. The full horror of the gas chambers was still unknown. We simply assumed that they were in a concentration camp somewhere in Germany, that they might be liberated when the war ended. By then, it was very clear that the war would end, that Germany was losing.

Meanwhile, we were preparing for my departure.

—

An old trunk had been obtained to pack everything I needed; sheets, towels, clothes. Harvard had sent a list. Grace, in New York was alerted that I did not own an overcoat, one would have to be bought when I arrived. The weather in Mexico City was much milder than in Boston or New York. Train tickets were purchased. I would go in Pullman from Mexico City, to St. Louis, Missouri, change trains there, and go to New York where I would stay with Grace for a week or so before leaving for Cambridge. The trip from New York to Boston would include a 3-hour lay over in Hartford, Connecticut so that I could meet with my pen pal. A lot of planning was taking place. Lucy decided that I should have my wisdom teeth removed before leaving. So one morning I had three wisdom teeth pulled out by our dentist — since they were nasty wisdom teeth growing side ways, the dentist who also taught at the National University, had some ten students to assist and watch. There were all these heads peering into my wide-open mouth.

In due time, I was ready. For the first time, I was leaving my parents for an extended length of time. Raffo was instructing me precisely: I was to study engineering. Engineering could be useful in business, yes, law could also be useful in business, but who knows where we might live in the coming years. The war would end and we might decide to return to France and what would I do with American Law in France? Engineering was a universal profession. An American engineer would probably be hired by a large European corporation — certainly after the war. Yes, I should study engineering. Well, yes, I like to draw — that is a nice passtime, but drawing or art has nothing to do with business. Business is how ones earn a living, I will want to marry someday, have children of my own, but meanwhile I should concentrate on preparing myself to know how to earn a living. My parents were

—

making huge sacrifices to send me to college, my father had never had the opportunities I was being given, he had learned to work just out of grade school. I will study engineering and if by any chance that turns out just to be too difficult or something, well I might see about architecture since I liked drawing, but at first, it had to be engineering. There was no point in his doing all this sacrifice if I did not study engineering.

At that time, my parents knew little about the social sciences — something like economics was not in their vocabulary. In France, as in Russia, engineers often occupied important positions in corporate management as contrasted to the role of lawyers in the U. S. hence the emphasis on studying engineering. I did not know better, either. I assumed that my parents knew. If they said I should study engineering, then that was it. I did not know there might be something called aptitude. I assumed that if my cousin Roger had always done better than me in school it was that he studied more, not that he had a better aptitude for the subjects and expectations of the French school system. Be that as it may, I understood that I would study engineering. I did not explain to Raffo that we had to hire engineers to pass Vera's physics course. But he would have pointed out that I did not study enough. I went to too many parties. Luckily, he did not know about the taxi-girls. If he was to make the sacrifice of sending me to Harvard, I had to be prepared to study hard, or else.

My sexual education was left for the future. There were no more allusions to "not doing it" with nice girls, and suggestions of the potential role of "boniches or artistes" But I had kissed — or more exactly, been kissed by Andrée Stassart, I now vaguely understood what "doing it" might mean or imply. After all, I had been told but since I had not liked the idea at the time, promising not to "do it" was

—

really not difficult.

    As I prepared to leave Mexico in early February 1945, I still thought of myself as French. I had a French passport, plus a photograph of De Gaulle and I still had my photograph of Rheims Cathedral to decorate my room at Harvard. My identity was evolving. I was known in school as "Frenchy". I did not play football — that is American football. The best way to explain this weakness was to assert that in France, we played soccer and that I was French, therefore not expected to play football — but presumably talented in the amorous arts — although dedicated to the cause of "not doing it" with nice girls. I danced well and gave a few good parties. Those were my main social assets. My religious stance was somewhat vague. When asked, I would answer that I did not know or that I was "Protestant" or "French Protestant" since I had been baptized in the Reformed Church of France. I saw no need to emphasize my being Jewish, having long learned how to urinate while masking my circumcision. Moreover, I had already discovered that in contrast to France, many non-Jewish boys were also circumcised — for health reasons, no less. Americans did it to be clean, so be it, clearly I was destined to be American! My view of Zionism was fairly negative. In the early forties, the Jewish community of Mexico was actively working for a Jewish homeland. I had attended some fund raisers — probably because Saul Carasso must have asked us to go. Lucy of course was strongly anti-Zionist, although she realized that many refugees from Nazi Germany had nowhere to go and that between being arrested by the Germans and going to Israel, going to Israel was preferable. But she did not think statehood would solve anything. She was bored by formal religion — or by churches as organized ways to be near God. Raffo was less sure. He saw himself as Jewish, Juif oriental as he would say. For him, a Jewish state in

—

Palestine made sense; it was a re-creation of Salonika, only bigger. As for myself, I was mostly guided by my preference for non-Jewish women. I argued that wars of religion and persecutions would continue as long as we did not recognize the universality of religions. I was for inter-marriage, Jews marrying non-Jews. There had been several Jewish girls around at the American High School who had liked me but I had not reciprocated. I was feeling emancipated by Andrée Stassart and my first kiss.

The tickets on the Pullman were purchased, and one day in February 1945, Lucy and Raffo took me to the railroad station to board the train to St. Louis — my first destination in the United States. There, I would transfer to a train going to New York City. I forget exactly how long it took from Mexico City to St. Louis — maybe 3 or even 4 days? At night one slept on the beds of the Pullman car, which were made by the Mexican porter after sunset. During the day, there was the dining car or the last car of the train where one could stand in the open. It was the dry season in Mexico — colder as we went north. At the US border, my student visa was accepted, my trunk inspected, and I finally entered the United States. In St. Louis, I changed trains and made sure the trunk went with me. I think I saw bathrooms that said "whites only", and others with the word "colored" at the door. I thought that was pretty stupid, but I went into the "whites only", although it was not self-evident to me since I was slightly pigmented. To the wars of religions, I was ready to add racial turmoil as another unnecessary human frailty — although I was not as attracted to black girls as I was to non-Jewish white girls.

At Grand Central Terminal in New York, my Aunt Grace and uncle Jacques Scialom were waiting for me. By then it was really cold, and I wore all the sweaters I owned.

—

We went to the apartment at 88 Central Park West. Renée was already at Mount Holyoke College. My new and young cousin Jimmy was in a playpen. The next day Grace took me to a department store to buy an overcoat. It was very cold — at least contrasted with Mexico City. I left for Cambridge one or two days after arrival. I think that Jacques took me to see his office downtown. I do not recall visiting any museums or skyscrapers. New York seemed a huge city compared to Mexico City, and I was looking at skyscrapers for the first time. My only reference was the Eiffel Tower. In the 40's there were no skyscrapers in Paris, or Pau, or Nice, or even in Mexico City. It was cold and people rushing out of the subway would collide into you and elbow their way around you. I cannot say I liked what little I saw of New York. My aunt seemed tired, less joyous than I had known her in Pau. My grandmother had died a few years before and my aunt's only preoccupation was Jimmy. Did Jimmy sleep, did he eat, did he smile? There was no other topic of conversation

The trunk was sent ahead, and I took the train to Boston — stopping for 2 1/2 hours in Hartford to meet my pen pal. I kept humming "our" song, "I'll be loving you always, with a love that's true, always . . ." We met at the station. I must have called her from New York to arrange how we would recognize each other. I had liked her voice on the phone. Now we were meeting. She was there with her mother, who had brought her. We would go to an ice cream fountain where her mother worked, to have lunch — sandwiches — and then we would return to the station so that I could catch the next train to Boston. Her mother was very kind, but I do not remember my pen pal. She was not what my imagination had concocted. She was smiling shyly, and not too good at conversation. We ate our turkey sandwiches, our ice creams, and off we went to the station. I said goodbye, she said goodbye — no one said to write to

—

me, I never heard from her, nor she from me. My pen pal did not survive our meeting.

In Boston I found my trunk, had it hauled to a taxi for Cambridge. The cab driver was Irish. I asked to go to Plympton Street in Cambridge. He left in a huff, drove what looked to me like long circles and finally arrived at Plympton Street where Adams House was located. There were doors that said Adams House on both sides of the street. The cab driver undid the trunk and let it slip onto the middle of the street. Plympton Street is rather narrow, so the trunk effectively blocked the traffic. He took his money, gave no change, and left leaving the trunk, suitcase, and the "to be" freshman right in the middle of the street — so much for Bostonian hospitality. It was cold but I wore the new overcoat. In due time someone helped me shove the trunk on the sidewalk. I was able to find the building superintendent who told me I was to go to the "D" entrance on the other side of the street. The trunk was shoved once more; some students appeared and gave me a hand. We managed to get the trunk into "D" entrance. I had to find the keys to my room — I was to move into D-23. Keys were finally produced, the trunk was lifted unto stairs and dumped in a largish room. There seemed to be no heat. I thought I heard mice scurrying around. (They were mice as I was to find out.) There were two bedrooms giving on the living room. It was designed for two students but three of us were assigned to D-23. Since I saw no one had arrived, I took one of the rooms and shoved the trunk into it.

I had arrived at Harvard for the spring term of 1945.

—

III

HARVARD COLLEGE

Harvard in 1945, was a university at war, much more at war than the rest of the country. You could sense it by the large number of men and women in uniform. There were many fewer incoming freshmen and the departments were depleted of younger faculty and graduate students. Many who might have gone to Harvard were being drafted out of high school or volunteered or opted to defer college until after the draft and the war ended. In addition, there was an influx of war related research while at the same time a flow from Cambridge to Washington where expertise was in demand. There was more awareness of the war at Harvard than I had sensed in Mexico or even during my brief stay in New York. In any case, there was much more concern, particularly among the incoming freshmen, many of whom were facing, sooner or later, a call from their draft board.

There are no fraternities or sororities at Harvard or at Radcliffe. In 1945 Radcliffe College also in Cambridge was the women's college affiliated with Harvard. Normally, the freshmen would first arrive and be housed in dormitories within the Yard, namely the older part of the campus. After one year they would choose or be assigned to a house. But in 1945 our small cohort of freshmen was sent directly to houses. The houses are located outside of

—

the Yard, between Massachusetts Avenue and the Charles River. They were built in a Neo-Georgian style with red brick and charming turrets. They are large housing complexes where students usually stay for the rest of their undergraduate years. The houses are therefore more democratic than fraternities or sororities because all students can be housed in any one of them. They are all more or less equal in terms of resources and facilities, and there is no social selection of students. They not only include undergraduates but also a sprinkling of proctors, usually young faculty who live among the students and a House Master who lives with his or her family in a suitable accommodation within the house complex. At the time, Adams House had the distinction of having an indoor swimming pool that had been used by Franklin D. Roosevelt. It also had a small library, a dining hall where one had to wear a tie (ties were available at the door if you had forgotten yours) and a dark room for photography. I think there was also a squash court, but I am not sure. The rooms were set by entrance (A, B, C, D) with one proctor per entrance, and consisted mostly of a "suite" with a living room with a fire place, a bathroom, and two adjoining small bedrooms large enough to contain a single bed and a desk. These rooms were cleaned by Irish women who were referred to as "biddies" — the Irish diminutive of the name Bridget — presumably because many of these cleaning women were named Biddy. The proctor, with or without wife, lived in one of the suites and was expected to provide intellectual enlightenment and assure that the rules of the House were observed. More serious control was exercised by a building superintendent who took care of everything — removing drunken students from hallways, repairing leaking faucets, changing electric fuses, and most important of all, making certain that no female was present within the living quarters after the curfew hour of 8 pm.

—

Prior to 1943 freshmen spent one year in the Yard before moving into a house, but in 1945 we were assigned directly to the two houses still operating, with the choice of moving to a different house at the end of our freshman year. I was assigned to Adams House, a more old fashioned and fastidious house than the more recent houses that are nearer the Charles River. One advantage of Adams was proximity to the Yard where most classes were held. One needs only cross from Plympton Street across Massachusetts Avenue to enter a small gate onto the Yard inscribed on the arch: "Enter to Grow in Wisdom." The other houses, Lowell, Kirkland, Leverett, Winthrop, and Dunster, are all closer to or on the Charles River. I always assumed that those of us who were assigned to Adams were perceived to be "distrait" — distracted — that is incapable of getting up and getting to class and therefore housed as close as possible to the Yard.

I arrived at the end of February and had a few days to become acclimated. Registration for the spring term was to take place on the first days of March 1945. Most of the students in my class, the class of 1948, had arrived in Cambridge either in July or in November of 1944. I had originally been admitted for the term beginning 4 November, but had to postpone due to the visa delay. I thought I would be the only "late" freshman of the class of 1948, but that was not the case. Because of the draft which continued well into 1946, Harvard was losing freshmen as fast as they were being admitted. Thus, admissions continued each term, and I was not alone. Of the 1150 freshmen who were admitted in July, November, and March, and who composed the original class of 1948, only 434 graduated in June of 1948. Most of the others graduated later, when they returned from the war.

. The college assigned an adviser to each freshman.

—

My adviser was a professor of music. He received me in good style, with a glass of sherry and was very jovial. When I mentioned that I was to study engineering, he was quick to tell me that he had no idea how I should go about it, but of course, wished me well. He said I might want to change adviser, if I wanted advice, but if I only wanted to chat and obtain his signature on my class lists, he would be delighted to remain in function. Thus, he remained, although I saw him rarely — usually leaving papers with his secretary to be signed and picked up later.

My first term required taking a course called English for foreigners. This, instead of the grueling English course required of all English speaking students. English for foreigners was given by a Greek man who, I assume, by virtue of being foreign had the credential to teach other foreigners. His accent was deplorable. Being cautious, I took a course in French Literature, one in Philosophy, and the corner stone of any engineering career: Calculus.

In Mexico, I had been able to avoid too much work, but at Harvard I was not going to survive if I did not plunge. I had to study. There was a huge amount to read, even for the Greek man, and then the dreadful calculus homework.

I also began to find my way into student social life. There were lots of freshmen dances advertised, and my roommate Baldwin and I would go in hope of meeting someone we might dance with. These dances tended to be attended by Cliff girls who had the reputation of being very intellectual. They supposedly wore glasses, and were not very pretty. Presumably one had to go out of Cambridge to find attractive, desirable college girls. Vassar girls were supposedly the most beautiful, rich, and fun for parties.

—

Smith girls were not as pretty or rich, but great fun. For those colleges a car or access to a car was essential. Closer to Cambridge there was Wellesley College, and I was told by some of the French students that Wellesley was my best bet. I should look for someone who dated there, and get a blind date. It was feasible on public transportation, although as in all other matters, a car was far preferable. On foot, there were only Cliff girls, but they were surrounded by men — not only from Harvard, but also MIT down river, and therefore in great demand. Townies, namely girls from Cambridge High did not count. They were stupid, would pronounce "Baston" and not "Booston", and their parents were around to create trouble if by chance something happened. Being cautious and clearly with no knowledge of how to get to Wellesley, I dated a Cliff girl I had met at a dance. But this did not get me very far. First, it was cold in March and April, and after a movie or a dance, taking a Cliff girl back on foot meant that you had to cross Harvard Square, go through or past the old cemetery and then finally reach the Radcliffe yard across from the Cambridge Common. By then we were both frozen, the girl had to check in and one could hardly ask or obtain a kiss.

Somehow I survived that first term obtaining 3 C's (satisfactory, remember) in English, French literature, and philosophy and a B (honor!) in calculus. With my two roommates we had sent a letter to the movie star Dianna Durbin asking for a photo, and she sent one signed "to the boys in D-23." I kept it because I had had the idea to send it in the first place.

I was to stay in Cambridge that summer since I had started one term late. I would not go to Mexico during the 2 or 3 weeks interval between the end of the spring semester and beginning of the special summer program, because the

—

trip was too long and too expensive. I arranged with the Boy Scouts of America in Cambridge to be a counselor at a camp in the state of New Hampshire, north of Laconia on Squam Lake. They were not going to pay me anything, but they would transport me there, house and feed me, and bring me back in time for the summer term.

We spent one week setting up the facilities, we erected tents, unfolded beds, and prepared the dining facility, it was a good deal of work. This was a boy scout camp and all the counselors were college students like me who were looking for inexpensive vacations. We had a little free time on the first weekend. We drove to a little town called Ashland where the high school was having a dance. I remember I was a huge success in Ashland, a college boy, and someone who could dance. In Ashland, in contrast to the Boston area, being French was an asset whereas in the dominant Irish culture of Boston or Cambridge, the fact that one was foreign provided grounds for suspicion, if not fear or hate. But in those parts of New Hampshire, Vermont or Maine, there were many French names, and while none of the girls I danced with spoke French, they thought I was a prince. I was not used to such a good reception.

The campers came and we did the usual camp things: hikes, swimming, boating, knots, games, fires, singing. The site was very beautiful : pine forest all around the periphery of the lake and in 1945 that lake was deserted, silence and dark woods surrounded us everywhere, there seemed to be no one else, there were no motor boats, no mobile campers, no radios, hard to believe today!

We were still at war and that explained in part how one could enjoy such pristine solitude. How a lake

—

surrounded by a forest of pine could be so mysterious, so dark in the evening light, how a canoe coming up in the dusk could make a plop, plop sound as it glided on the water. I think that it is at this camp in the summer of 1945 when I came to appreciate the North American landscape that I began to enjoy living in the U.S.A.

Boston was not a very friendly city, at least to someone who came from France and had become accustomed to the warm and fun atmosphere of Mexico City. Even on VE day, May 7, 1945, when the war in Europe ended toward the time of mid-term exams, I joined a group of European students. We decided we had a duty to abandon our studies and go downtown to the Boston Common. Presumably everyone would be in great spirits, we would join in the general rejoicing, and have a chance to kiss some girls. There were four or five of us, we reached the Common where indeed there were thousands of people singing, applauding, and dancing. As expected, there were groups of girls going around who would stop every serviceman and kiss them, and every serviceman did the same. But it did not work for us. We were not in uniform — we also looked foreign. The girls avoided us, we kept explaining we were Europeans that we were allies, but it did not work in Boston in 1945.

The food we received in the dining hall was a bland version of New England cooking. We ate lots of beets and lots of brown-looking pies. Chicken-a-la-king probably defines this cuisine, or Boston-baked beans with sausages. It was food, but no more. We had a somewhat white/brown/green diet, like white New England chowder, white bread, and white macaroni in cream sauce. Or we had brown stew, brown cake and spinach and some other greens cooked to death. There was no easy escape. The only good restaurant was Lock Ober in Boston, where you could get

—

an impressive cut of roast beef au jus, but Lock Ober was too expensive for our budgets. As far as I remember there were no French restaurants, you had to go to New York for that. Our only affordable escapes were a few Greek restaurants in Boston. There was nothing much in Cambridge, only a few drinking places such as Cronin's and Jim's that served large containers of beer, hamburgers and "French" fried potatoes. There was an expensive pastrami place. There were chain establishments like Horn and Hardart or Hayes-Bickfords who served the bland diet we obtained in the dining hall. Ultimately, I did find one small place where I could order undercooked (I had to be very specific about it being practically raw otherwise it came as shoe leather), calf liver with onions. Together with a cup of soup, vegetables, potatoes and a scoop of ice cream , the price was 75 cents.

But the camp on that lake felt different and I had a good time, not that the food was a great improvement, but the fresh air and my local popularity cheered me up.

The weekend I was to return to Cambridge coincided with the end of the first two weeks when many campers were returning home, their parents came to fetch them. It was therefore arranged that I would return with a young boy whose parents lived in Cambridge. That boy was probably 14 or 15, but it turned out that in addition to his parents, his sister had come to fetch him. She was just finishing high school — therefore about 17. We sat in the back, the sister between her brother and me, the parents in front. It was raining or late in the afternoon when we left, maybe it was cold; anyhow she asked that we put a blanket over us and as soon as the car started on the road, she held my hand under the blanket. I was quite pleased by this as I had found her good looking, and I therefore began caressing her arm, she responded by getting closer and we

—

were only ten minutes on the road that we had already exchanged a kiss. Meanwhile the parents were getting information about camp life from her brother and asking me about the camp; where I came from, what I was studying. I was kept busy while the sister was getting closer to me, her legs touching mine, her hand traveling up and down my front, her lips biting my ear. It got dark after a while, the parents tired of conversation, the brother dozed and the sister began kissing in earnest, this was more than I expected and I could feel that she was getting very excited, even to the point she took my hand in hers and guided me up her leg to her . . . . well, of course, in those days I was very ignorant about woman's anatomy, so my hand reached a hairy and wet area which surprised me because I did not quite understand why it was wet, but she insisted I keep it there, she rubbed herself against my hand while kissing me more passionately. I became concerned as she was agitating herself under the blanket. While it was dark, there were lights of oncoming cars. There was my camper, my Boy Scout camper on the other side of the seat who, I could not imagine, would not feel all the movement going on next to him, and just in front, still talking to each other, the parents were only 3 or 4 feet from their passionate daughter. For some this could be an additional thrill, the danger of this incongruous love making arrangement, but I was unprepared and not up to the task. Not to mention that I could hear the voice of my father, "You are not to do any such thing to "nice" girls". We returned to Cambridge, ending my best 3 weeks in the United States. As we parted, we exchanged names and she gave me her telephone number. I never called her.

That summer I was back with my Greek English for foreigners' teacher. I took an intro course in economics and one in math. I received one C and two B's. I also met Nancy Smith, who was studying at Tufts where Mr. and

—

Mrs. MacJannet of the MacJannet Camp at Talloires were now working, having left France during the war. Mr. MacJannet was an advisor at Tufts. The MacJannet's gave garden parties. They had asked me to come, as there were French students from Tufts, some French teachers, and Nancy Smith who was studying international diplomacy. Nancy was pleasant, we liked each other, and started dating. Nancy's mother had a summer house in Scituate, a beach town just south of Boston. We saw a lot of each other either at the MacJannets or very often at the house in Scituate; she had access to her mother's car.

The house was on the beach, it was used only in the summer, and closed in the winter. You could see the sand between the boards of the first floor rooms. Madame Smith mère would provide lunch and I would spend wonderful weekends at the end of that summer discussing literature or politics, and from time to time a kiss here and there. But with Nancy it was a rather platonic relationship, we were just friends.

Before the fall term, I went to New York to visit my Aunt Grace. One of the French teachers at Tufts, whom I had met at the MacJannets, had spent the summer at Tufts teaching, but lived with her French husband in New York, where they both held appointments in a local college. She was "old", that is, she was probably 30 or 35 to my 18 years. She had asked me to call when in New York, which I did. I found her interesting and very kind, and more importantly she had kept close touch with events in France and spoke with feeling of the life of the émigré to the United States and of the poetry of the French country side. She invited me to come around 11 am. for a talk and lunch. I arrived at her apartment where I found her alone. Her husband was gone for a few days. We talked, I asked about books I should read, about what was happening in France

—

now that the war had ended: life was very difficult, still, as the economy was in shambles but it was wonderful because it was France. She served me an omelet and salad, she hovered a bit around me, but I was intent on learning. She was so much older, so much more knowledgeable, so much above me intellectually, that I thought only of our conversation. As I prepared to leave after the lunch, she became sad. As we parted we shook hands as if I was her departing lover of many years called to serve in a dangerous mission abroad, she looked in my eyes for a long time and said very simply "alors au revoir". Once in the street I though: could it be? Did I miss something?

In the fall we sophomores could move to our permanent house. When I arrived at Harvard in early 1945, only two houses were operating with undergraduates; Adams and Lowell. But with the end of the war in Europe, many students who had served before finishing their undergraduate degrees were returning and the houses on the Charles River, Eliot, Leverett, and Dunster were being re-opened. One roommate promptly left for Eliot where he would room with friends. Baldwin remained with me in Adams, we moved to room C-35 on the other side of Plympton Street because it was in the main building where the library, dining hall, swimming pool, and photo dark room were located. Ultimately, Baldwin would move to Winthrop House also on the Charles, but I remained at Adams for the rest of my stay at the College.

Adams C-35 was on the third floor. We had a private apartment house in front of our window. One could observe the comings and goings of the inhabitants. An Asian couple was living in the apartment facing us. They would lower their shades in the evening and light up the room. But they left the shade one third up, probably to let more air in. We spent many late evenings waiting for the time when she would undress. We could only see her partially as she removed her dress and her panties. We felt it would be wonderful to live the way that unknown man did with a woman who would, every evening, remove her dress and panties and join him in bed. But we were mere students, we could hardly pay for a visit to a restaurant once or twice a month.

I took an engineering drawing course, a math course and a physics course (mechanics, heat, sound) and another economics course since I had done well in the summer without much effort. The engineering drawing course required a lot of home work: one performs endless projections on paper of an object seen from side, top or bottom. This was best done late at night. I had bought a Hallicrafter short wave radio so that I could hear news from France. I would work on my drawings until 3 or 4 in the morning, tuning into short wave, with my door closed while Baldwin slept, and I would catch London, Paris, or radio El Mundo RL1 in Buenos Aires. I had this wonderful sense of being linked with the world, while alone with my lamp and my tedious projections.

In one of my classes I met Francis Cahn; he was a freshman from France who had gone to Argentina before the war. He had attended the Collège Français in Buenos Aires. He spoke both French and Spanish. He roomed in Dunster with a Spaniard, José Ballester who also lived in Buenos Aires, and an American from St. Louis, Missouri, James Arthur Sevin. Later, we would remember, Francis and me that we had played together in Menthon St. Bernard in the 30's. Dunster is located on the Charles and is the last house of that row starting at the Anderson Bridge by the Weld Boat House. At Dunster, the House Master Clarence Haring, a professor of Latin American history and economics, was far warmer and bon-vivant than the rather

—

formal professor who had accepted, with his somewhat sad wife to be Master of Adams. So while Adams tended to be a serious place where few parties were organized, Dunster was a very different house where many weekend parties took place with dancing and dinner. Cars were available and these drove into Cambridge with radiant dates from far away colleges like Vassar, Smith, or Mount Holyoke. I did not wish to move from Adams because it was convenient to the yard. Instead, I became the fourth member of that trio, I had the advantage of both houses, often visiting Cahn, Ballester, and Sevin, going to the Dunster dance and eating at Dunster instead of Adams.

Jim Sevin had a car. He was the son of a very successful surgeon in St. Louis named Dr. Omar R. Sevin. He had come from St. Louis by road with his convertible. Both Sevin and Cahn were very keen on finding girls. They were like me in that respect, except far more experienced and practiced. Ballester did not join us. He was already going steady with Martha, and Martha, his novia from secondary school, was in Buenos Aires. Pepe only waited for Martha's letters, and he wrote to her continually. He was studying chemical engineering and he spent his four years at Harvard writing to Martha, receiving her letters which he kept very secretly in his room and he never showed us any of them. He married Martha after he returned and had many children, became an important businessman in Argentina. But Pepe was supportive of our efforts. He was to remain pure and aloof, he still wanted Jim, Francis, and me to succeed. Maybe he enjoyed the thought if not the action, but he helped when we organized room parties, preparing drinks, watching us dance, receiving and guiding guests.

We formed a group of expatriates, foreign students who spent time together. Some were at MIT down river.

—

Victor Sciaky also from the Collège Français of Buenos Aires would join us. We adopted Jim Sevin as a US ambassador to our foreign colony. We would take week end trips to the Cape or to Marblehead, buy cooked lobster for nothing at the beach, lit a bonfire and enjoy a few hours away from the text books.

Since Jim had a car, I had been in touch with my cousin Renée at Mount Holyoke in South Hadley, Massachusetts — about a 2-3 hour drive from Cambridge. I asked her to look for dates for us. At first nothing much happened. Meanwhile I had met at a dance, a young woman from New York named Leslie who was attending a small college or finishing school, north of Boston. She was Jewish, short, dark, very vivacious, elegant, and not the greatest mind in the world, but certainly fun on the dance floor, and fun when it came to kissing. That spring of 1946, I dated both Nancy Smith and Leslie who was very happy to find rides and come to Cambridge for dances. She would propose that I go to New York with her, but I did not have the kind of money she was able to spend, either on clothes or on travel. Moreover, her studies at her college did not seem to require too much of her time and attention so while she dated me, I knew she was very busy with other college boys. Yet I enjoyed her spirit, living life as a continual party — she was an antidote to any tendency to depression I might slip into. I went one weekend in March 1946 to her college, north of Boston, for a dance and slept in someone's room. It was sunny and the snow was thawing everywhere. We were outside on a patio drinking beer, a group of college girls and their dates, the winter was over, the sun warm, the spring was with us and we all sang together. And I thought that I was having a marvelous time and that I should like my friend, although I knew I found her shallow, too consumed by her passion for clothes, and what I thought to be superficial excitement.

—

I continued to see Nancy Smith, we were good friends, had long talks about our life's prospects. During the fall of '45 and spring of '46, we attended some lectures together, went to see how the house in Scituate was faring in the winter or went to movies. She was to graduate summer 1946 and was planning to go west to California.

In the fall of 1945, I managed only 3 C's in the science courses I was taking, and a B in economics. The sad part is that I had an innate affinity for economics, I obtained my B's with no effort, while the science and engineering courses took a heavy toll. But I did not really know one could make a living studying economics. My friends like Ballester, Cahn, or even Sevin were studying the hard sciences. Cahn was very slightly better than I in class, while Ballester, undisturbed by the pursuit of girls, plowed steadily in his chemistry.

I had also met at Adams another Belgian-Argentine, Claude Enrique Luis Pablo Dechamps also, like Cahn a graduate of the Collège Français of Buenos Aires, who was also studying engineering and taking many economics courses. In that culture it seemed to me that I had to study engineering, because my father had said so and evidently the fathers of Claude, Francis, and Pepe had instructed them similarly. Had I known better, I could have majored in economics, done very well and maybe gone directly to graduate school. Moreover, economics at Harvard in the late forties included towering men such as Hansen (the business cycle), Schumpeter (political economy), and Leontieff (input-output analysis). I did manage to take courses with Hansen and the elegant Schumpeter. But I could have done so much more with my Harvard education if I had paid less attention to my father and taken a plunge in a field that was just beginning to have considerable

—

influence in both private and governmental decision making. But I did not know, I was doing what was required, I did not invent a career for myself, not at that time..

Summer of 1946, I went back to Mexico City for a vacation. I did not attend the summer school. Since Jim Sevin was driving back to St. Louis at the end of classes, I left with him in the convertible. I would stay several days in St. Louis with his family where Jim was promising to introduce me to the most beautiful girls he knew — all his friends from high school. After my stay, I would board the direct train to Mexico City and get there in a few days.

We rode somewhat dangerously. Here we were in a convertible doing 80 miles an hour on straight two lane roads without air bags or even seat belts. But the roads, once we had left the eastern congestion, were quite empty, and we avoided the big cities aiming west and south through Pittsburgh, Dayton, Indianapolis, driving without stopping through the night and arriving exhausted the next day.

St. Louis was magical. Doctor Omar Sevin's house was large, made of brick, we would arrive just as the new strawberries appeared in the markets and Mrs. Edna Sevin would serve us huge helpings of strawberries and cream the likes of which did not seem to exist anywhere else. We would go for dinner to the Sevin's country club, and Jim was right, he knew and introduced me to the most beautiful girls I had seen in a long time and after 2 or 3 days in this paradise I hated to leave to return to Mexico. Jim would tell me over and over what a great country the United States was, how I should not think of returning to France or Mexico, how I should settle in the U.S. We would return from a dance at the country club, the convertible open in

—

the warm summer air, and as we went up and down little valleys in the dark, Jim would repeat, "this is a great country, Guy, you should come and live here…"

Mexico City : A Rite De Passage

My parents were at the Mexico City railroad station. I had not seen them for a year and four months, but they had not changed and I quickly rediscovered that I was a child living at home with his parents who wanted to know at what time he would come home and where he was going. But they were planning a trip to Europe, their first visit there since our departure in 1942. They wanted to go to Paris to reclaim our possessions that had been left in the Ave. du Général Détrie apartment. Madame Azouvi, our friend from the Serpa Pinto would supervise my stay alone in the house at Oklahoma 27.

Before their departure, my father decided to seriously take his responsibilities toward his only male son. In the tradition he knew, it was his responsibility to arrange for my sexual initiation. I was now 19 and still a virgin. He had spoken to his partner Horace who also had a son, Horacito about my age who needed the same rite de passage. An older boy, a cousin of Horacito was instructed to take us to a whorehouse so that we would understand what this activity was all about. Presumably the older cousin had some experience and he knew a "clean" whorehouse where one could bring these two novices and where the women would be kind and patient with our fumbling.

Thus, we went somewhere in town behind the Zocalo, entered an old colonial house, went in a rather dark room where three or four rather heavy women were sitting around without too many clothes on. The older cousin

—

assigned each of the novices to one of them and up we went to little bedrooms upstairs. My lady asked me if it was the first time, I sort of shook and said yes, she then instructed me to disrobe while she disappeared behind a screen. I had started to remove my shirt when she returned, naked and exclaimed how slow I was. She promptly undressed me, placed my clothes on a chair and asked me to lie down. For a short while, she massaged me here and there, but I felt cold and nervous. I did not like her nakedness or the general smell of the place. After a while she lay down near me and instructed me to climb on top of her which I did as told. She took hold of my penis, did some massaging and guided me into her. All this seemed quite unpleasant to me although it is true that I had an erection, but I felt I did not know this woman, she seemed older and tough. After a while all this seemed incongruous. After five or ten minutes she must have tired. She said that it was normal, I should not worry, first time boys often had no orgasm, that I should come back, meanwhile the session was over, I should get dressed, I could pay her now. I thanked her not knowing exactly whether this was good or bad and whether I should worry about something. I paid my 50 pesos.

I met Horacito and the cousin in the dark room, we left and drove directly to an empty lot between two buildings where the cousin instructed us to urinate so as to wash away any infection. Thus, he completed his duties and he drove each of us home.

I told the cousin what had happened or more exactly what had not happened. This was repeated to my father who immediately insisted on a prompt second try. He calculated that if I was not capable, therefore not capable of bringing grandchildren into their life, and more importantly a boy to carry on the name, then this would be matter for urgent medical attention. He did not want to leave for Europe with this doubt in mind. Dutifully Horacito and the cousin were mobilized again, this time the cousin said that I should choose the woman, someone I liked.

We went back to the same place — we were well received, like steady customers who are well known and well liked. My last woman came up to say how glad she was that I had come back to try again. The first time was always so difficult, she knew, "la primera vez, no se puede" but now it would be different. The cousin said that maybe I should try with someone else. She offered to help; with two of them working I could not go wrong could I? Somehow there was more jollity this time than the last, it was a bit like a second visit to the doctor, when one knows him or her a bit better, and one is better able to describe one's ailments. I looked around and chose a somewhat younger and slightly less corpulent woman who seemed to have a more dreamy expression and the three of us went up to the little bedroom. This time my manageress decided to undress me while the dreamy woman got ready behind the screen. I was laid down between the two of them and they massaged me, it was clear that they were not going to allow a failure, "viene, viene, pequeñito", they called for me to rise and of course they succeeded. This time I climbed on the dreamy girl, she guided me in and began her gyrations. Her companion meanwhile was satisfied she had done all she could for a good cause, "los dejo", I leave you she said and she left. While I waited, I thought it would be like the last time. But very soon, I felt different, there were currents awash, I did not know what to expect really but it was a blinding experience building up. In no time I had this sensational experience, I was awed by it, this was what it was about, I understood at last, I had had my first orgasm.

All this was duly reported first downstairs by the

—

dreamy girl who now took the role of the nurse who has saved a patient. "Con migo, este si puede", with me this one does it, she was telling everyone. All the women came up to congratulate me as if I had passed a difficult exam. The cousin was pleased, Horacio, his uncle would be pleased, so would my father. They had guaranteed future potency and generations of Benvenistes. Now all that was left to do with Horacito was to rush to the empty lot, line up and urinate.

My parents left for France a week or so after this episode. I was left in the house with the two maids. No parties, I was told. If there was any trouble, I was to call Madame Azouvi, the friend of my parents who had traveled with us on the Serpa Pinto.

I remember vaguely making an attempt to have the younger maid join me in my bedroom, but this did not go very far. She pretended not to understand me and I was far too shy to insist. In any case, my freedom at home did not lead to any wild parties for the simple reason that within a few days I had quite a fever. I called Madame Azouri, she came, and called the doctor. Dr. Becker said that I had typhoid, actually Para-typhoid A, a more benign form of this illness. Moreover, since I had had typhoid shots prior to coming back to Mexico, I would have an easy time of it. I would be in bed for several weeks and would be taking sulfa drugs that would make me very weak, he insisted there was no danger, no need to ask my parents to return and that I would be fit by the time I had to leave Mexico for Cambridge.

By the time my parents returned I was fine. Madame Azouri had kept me supplied with books. I had taken the sulfa drugs, had been very weak, but it was over in due time. When they arrived I had just about enough

—

time to go to a dance or two.

During that short window of time Raffo decided that I should learn to drive a car. I was 19 and of course I would not own a car until I had finished college and began to work, but meanwhile, I should learn how to drive. He gave me the lessons in the large black Buick he bought from Monsieur Carasso. Raphael, the garage man down the street was also asked to give me intensive driving lessons. In the 3 or 4 weeks remaining, I became quite capable to drive. Just before my departure for Cambridge, Raffo had me drive the black Buick to the "Desierto de los Leones" — a site just out of Mexico City — maybe 30 or 40 miles? It was a road in woods, climbing above Mexico City. Coming back at dusk at a turn, I saw and hit a pig running across the road. It was a horrible experience, pigs scream like people and the impact on the car gave a vivid feel what it meant to hit someone. After that experience, I was always a careful driver and never forgot hitting that pig in the Desierto de los Leones Raffo told me much later that he had been scared I would swerve too wide and crash the car, but I had not. The owner of the pig saw the accident, managed to remember the license plate number, was able to obtain my father's address and ask for compensation, which he obtained. But at the time, in the dusk I had not stopped, I did not want to stop. I had no idea what kind of reception we might receive if we did.

Back To Studies and Other Activities

In the fall I had to take chemistry, some math, a course on electricity, and I decided to take a philosophy course on logic, something about arguments, truth, and so on. I thought the chemistry course was the worst, the experiments took a huge amount of time and I could not remember all those compounds, how they combined, it was

—

too much for me. Pepe Ballester and Francis Cahn were taking it also — Ballester was good at it, so he helped us both. He did so well that I obtained a B in that course and C's in the three others, but I knew I could not do chemistry, and avoided taking too many such courses.

Nancy Smith had left Tufts, I had written her about my experience in the whore house in Mexico, but she was somewhere west, of no avail to me. My friend Leslie from the small college north of Boston was still around as she dashed back and forth to New York. I had told her I was no longer a virgin, and she seemed keen on seeing me. She called one week to say she would be in Boston that she was staying in a downtown hotel on her way back to her college from a week in New York. She had also told me she was quite serious about a friend of hers in New York, but still she would like to see me. What about meeting for lunch in Boston? I could pick her up at her hotel. Could I come early — about 11 am.? She wanted to talk, go to lunch, and leave early for her college.

I arrived, called from the lobby, she said she was not quite ready, could I come up to the room while she got ready. I found her in stockings, a blouse, no skirt doing her hair. She seemed quite happy to see me, happier than she had been on prior occasions. She kissed me, or I kissed her and very rapidly we were on the bed kissing with considerable intensity. But there was that voice of Raffo in the background: "never, never do that with a nice girl". In my mind "nice girls" did not want to do that unless they were married. What I had learned from the summer experience was that it was possible for the man to have an orgasm without penetration. That is, once I had had that first orgasm at the whorehouse, I had managed (age 19) to discover that I could induce the same, or at least a similar sensation by my own doing. This had led me to realize that

—

it was also possible, with a "nice girl" to do a lot of kissing and petting and my new theory was that a "responsible" boy could have an orgasm, but outside, thus saving the virginity of the "nice girl". I thought that "nice" girls would or should prefer this, since they were always the ones saying "please no", "please don't do that.

I knew there were girls who were known to be "nymphos". These girls wanted to make love although they were supposed to be "nice girls". Some "nymphos" would make love to two or three boys in succession as was the case of a Radcliffe girl who spent much time in a suite on another floor in the Adams "C" entrance. This Radcliffe girl would come to a pre-dinner, pre-dance room party with two other girls, as there were three boys in that suite. When the other two couples left for the dinner and dance downstairs, and girls were no longer allowed in our rooms, she stayed with her date. He had bought some food and one of his roommate's would manage to bring something from the dining hall so they would not go hungry. This would be a Saturday evening because there would not be any cleaning biddy the next morning. We were told that they would drink, eat what they could, and make love, so much love that the boy would be exhausted, even asleep when his roommates came back having delivered their dates to their dorms before their curfew. At this point, we were told, this nympho wanted more and the two roommates would oblige. She was finally satisfied and she would sleep until Sunday noon. She would be evacuated in the early afternoon when girls were again allowed to visit and it was safe for her to go down the stairs. She would pass the office of the house superintendent and return to her own dorm where, presumably, someone had signed her in the night before, when the doors of the woman's dorm were still open, before curfew time, when no one paid too much attention to who was still out. We would watch for her

—

departure when we knew she had stayed the night to see how she looked. My memory is that she looked tired but happy and still seemed a "nice girl".

It was not clear to me why "nymphos" had this sickness, for surely, it was a sickness. I thought, that girls liked kissing and petting, but that "doing it" was really a man's desire or need. We knew nothing about female sexuality, much less about the possibility of a woman having an orgasm. The sex thing was for men. Women suffered when men penetrated them. This difference was easily explained in Darwinian terms. Women had babies when men took them. Therefore, nature endowed men with a desire and pleasure to do so. But women did not need desire to be taken by a man. What they liked was the kissing, petting, but not much more. Penetration was painful to them. That was my theory at the time.

This was why "nice girls" waited until marriage to give up their virginity, why we had these messages "please not now, please no, please stop". It was known that given enough drinks, "nice girls" might let you go beyond, and the amount of kissing and petting was in proportion to the amount of drinking the girl took in. The strategy therefore, was to attempt to give the girl enough drinks before dinner so that she would be sufficiently smashed during the rest of the evening to allow more action. The rule among the girls was to drink no more and no less than the boys since a boy had to be sober enough in front of the proctors and the master of the house when they went to the dance. The boys could not get too drunk, and therefore rarely succeeded in getting college dates to drink too much, although some could hold their liquor better and girls were known to fail. In any case, I thought that girls did not want to be penetrated, period. At least not when not married. Maybe in time they could become used to the practice. I knew that

—

Madame Castro in Mexico had been very happy at the Hotel Hamacas with a lover, so maybe they did like it? When they were older? It was a confusing subject.

Boys who had cars and enough money to rent a hotel room for the weekend were in a different ballpark than mere foreign students, on foot, and with no money. Hotels of course were not free of problems. One was supposed to register as man and wife if one wanted to access a good hotel, or take two separate rooms (which meant double the money) and manage to go from one room to another. In the 1940's many hotels had someone at each floor in the evening hours making sure people went to their own room. Registering as man and wife could lead to legal and police problems. All this was out of the realm of the foreign student contingent.

This brings me back to my kissing Leslie in that hotel room around 11:30 am. when hotels did not check who went in what room. I did what I thought was right, that is I did not do more than come carefully in a hotel towel and to my utter surprise was given a verbal harangue I did not expect: What had I done? I had said I was not a virgin, why had I not taken her? Did I think she did not want to make love? I said meekly that I thought she wanted to protect her virginity — what virginity? What about children? She knew when she could do it — she was furious. I was clearly a drip, we had lunch and after that episode, she never answered my calls.

Somehow, that fall term, someone from Boston placed my name in the list of invitees for the cotillions and other social dances in Boston. I have no idea why I was selected. Benveniste was not perceived as Jewish and I guess it was assumed I came from good Latin American stock. Neither Ballester, Cahn nor Sevin were selected, but

—

I was.   This was a different dancing opportunity: the Boston society debutante milieu, all very proper and decorous with big bands hired for the occasion. The girl had a dance carnet in which she would write your name after you asked if you might dance with her as she stood with friends. Chaperones were not far away, elegant ladies, men in tuxedos. As a result of my attending three or four of these dances, I met a very agreeable pretty girl from Newton, who had a car, was alone and could take me back from downtown Boston to Adams House on her way home since Newton is west of Cambridge. She was studying at a finishing school. She lived in a huge mansion — with a very large garden. She was quite unassuming, curious to know a foreigner, very willing to drive me around and very happy to give me many of her dances at the various social parties where we would both be invited. All this would have lcd to a very pleasant relationship if I had not become a socialist.

I had become a "Late Sophomore". As I actively searched for truth, I came to the conclusion that the unequal distribution of wealth was clearly the greatest cause of mankind's unhappiness. This very nice Newton girl was willing to agree with me that unequal distribution of wealth was a problem. But she was not as ready as I was for her to reject her family or her large bedroom, much less her car which now took me back and forth to the never ending Boston cotillions. There is some kind of madness in youth, I may have been a theoretical socialist but it did not occur to me that I should ask the biddy to quit doing my bed or that I could tell my parents to stop sending me money. Yet I would make long speeches to this very friendly, well meaning, not stupid society girl, so many speeches that one day her father called me and asked me to leave his daughter alone.

—

After his call I was no longer invited to social dances, cotillions or debutante balls. My Boston social career had ended. We were in late November, Christmas was approaching and another good soul gave Ballester, Cahn's, and my name to the Cambridge Rotary Club. We were foreign students who would not be able to go to our homes for Christmas. The Rotary Club invited us to attend their monthly meetings and invited each of us to a Christmas dinner at a member's home. This was very well meaning but our experience at the monthly meetings told us to expect an utterly boring Christmas. Somehow Ballester managed to get out of his invitation. Francis Cahn and I were stuck. Cahn decided we should go away. We would go skiing in Vermont. I had done some skiing in France, we could rent skis in Cambridge and arrange our Christmas in Woodstock, Vermont. We escaped the Rotary Club kindness without hurting anyone's feelings.

Going Steady

Spring 1947 found me dateless, or without a girlfriend. This was doubly painful as I was about to turn 20, no longer in my teens. Nancy Smith had left the area. Leslie had given up on me and now I had been told to leave the Newton girl alone. So, I was in a quandary. Luckily my cousin Renée who was at Mount Holyoke came to the rescue. As it turned out, at about that time Jim Sevin found himself in a similar predicament. When he heard I had a cousin at Mount Holyoke, he suggested I call her again to see if she could arrange blind dates for the three of us. Francis, Jim and I would drive to South Hadley and attend a party at Renée's house. Dates were arranged with two girls who lived with Renée in what was called the French House — namely a house where all the girls were studying French — and where French was used during meals and where I met Betty Hall. In exchange I arranged a blind date

—

for Renée with Francis Cahn. That relationship did not
continue but Jim liked his date, I liked Betty, she seemed to
like me and from then on we began double dating. In fact
Betty and I continued dating until our graduation in June of
1948 and I saw her again that fall when I attended the
Wharton School of Commerce and Finance at the
University of Pennsylvania, as she was then living at home
in the outskirts of Philadelphia.

Betty was the daughter of a Navy officer. She was
by all definitions a "very nice proper girl" who liked to
dance, discuss books, speak French, and would say "please
do not do that, please stop" at all the proper times and
places. Actually, we were very close, had similar tastes —
maybe Betty was less of a socialist, but she was keen on
new ideas and we had many good times together, her
background was certainly more severe or rigid than mine.
Yet, we saw each other quite often, studies, classes, and
exams permitting. Most of the time Jim Sevin and I would
drive to Mount Holyoke, but Betty would also come to
Cambridge, and in fact in December of 1947 she would
also come with Francis Cahn and me to ski in Woodstock,
Vermont. During all of that time, we had a "proper"
relationship. We kissed, if I went further, she said "please
stop", I did and later took care to release energy in solitude.
But I liked going steady, one did not have to worry about
who to invite when big dances were announced.

Also Betty at Mount Holyoke was conveniently far
enough away to leave plenty of time for studies. That
spring, I was taking five courses instead of four, to catch
up. I had arrived at Harvard one term late and taken three
courses during the summer of 1945, I had to take one extra
course to reach the 32 courses needed to graduate in June
of 1948. I was stuck with chemistry, two courses of
Physics (atomic and electricity) a course in math, and one

—

on statistics. Yet that term, thanks to my healthy friend Betty, I managed two B's and three C's. Similarly in the fall of 1947, my senior year, I again took five courses — two in physics, two in economics, and one French and again made three C's and two B's — so Betty was a good influence. I had taken five courses as a guarantee on the advice of Francis Cahn. He figured since he and I might flunk a course, it would be desirable to enroll in one extra course so as to allow us to fail one and still have the 32 units needed to graduate.

The summer of 1947 was a repetition of 1946. I returned to Mexico City via St. Louis courtesy of Jim Sevin. Betty went home to Philadelphia. We parted, promised to write each other, promised to see each other in the fall. Jim drove at 80 miles an hour — we arrived in St. Louis, we were well received by Omar and Edna Sevin, ate strawberries (it was early June) — saw the gorgeous young women at the Country Club, and I left for Mexico City.

Prior to our departure from Cambridge — we left on June 6 or 7, arriving in St. Louis on the 8th or 9th , the entire student body was mobilized to go, on June 5 to the Harvard stadium to hear the Secretary of State, George C. Marshall make a major speech at the graduation of the class of '47. He told us that the problems of the post war were of enormous complexity, few understood there were not enough goods in Europe to allow the rebuilding from the devastation of war. Disturbances were possible and dangerous, people were desperate. The policy implications for the United States should be apparent to all. We had to help so as to permit the emergence of the social and political conditions necessary for free institutions. Without US assistance, what was to be called the Marshall Plan, Western Europe might go communist. It was night when Marshall made his speech, Francis Cahn and I, were

—

impressed. We thought that with U.S. aid, Europe would prosper and we would be able to return, so we thanked the closest US representative on hand: Jim Sevin. We thanked him as we left the stadium with thousands of other students and dignitaries.

Mexico And Acapulco Beaches

It was vacation time again. In Mexico City I had met the cultural attaché at the American Embassy — a very young man in his twenties, married — I think he was a writer. Through him, I met a painter and a young woman my age from Venice, California who lived in a maid's room on the "azotea", the roof of an apartment building. Her name was Annie Ludlum. She was trying to write and was madly in love with an Englishman — another painter? He did not care much for her, and would disappear for several days, he would not call her. All this meant I was someone available, to visit her and try to hold her hand while she cried, but I was no substitute for the handsome tall, blond Englishman. Yet I envied her, or I envied her freedom. She did not have to be home at precisely 12:30 for lunch and at 7 o'clock for dinner. She did not have to explain to her parents what she was doing all day, not to mention she could make love right there in her small maid's room anytime she wanted even if she did not want anything from me but sympathy. I longed for independence, for being on my own. I felt it was so unfair that at Harvard I had so much studying to do that I was never really free. Now, here I was in Mexico with lots of time on my hands and I was obliged to fall into the daily routine of my parents. And there was this girl from Venice, California who received some money from home, lived this romantic life on a roof top in Mexico City with the sun, the maid's shower and this even more independent Englishman who came and went as he saw fit. These people were

—

living — but I had no idea what to do about it.

The cultural attaché told me about a group from Ohio State — boys and girls who were in Mexico City for the summer school at the National University. He introduced me to the young man who had brought them to Mexico who suggested I follow some of the classes on Mexican culture. I did and I met Joan Butler from Cincinnati. We began dating. We would go dancing in the afternoon at a club not far from the university summer school. At Lucy's suggestion, I invited her several times for lunch at the house. Joan smoked, and Lucy who did not smoke at the time tried some puffs from Joan, liked it and began smoking from that time onward. She always blamed Joan Buttler for that habit. Lucy was 43 in the summer of 1947 — her smoking lasted 46 years until her death at 89, yet it never seemed to affect her lungs.

When summer school ended, the director of the Ohio group asked if I wanted to join them for ten days in Acapulco. They were going by bus — the bus fare was small and they were staying at a hotel on the Caletta Beach where each of us would be charged six pesos per day, food included. At the time the dollar was at 4.85 pesos — so this was about $1.25 per day for a bed and three meals. Lucy agreed and I left for Acapulco. The hotel was right above the Caletta Beach — it was an old hotel with little rooms that gave on long corridors but without doors. A simple curtain served as a door and guaranteed privacy — the bathrooms were down the hall. It was replaced later by a much larger modern facility. At that time, 1947, meals were served in a large "comedor" an open dining area on a sheltered terrace overlooking the beach. The menu was simple — fish, fish, fish and rice or beans. The weather was hot, the water warm and Joan and I would kiss in the moonlight halfway into the dark water and then run back to

—

the hotel to change and eat our fish in the balmy air and evening lights covered by buzzing insects.

We kissed, we would lie on the bed in our bathing suits and be very excited but always stopped short of intercourse. Ten days in this hot house, with daily swimming, walking, eating fish, pulling the curtain to see if she was asleep did make me realize that while I liked Betty Hall, I also liked Joan Buttler. She was leaner than Betty, probably a less "nice girl" in that she did not come from a very strict Navy background. She obviously liked me, but it was also clear that Ohio State was too far from Harvard and just like I had Betty at Mount Holyoke, she had a steady back at Ohio State — our relationship was to be short-lived. There were vague thoughts that I might come for the big dance at Ohio State in the fall — but I would have to be sure not to tell anyone of my Jewish background. In her sorority one did not date Jews. I never went to Ohio State. Later, I wrote Joan that while I did not practice the Jewish religion, there was no way I could hide where I came from. Thus her main contribution was to teach Lucy how to smoke — and make me aware that some antisemitism was still lively in the USA.

Harvard Zen

Back at Harvard that fall, I dated Betty, except out dates were limited by distance, classes, and weekend activities that kept us apart. I met a nurse from one of the big downtown Boston hospitals. This turned out to become a platonic, poetic and philosophical relationship. Maybe we met at a lecture I attended? The fact is that we were both interested in mysticism — revelation, the sudden flash of intuition that makes you understand the immense beauty of the world — that flash of recognition that one experiences very rarely — what the Japanese Zen

—

practitioners call "satori." I have no idea how it came to be that this slightly older nurse, working in the operating room of Peter Bent Brigham Hospital came to discuss this topic with me. It happened rapidly — by this I mean that we met and immediately began talking intensely about our life, our experiences when we had felt something much bigger around us. We talked a lot about ourselves, revealed much to each other and immediately established a closeness I really did not have with Betty Hall. In two weeks I knew more about this nurse than I knew about Betty, she was much closer to me, more like a sister or certainly a friend. But while we were not particularly sexually engaged — although we did kiss — we were more than friends or even sister-brother. There was a closeness to our conversations that I had never experienced with anyone before — here, there was no need to kiss because we seemed to kiss with words. But the relationship did not last. I do not recall why it ended — either she left Boston for a better paying job in another city — or did she have someone she was supposed to marry? I know that we were separated by events that had nothing to do with our intense discussions. She did give me a copy of *Le Petit Prince* by Saint Exupéry — I forgot what I gave her, and we parted promising to keep in touch. Maybe we wrote each other for a while and then I lost track of her. All I know is her first name — Marilyn.

I had the great Professor Joseph Schumpeter teaching Econ 61, the Economics of Socialism and Capitalism. It was an experience in elegance. Schumpeter wore gray suits, a gray hat and gray spats on his shoes. He often used a cane, more as a part of his costume for he would remove the hat and place it with the cane on a chair and start lecturing standing in front of the packed classroom. This, in contrast to another economist of great renown Alvin Hansen with whom I took Econ 45, the

Banking System. Where Schumpeter talked in a loud heavily accented Viennese style, Alvin Hansen sat behind a desk in shirt sleeves with a green shade on his forehead. Schumpeter was the man of the conference, of the large ministries while Alvin Hansen was the clerk at his desk pushing fact after fact. The great Schumpeter was only pleased to allow me to take my final exam in French and he gave me a B while Alvin Hansen could only find a C for my efforts. Yet that term ended with my obtaining two B's and three C's. Clearly, a gentleman's grades, and I thought I should always try to be as elegant as Professor Schumpeter, but unfortunately no one wore spats, even in 1947. Schumpeter wore the suits of 1930 or even the 1920's. The spats looked so good as they covered the sides of his shoes and part of the front, linking his shoes to his suit and hat, all in perfect gray with a gray tie and a large pin to hold everything together.

The winter of 1947 was dreadfully cold, too cold to snow. Going to classes was painful. After a few minutes outside, even with the heaviest overcoat, sweaters, earmuffs, and wool scarf, my face still ached and I would run into buildings to warm up and venture out again. We, the Latin American cohort, were not quite ready for that kind of weather.

A good friend of Betty, I had met at the French House at Mount Holyoke spoke of going to California for the vacations. She had a contact with someone close to Aldous Huxley. She had been invited to go to California to be with Huxley, She suggested we go with her. It would be warm; we would be in the desert. It would be some kind of encampment at Huxley's house in Llana in Southern California, not far from Palmdale. It would be romantic, Huxley would be around, and we would discuss books and ideas. I had read several of his works including Antic Hay,

—

Point Counter Point and Brave New World. The thought of warm climes, books, ideas, in the desert of California on the other side of the continent was appealing to say the least. I knew the East Coast but had heard about the distant California, where people were more relaxed, open and welcoming. But there was no way we could join her. I simply could not afford the flight to Los Angeles and Betty was not that interested.

Pepe Ballester and I had been selling programs at the football games and I had been able to save enough to contemplate going skiing again in Vermont during the Christmas holiday. Since we could not join Aldous Huxley in Llana, Betty agreed to go with me and Francis Cahn. She came to Boston and the three of us rode on the train to Woodstock, Vermont. Woodstock in 1947 was not the large scale resort it is today. It was still a quaint New England village — mostly white with some red barns. We had rented two rooms in a bed and breakfast place — although I do not recall they were called bed and breakfast — maybe it was just called staying in private houses. It was all very proper, Betty slept in one room and Francis and I in the other. We went skiing, using rope tows that did not cost much, we found a lady in town who had chickens. Given the cold and exercise on the slopes, we decided to eat a raw egg every morning. We bought three eggs (one for each of us). We would suck the content in one clean swoop. We only bought one egg per person because none of us really liked the raw egg although each claimed it was stunning and that we felt so much better after eating it. We thought the egg was our miniscule substitute for California.

Spring of 1948 was to be my last semester of college. Bill Crawford, a sophomore who lived in Dunster, told me about a 1931 Buick he had in New York that he would sell me for $200. This was wonderful I would be

—

able to spend my last semester in college with my own car. I had saved enough to manage it. I took some money intended for my college expenses and my savings, went to New York and drove the 1931 Buick back to Cambridge. It was one of those box-like cars with a running board on both sides, it had a crank to start it, although I think it also had a battery and starting motor. But these did not work, so one cranked it and it would put-put-put along. It also consumed as much oil as gas. Each time you bought gas, you had to buy oil. In 1948 gas was very cheap, but not lubricating oil, so driving it back to Cambridge was demanding on my purse. I wrote to Raffo and Lucy about this wonderful buy and could they kindly send a few extra dollars to help handle expenditures. Unfortunately, Lucy did not want me to drive because she was worried I might have an accident, and Raffo was against my buying a car because I did not have a job. One bought a car or got married when one could support oneself. I was to sell the car immediately. In fact he was not sending the next installment of my money until I could assure him I had sold the car. Luckily the 1931 Buick looked grand even if it burnt oil like mad. I was able to sell it at a very slight profit to another undergraduate. But my dream of owning a car for that last semester had ended. Betty and I made the best of it. Sevin still went down to Mount Holyoke and she found ways to visit and attend Dunster House dances.

I only took four courses that spring, two science-engineering courses, one philosophy and one economics — three B's and one D. I had succeeded — I was going to graduate. Meanwhile, I had been interviewed at the Harvard Business School and I had applied to the Wharton School of Finance Business and Commerce at the University of Pennsylvania in Philadelphia, and to the Stanford Business School. My thought was that I did not think I really had either talent or pleasure in engineering. If

—

I could combine my engineering education with a business degree, I would be able to obtain employment in the business end of engineering firms — say like General Electric, Westinghouse, and so on.

My father saw no need for a "business" education since to do business all you needed was experience — "faire des affaires" was what life work was about: It meant buying at one price and selling at a higher one. But he understood vaguely that places like General Electric might be more complicated. He reluctantly agreed to another two years of "sacrifices". Lucy, as always, was supportive. She had a bridge group and one lady member, Madame Maryssael was married to Gustave Maryssael, the general manager of the Mexican Light and Power Company. She consulted Madame M. who consulted Monsieur M., their verdict was that a business education was a very good plan indeed.

I thought I would do well in a business school since I had no trouble getting B's in economics while hardly opening the textbooks! But I was unsure I would be admitted as my grades were not sensational. I applied to three schools hoping at least one would admit me.

Betty was going to graduate and our relationship was in limbo. Since I was going on to obtain a master's in business administration, it was clear that I was not able to marry her. She was unclear what she would do — except return to the suburb of Philadelphia where her parents had retired. I do not know really what she thought about me, whether she ever thought she wanted to marry me, although we were very close, very good friends that last semester in Cambridge.

I did not attend my 1948 graduation. These

—

ceremonies were intended for the families of the graduates. Since my parents were not anxious to come to Cambridge for the occasion, I saw no reason to attend the festivities. Moreover most of my friends were not graduating and even if they did — with the exception of Jim Sevin — their parents would not come either — and in any case if I wanted a ride to St. Louis with Jim, I had to leave sooner. Thus, Betty and I attended a last dance at Dunster House, and I left with Jim for St. Louis and Mexico City.

Before leaving I had heard from the Harvard Business School. They wrote that while they would like to admit me, they thought I should gain some working experience before starting — say two years of work and then back to school. That did not fit too well with my own planning. First, I was unsure where I could find employment for one – two years except in Mexico and that meant going back, packing and then possibly coming back two years hence. Would my father still be willing to support me then? Also, the Wharton School in Philadelphia had admitted me. This meant that Betty could go back home and that I could move to Philadelphia, go to Wharton and continue dating Betty. Obviously the gods were smiling upon this relationship. I had not yet heard from Stanford, but I promptly accepted Wharton.

Bill Crawford who had sold me the Buick, once more came up with an easy solution. His parents lived in Germantown, a suburb of Philadelphia, in fact his father taught at the University, was a specialist of Latin American literature. His mother was a principal in the public schools. They would be delighted if I moved into his room. They would charge a small amount, I could live with them and could ship all my belongings directly to Germantown before going to Mexico. I do not remember if I met Professor Rex Crawford or his wife that spring. One of them probably came to Cambridge and it was all arranged.

—

I left with Jim Sevin, my trunks and packing boxes went into the Crawford basement, and Betty returned home.

Mexico, Visit To Necaxa

Lucy had spoken to Madame Maryssael, Madame had spoken to Monsieur and an appointment was arranged. Monsieur Maryssael was Belgian. Mexlight was owned by Sofina, a Belgian Trust that also owned, at one time, the Barcelona Traction (tramways), the Mexican Tramways (sold to the government), Brazilian Traction and CADE, Compania Argentina de Electricidad. Claude Enrique Luis Pablo Dechamps, my only Argentine/Belgian friend who was graduating, was the son of the chief engineer at CADE. I knew little about the politics of electricity or tramways, and was happy to be introduced to Monsieur Maryssael, who promptly suggested I spend half of my summer time as an apprentice in the company. They would pay me some minimal token amount. He suggested I spend three weeks in their laboratory where they tested equipment and three weeks in Necaxa, at their main hydro electric facilities in the State of Puebla. Within a week I reported for apprentice duty in Mexlight's laboratory.

The director of the laboratory was an older German man who had been in Mexico for many years. I frankly forget what we did in the lab. I think I was assigned with others, to find out why a distribution transformer had failed. I really do not remember too well. The director was a theosophist, a follower of Madame Helena Blavatsky — a person most concerned with reincarnation and the deeper understanding of astral and spiritual matters. He spent most of his time with me, explaining these mysteries and seemed totally uninterested in what I might learn or find out about the failure of distribution transformers. He liked to speak English — I think he read Madame Blavatsky in

—

English. The rest of the staff in the laboratory had long ago managed to deal with his constant preoccupation, they had real jobs to perform including writing the report on the failed transformer. I was only an apprentice and in addition somewhat interested by these discussions. I therefore spent three weeks listening to my German "older brother". In due time I found the discussions somewhat beyond my comprehension and was not too unhappy when they ended. I met with Monsieur Maryssael again, and went to Necaxa.

Necaxa is in the State of Puebla to the northwest of Mexico City. It is an impressive site in the mountains. There is a dam, a reservoir, a fall of several hundred meters down to the first plant, at Necaxa, followed by another waterfall to a plant at Tepexic. A third plant at Patla did not yet exist in 1948. These first two hydro electric plants were built at the turn of the century by English engineers. They also built an encampment with housing for the engineers — handsome houses with gardens and an "English" club with housing for visitors on short stay. The encampment is at the dam above the plants where the climate is pleasant and cool. One takes a small rail car down to the plants. Below Tepexic and Patla, the climate is tropical and you are in the rain forest. Between the plants one climbs straight up on the rail car, mostly through banana plantations — or where it is too steep through heavy jungle.

Since Mexlight maintains a path along the rail track so that repairs can be made, this path is the constant and preferred mode of Totonac Indian locomotion up and down. Men and women carry wood, bananas, plastic utensils, charcoal, and chickens. They go back and forth from the lower levels of the Sierra up to the little town of Huachinango, not far from Mexlights' encampment. It seems strange to be going up in the small open rail car,

—

passing this multitude of climbers or descenders who sometime walk a few inches away from you and who never speak or even seem to notice you. Many of the women wear wonderful blouses embroidered usually in red on white background, dark blue skirts with the huipil, that triangular cloth that serves as a top. In 1948 many or most women are barefoot, while some men wear huarachas, sandals made out of old tires. Most of the men carry machetes. Sometimes we passed men who were drunk and the operator of the rail car would push them away.

At the club I am quite alone. These three weeks will be weeks of solitude. The chief engineer of the plant does not care much what I do. The club is now empty. The engineering staff at Necaxa is now entirely Mexican, therefore family oriented not English club oriented. Except for a few visitors, engineers surveying the power lines between Necaxa and Mexico City there for one night, I am the only guest. I have some books to read. The cook prepares breakfast, lunch, and dinner. I even learn some Nahuatl to talk to her: omé piotem, two eggs ranchero every morning. Many Indians around Necaxa are Totonac and speak Totonaco. But we converse in Nahuatl the language of the dominant Aztec of the Mexican plateau. The breakfast in the State of Puebla countryside is a big meal. She will serve ham, tortillas, chili, beans, eggs, some barbecue lamb, if I want it.

One night I was invited to go down to the Necaxa plant as one of the turbine's had been stopped for maintenance. The water above is dammed, goes into a level tunnel until it reaches a site perpendicular above a turn in the river where the Necaxa plant is sited. Here, the water enters the quasi vertical penstock and that mass of falling water drives the turbines located at the foot of the cliff. We enter one of the turbines which seems to be an

—

immense cavern illuminated only by the lamps we carry. In front of us is the dark opening, the dark hole that goes up to the tunnel and then back through the tunnel to the closed entrance at the dam. The engineer laughs: "If someone opens that gate by mistake, we are done for — but it would be quick and neat "no se preocupe" (do not worry). Behind us we see the huge blades of the turbine. The workers will be scraping them clean — otherwise the water does not flow well and the turbine will vibrate. We have finished our visit, the gate remained closed, and we return to the camp in the dark on the little rail car and pass a few climbers who must have night vision.

After Necaxa, I return to Mexico City. Annie Ludlum, the girl from Venice, California is still living in her maid's room in the "azotea" the roof top. But her Englishman is gone. She seems to be involved with a Mexican businessman who may be helping her. I see some old friends and spend a weekend at John Mohr's parent's house on Lake Tequestitengo, south of Cuernavaca. We try to hunt, do some fishing but we are much more sedate. We have become much older; I am a college graduate, John a student at the medical school. We are already starting to talk about old times. Weeks pass quickly, and once again I am in route, but this time I take the train all the way to Philadelphia.

—

IV

FLUNKING AT WHARTON

The Crawfords live in a large house, there are books everywhere. Rex's mother in her eighties lives in one of the upstairs (third floor) rooms; I live in another under the roof. A desk is built with a plywood plank; I unpack my trunks that were stored during the summer. Photographs of Betty Hall, my photograph of the Rheims Cathedral, the shortwave radio is connected, an antenna installed on the roof. I eat most meals with them, pay a flat fee, help with chores like bringing coal from the basement for the cooking range. Dorothy, Rex's wife, is a school principal. Rex teaches Latin American culture and philosophy. This is fall of 1948.

I rapidly decide that Wharton is not intellectually challenging enough. I register for five courses at Wharton, but to enhance myself, to "learn", I decide to audit five other courses at the University including philosophy, French, literature, and a course with Rex. I become friendly with a young woman philosopher and attend seminars she is giving. There is a professor of French who is a member of this group. They all seem to think that I am doing the right thing, Wharton is a stupid place: no intellectual life there.

Early in the fall, Betty introduces me to her parents.

—

As I mentioned earlier, her father's career has been in the navy. They are rather cold and distant when I meet them. I do not think they approve of me. They want their daughter to marry a navy man and while they thought it was okay to study French in college, they have no intention to have their daughter marry a foreigner. So our dating that fall is already under the shadow of Betty's parents disapproval. Betty will ultimately marry a navy man, and divorce him in due time.

At a party given by the Crawford's I met a psychiatrist — a woman. She was still finishing her residence for her MD and living in a mental hospital where she worked. We met at a party given in honor of a German musicologist specializing in Latin American music, just returned from Bolivia with what was then rather unknown, namely music recorded in the Altiplano. Very few people had heard this music and it was fascinating to listen to his recordings.

The psychiatrist was older than me. I was 20 at the time and since she was finishing her residence and had completed some years of analysis, she must have been in her early thirties. She seemed to be interested in what I had to say about the music, she gave me her phone number. I called her and soon enough we had a date at her hospital where she lived at the end of a corridor.

This is where she has invited me to visit her. I take a tramway and find the hospital. To reach her room, I have to navigate the ward, there are people screaming behind some doors — it is unsettling. The psychiatrist finds me cute, she shows me her room, then she kisses me and starts undressing me. I find all this a bit surprising but she reassures me. It is okay, she is a doctor, she knows all there is to know about boys and girls, and I need not worry.

—

We are to enjoy ourselves, she undresses me, then she undresses, and in no time we are making love. It is all sanitary and healthy. I cannot say I like her — in fact I hardly know her, we listened to the altiplano music together, she gave me her phone number and asked me to call her. That is all. Now we are in bed together. She is short and stocky, dark hair, very Jewish looking. I do not remember her name, it was a Jewish name. After love making, we stay in bed for awhile, then she dresses: she has to visit patients in the ward. I am to leave when I am ready before the last tramway. Once again I navigate the corridors, I hear the screams, catch the tram and I am smiling, happy, all the way to Germantown.

With Betty Hall, I have a new problem. I tell her frankly that I need to make love to her. The psychiatrist has destroyed the myth my father taught me. I am no longer interested in making love with a whore. Making love to a friendly woman — an intelligent Jewish woman even if a bit stocky is a totally new experience. I see no reason why I cannot do the same with Betty. To be sure I would much prefer to be in bed with Betty to being in bed with the psychiatrist. I would like to marry Betty and live with her but I cannot see any reason for waiting. All this is clear to me. Betty has a different opinion. She is not ready to abandon the values she respects. One should wait. She is the daughter of a naval officer, and this officer is not interested in a foreigner son-in-law, he wants a young navy beau for his daughter. Betty is torn and now in addition, she is repulsed by my actions. We break up. She will not make love with me, especially after this psychiatrist business. It is all too sordid. I never see her again. She never forgives me.

At the University, I am taking a double load of courses, ten in total: five for credit at Wharton, and five for my enlightenment elsewhere in the University. In one of my Wharton courses: "The Regulation of Public Utilities", the research assistant is a graduate student named Sydney Miller. He invites me to have dinner with him at his home, the invitation is for Christmas 1948. I will meet Mrs. Miller then. At home, I am reading Marcel Proust, I have bought a 15-volume set of *À La Recherche du Temps Perdu*. In the book Albertine is lost, she is killed in a stupid horse riding accident. I have lost Betty and I am upset about it. I am writing rather dark and somber poems about lost life or lost hope. I am not doing too well. Once a week, I take the tramway, navigate the hospital corridor, find my Jewish psychiatrist who always undresses me, takes me into her bed, followed quickly by her departure, my getting dressed, walking the corridor and hearing the screams.

One night, Rex's mother falls in her bathtub. Rex is alone in the house below, his wife Dorothy is at a conference. He calls me to help him move his mother out of the bathtub. She is in pain. In fact, we find out later that she broke her hip. Moving this old, nude, wet, frightened woman in the middle of the night is not easy. Rex covers her, she screams, we somehow manage to put her in bed. I urge Rex to call an ambulance, my boy scout training tells me one does not lift people with severe pain out of bathtubs. But Rex is adamant: an ambulance would cost too much, she has nothing wrong, he wants her in bed. The next day, he finally decides to call a taxi and has me help him take her to a hospital when it is obvious she cannot move, even as I point out I have to go to classes. When it came to money the Crawford's were as tight as they come. But in all other respects they were most kind and gracious. Maybe Rex did not like his mother, or did not enjoy having her in his house. She was kind, patient and stoic with that sweet smile some old American ladies seem to keep: a smile from their youth, a vestige left on a wrinkled face. I still see her in the bathtub, in the dark, it was my first encounter with the nudity of old age.

My ten courses take time. For me, the University courses take precedence over the Wharton courses. Before the Christmas holidays we have finals. I find much of the content of the Wharton courses "stupid." There is much less economics that I expected a lot of "how to do it" preaching taught directly out of professional experience by accountants, personnel managers or financial advisers. The only vaguely interesting course is the one in public utility regulation. But the course seems to be condensed by only one sentence: "public utilities have the right to expect a fair return on the fair value of their property." After that you can spend the rest of your life discussing the meaning of these words.

As I take my final exam in personnel management , I decide that the questions underestimate that employees are something more than economic animals motivated by gain alone. To make my point, I decide to write answers to the questions in the form of a series of short poems, rhyme, and all. Here, the student is demonstrating to the faculty that poetry exists and motivates. But this brave effort for the enlightenment of the faculty is to no avail. The faculty is not amused. My effort is not even given a D. I flunk the course — I obtain a poetic E.

I am depressed. I do not like Wharton. I miss the world I knew at Harvard, even the science courses. I miss Betty. The psychiatrist is not helping. In fact, one evening after hearing the screams in the corridor and making love with her, I also start screaming. I scream that we are alone, that she is alone, that I am alone. This time, I am the one who leaves in a hurry and I tell her I do not want to see her

—

again. When I meet her again, much later, at a party, she tells me she thought I was near a nervous breakdown.

A New Significant Affair

We are near Christmas, and Sydney Miller, the teaching assistant, repeats his invitation to come to dinner as he has heard that I am staying in town during the holidays. He lives with his wife, Frances (née Crawford, no relation to my Philadelphia hosts), in a one room apartment. There is a cooking area in a corner of the room with a green curtain that is pulled when the "kitchen" is not in use. The couch converts into a bed. There is a table and I think they borrowed the third chair. There is a radio and I remember not much more. Sydney is finishing his PhD, Frances has hers already, but she is not working at the time. She is cooking, keeping house and both writing and typing Sydney's dissertation. Sydney would probably admit that she is "helping him" and no more. I quickly find out that Frances likes poetry, has written and even published poems. The dinner is good; most of the conversation takes place between Frances and me. We talk about poems, clouds, travels, and Sydney makes noises. I go hide behind the couch while Frances does the dishes and I write a poem in French that I will give her before I leave. Sydney seems pleased; the evening with the foreign student went well. When I leave, Frances gives me poems and her phone number. She is flying to the west coast the next day to spend Christmas with her mother. Sydney and Frances also own a small house in Carmel-by-the-Sea where her mother resides a few blocks away. We talk briefly about California. I mention I was once invited to join Huxley in the California desert, that I could not afford the trip. "Let's get together again sometime," she tells me.

—

When did I call her? I do not remember, early in 1949 I suppose. She is glad to hear my voice — yes, she would like to see me. I had no experience with married women; this was my first. Where should we meet — her apartment? The Crawford's house was not a good idea so I suggest I would visit her to return poems she has lent me. She invites me to come. When I arrive she tells me Sydney has just called her and she has to leave to join him somewhere. We have a few minutes together. I return the poems, ask about California and when she is about to leave, we face each other and I think I kiss her or did she kiss me? She also gives me a second set of poems.

Frances and I met in a park about a week later. It was cold. We went to a bookstore where I knew the owner. We held hands furtively while looking at the poetry selections. I was worried about Sydney. Suppose we were seen by a friend of his? I had read recently where a jealous husband had killed his wife's lover. I was not Frances' lover — but what about appearances? I had also heard about a foreign student who had been in some big difficulties because of his involvement with the wife of one of his professors . I felt unsure. Frances told me she was unhappy with Sydney. He had served in England during the war and during that time she had finished her PhD. in psychology at Stanford. They had married just before the war and had been separated for several years. She had new interests — Sydney had also changed. She could talk with me but no longer with him. I was impressed. I was 21 years old with this 28 years old PhD who wanted to discuss her life with me. She was joyous with me. She published poems. I had kissed her. I wanted to go to bed with her. I told her so. Sometime in February 1949, Frances arranged to borrow the apartment of friends of hers, on an afternoon when they were both at work and Sydney was at the University. I went up the stairs behind her, worried that

—

neighbors would notice we did not look like the couple who lived there. In 1949, adultery is not only a sin but an illegal act. We enter the apartment, there is a separate bedroom, a very small room large enough for a double bed made with clean sheets and invitingly open. We kiss, we talk, we kiss again, and finally I undress Frances and quickly undress myself. I realize I have never undressed a woman before. We make love. I would stay but the owners are coming back soon and Frances needs to return home. We remake the bed, put things in order, dress and leave. I realize when we dress that Frances wore blue, white and red undergarments. I am in love.

The second semester had started. Again, I was taking five courses at Wharton and auditing five more. The Wharton school bored me. Their definition of what matters seemed trivial to me. It was not clear that I would be able to complete my studies.

At another Crawford party I meet the relatively young and good looking Director of the Philadelphia Museum of Art. He seems genuinely interested in what I have to say. He invites me to have a private visit of the Museum: on a Monday when the Museum is closed. Anyhow, I find all this very interesting, I also find it natural that a director would give a private tour to a young man who has expressed deep interest in paintings, sculpture and of course poetry. I accept and meet him at the Museum. He explains how the Greeks would paint their temples and statues — what we see today is not how they looked then. He shows me painted reconstructions. I find the colors garish and cheap but do not say so. Then he wants to show me the ceiling in one of the painted rooms. If I will lie on the bench in the middle of the room and place my head on his lap for comfort? I will have a good view while he explains. I am all innocence. I still do not know what the

—

word homosexual means. I find it normal, maybe poetic to do as he says. What a nice elegant man I tell myself who spends several hours with a foreign student. He explains the ceiling while my head is on his lap. After a while he realizes that I have no idea what he is after. He finally gives up. He concludes the tour takes me to the door. I thank him profusely. America is a great country. No French museum director could ever be so kind.

I also visited the Stephano extended family. I had called them and they suggested I first come visit their cigarette factory, which until 1961, was still operating in down town Philadelphia at 1014 Walnut Street. From there they drove me to their vast mansion in Elkins Park just outside Philadelphia. The Stephano brothers, Constantine and Stephano were the people who bought my Grandfather's Turkish tobacco for their cigarettes. They helped my Grandmother after the death of her husband. Lucy had asked that I visit them. By 1948-49 the older generation was gone but the children had taken over the business and the mansion. Three or four families lived under one roof each in separate parts of the huge 19th century house. The sons and daughters had married and had young children. We were maybe 15 or more around the table, dinner was served by waiters presided over by a butler all in white gloves. I was impressed by these Greek immigrants, by their wealth, by their success. They took me into the basement where they kept a very large shortwave radio set with antennas on the roof. We listened to France and Greece. Later they drove me to the railroad station so that I could return to Philadelphia. It was possible to succeed in the United States. This was a great country. I was impressed. My friend Jim Sevin at Harvard was right, I should really live in the United States.

By late March it was clear I would flunk at

—

Wharton. I did not pay any attention or even attend any Wharton classes. A professor of French literature I had met at the Crawford's urged me to drop Wharton and work toward a PhD. in French Lit. But I could not see how I would explain such a move to my father. I called Claude Dechamps, my friend at Harvard who had remained there for a master's in engineering. He thought I could try to obtain a Master's with him; in fact he was looking for a roommate for the fall term. I then called the dean of the Harvard Engineering School and explained that I found the business school too dull. He was receptive. "Come up and see us, we shall see what we can do." I called Frances and she decided that we would go up to New York together. She would tell Sydney she was going with a woman friend. After that I would go to Cambridge. We left together, went to a hotel on Central Park where she registered alone and I managed to stay in her room although there was a guard on each floor — a matron. We spent two days in New York.

After that I was interviewed at Harvard and wrote my parents to inform them I might have to finish the next year in Cambridge. In a matter of weeks I was admitted "on probation" for the coming summer term. I resigned from Wharton before the end of the term thus avoiding being expelled and saving me the trouble of going to classes. Frances and Sydney were also leaving for California as Sydney had completed his PhD. They were going to Carmel to their small house but their relationship was strained. Frances was talking divorce. I pointed out that she should not divorce on my account. We decided to break off our relationship "to clear the air," to allow her to decide what she wanted to do about her marriage without reference to me. In May 1949, I gave my adieux to her, to my hosts the Crawford's and to all my Philadelphia friends, I packed and returned to Cambridge.

—

V

BACK TO HARVARD

Claude Enrique Luis Pablo Dechamps was looking for a roommate and attending the summer school. We took a room in graduate housing north of the yard, close to the Engineering School in Conant Hall. The price of the room was $90 per semester. We had a small living room and two bedrooms. We ate in cafeterias and managed breakfast on hot plates.

We had to take a course in machine design and another dealing with motors and alternating current. This second course had many hours of laboratory work where we spent our time connecting circuits and motors. It was quite hot and Dechamps tended to collapse and go to sleep. He was not "on probation" and could afford a C or a D but I had to obtain B's if I was to continue with the fall term in September 1949. So I did much of the work which meant that I kept getting jolts of 220 volts when I had to reconnect in a hurry. But we both got used to it — you place your left hand in your back pocket and only touch wires with your right hand — you wear heavy crepe soles and keep everything dry, and you still get jolted. That summer was work and few escapes, but I managed an A- in machine design, and a B in alternating currents. I had made it, I would be able to complete the one year masters at Harvard, and my father would never know how close I had been to wasting his money. In fact, I was so surprised that I had

—

obtained A's and B's that I briefly thought in late October that I might attempt to obtain a scholarship and continue for a PhD. in engineering, but nothing came out of that. When I finished the masters in June 1950 I had two more A's and the rest were B+'s, not good enough for a scholarship or to be admitted for a PhD.

I exchanged a few letters with Frances; she was in Carmel and in August, had obtained an "interlocutory" decree of divorce against Sydney L. Miller, Jr. One obtained an interlocutory decree on the grounds of "extreme cruelty" and had to wait one year before the links of marriage could be broken — the final decree was to be obtained on September 2, 1950. Meanwhile, Sydney was to go east, but not before obliging Frances to have sex with him: after all they were still husband and wife, right? which led her to accuse him of raping her, which was in fact rape but not before the law. In those circumstances they had some trouble settling their affairs, including selling their little house in Carmel.

One of my friends, a Frenchman, had invited me to his room for a drink. This was in the early fall of 1949, and this time there had been an explanation. Some men were homosexual these were the best and the brightest. Arthur Rimbaud, the French poet I adored, was one of these selected few, Verlaine also; and I could also be one of them. I could join; all this being said, as we gently sipped drinks on a sofa. We met twice on that sofa. But I quickly discovered I was not one of them. The final penetration did not appeal to me at all and I refused twice. We remained good friends and met again many years later when my homosexual tempter turned out, in a new life, to be married with children having forgotten or renounced his past. While I liked homosexuals, felt close to many, in the final analysis I was not one of these best and brightest. I wrote

—

to Frances to say that I had met a man, had had a tentative new experience, but nothing was changed with me. She answered and our correspondence continued.

Fall of 1949 Dechamps was dating a blonde débutante, or aspiring débutante from Boston, she came to the room on several occasions and I "graciously" went to the library to study. I do not think Dechamps liked her that much — for what ever good looks she had seemed quite superficial, the kind of person you know will become old at 29. There mind will age badly. Personally, I had little contact with her as I had no girl friend and did not double date with them. At some point she informed Claude that she was pregnant and they should marry immediately. Dechamps was taken aback but after her mother and father met with him, he informed me he had decided to marry her. He wrote about his engagement to his parents. A week or so elapsed and one morning our door bell rang and Claude came running into the room, white as a sheet. It was his mother. She was on our door step. She had flown unannounced from Buenos Aires as soon as she had heard of the impending marriage.

Madame Dechamps mère took over. I think if my memory is right that she was Russian and married to Monsieur Dechamps père, a Belgian who worked for CADE the electric utility in Argentina owned by SOFINA — the same company owning Mexlight. She hired a lawyer, dragged Dechamps and me in front of a dean and the lawyer to record our testimony that nothing had ever taken place in our rooms. In no time she had Claude break up with his blonde débutante, who as it turned out later, was not pregnant, she had never been "enceinte". Within ten days, Madame Dechamps had left for Buenos Aires, leaving Claude somewhat reconciled to the idea that marriage was not for him, not yet in any case.

—

In November, Frances and I agreed to meet again. We would meet at Christmas time in Chicago where Frances and her mother were planning to spend the holidays with Elizabeth, her sister who was working there as a psychiatric social worker. Thus, at the end of that first semester I took the train and met Frances at the Chicago Union Station. I had spent the night sitting in coach and found the city as reputed: cold and windy. But Frances looked dashing — she was free from Sydney — we would be staying at the home of friends of Elizabeth, the Mayer's — Milton and Jane, while her mother stayed in Elizabeth's small flat.

We were meeting to consider whether we would get together again, but we never really discussed what to do. It became self-evident that Frances would not return to California with her mother, she would come to Cambridge, find employment and we would live together. Madame Crawford was not exactly happy with this, but her daughter was nearly 30 years old and was a married woman. The Mayer's and Elizabeth were all in favor. We went to parties, ate Olympia oysters at The Well of the Sea, and Frances flirted with Sidney Harris a well known columnist with the Chicago Daily News who also happened to be Elizabeth's lover. This second Sidney then tried to seduce the younger sister. He gave us tickets to go hear a concert given by Mugsy Spanier — not before telling everyone what a good looking PhD that little sister was, not before making me feel quite foolish in the sophisticated world of his Chicago.

After the New Year, we left for Cambridge. At first I stayed in Conant Hall while Frances took a hotel room. Now Claude had to go read in the library. But this did not last long. We found a furnished studio on Mass. Avenue

—

— one room with a kitchenette — rather gloomy with heavy plush furniture, but it mattered little. Frances had the name of someone at Massachusetts General Hospital where she was hired to administer Rorschach tests to patients who had had a lobotomy. It was winter, it was cold but it was wonderful. We were in love, and I decided that I should paint. I went and bought five or six oil colors including red, blue, yellow, white and black, a few brushes, a 20 x 24 inch board — actually it was smaller — maybe 16 x 18. Anyhow, I did a painting — it was my first.

In Mexico, I had met Guido Sandri, the nephew of the hydraulic engineer of Mexlight. He and his roommate Knüt Hansen, the son of a well known writer, were just starting as freshmen at Harvard. They were both younger, but interested in poetry and painting. We gathered on many occasions going to dinner at inexpensive Greek restaurants or from time to time, for dinner in the furnished room. They encouraged my painting. I was influenced by Picasso's blue period. I liked his series on the "saltimbanques", especially his two saltimbanques showing a nostalgic young woman at a café table with a harlequin. I was also taken by the despondent emaciated young mothers he painted at that earlier time in his career. My early paintings clearly show my feeble attempts to replicate the twisted hands from the Picasso originals. I must have done a half dozen canvasses in Cambridge before the end of the term. Most are no longer. I think I must have painted over them later when I started again in Mexico City. Bourgeois economy was instilled in us.

Next thing I knew, my mother was coming to discourage my intensive relationship. I was much too young to live with someone older — and be talking of marriage. My father threatened to cut all funding, I was to return to Conant Hall and stop seeing that older woman. So

—

sure enough Lucy came, just like Madame Deschamps had come, but in contrast, there was no lawyer to hire since no one claimed anything. She told us that Raffo would not pay for my living out of Conant Hall and after repeating this several times, she returned to New York to see her sister and do some shopping before returning to Mexico City.

Raffo dutifully cut the funds — but my tuition was already paid until the end of the year. He had also paid an advance deposit to Harvard required of all foreign students. Elizabeth, Frances's sister signed a deposit guarantee and I was able to recuperate that money in cash. This sum, together with a $100 donation I obtained from the Harvard Engineering School and Frances' meager salary. was enough to finance the remaining months in Cambridge — although restaurants had to be sharply curtailed.

I began looking for employment, the Engineering School arranged an interview with General Electric and I received an offer to train for 18 months at a token salary of about $150 a month. This meant moving to Schenectady, New York, where it was not clear whether Frances could find a job as easily as she had been able to do in Boston. I wrote to Monsieur Maryssael at Mexlight and he offered to hire me at a starting engineer salary of about 25 – 30 pesos per day, about $100 a month. Later, my first contract with Mexlight would be for 34 – 40 pesos a day, no great bonanza. We wrote to Paul V. Murray, the head of Mexico City College to see if Frances might be employed. He offered to help out as long as we understood they did not pay much.

Raffo calmed down. He had done his duty, If his son wanted to marry, let him do so. They left for a trip to France, came up to New York where we all met and made

—

peace. Later, when my parents returned from Europe, I went back to Mexico City alone but with all my belongings. Once again I did not attend my graduation. Frances went directly to her mother's house on 15th Avenue in Carmel. I stayed in Mexico City for a few weeks, filled forms for employment at Mexlight and stored our belongings. I was glad to leave for California, flying from Mexico City to Los Angeles, and on to Monterey. I was reunited with Frances in Carmel at the beginning of July 1950. I had finally arrived in the Golden State.

By now matters were settled. Frances and I would marry in Mexico City in September or October. Raffo was assured that I would accept the job offer from Mexlight and that I would start work at the same time. This satisfied him: I would be married at a time I was gainfully employed. This also facilitated obtaining working papers for Frances. She would come to Mexico as a tourist, would marry there and at that point would apply for permanent immigrant status as my wife. She would be able to stay in Mexico City while the paperwork was processed and would only have to go to the border to obtain the immigration documents once they were granted. Meanwhile, she would be able to work on temporary permits. All this of course did not please Mrs. Crawford who wanted Frances to be married in Carmel as soon as her divorce with Sidney was final. Luckily this was not going to happen until September 2, 1950, and she relented to postpone the ceremony for mid-September in Mexico City.

Madame Crawford would have nothing to do with the sinful life of her daughter. There was no question of our sharing a bed under her roof in Carmel while still unmarried. Major Wallace Crawford had been discharged from the US Army. He was away. His room behind the carport was empty. I would sleep there while Frances

—

moved into a room in the main house. This made our love life difficult, although Frances would sneak out once her mother was asleep and we were relatively safe in the room of Major Crawford since it was separate with a little patio between it and the other rooms.

One night Frances had left to return to her bed when I awoke with a pain in my back. I turned the light on to find a crushed spider below me. I rushed to the main house as the pain was getting worse, but the door was locked. So I banged calling that I had been bitten — pronounced beaten. Finally mother and daughter came out, the spider was examined in full light — a black widow. Phone calls were made to the hospital, Frances and her mother hurriedly drove me there to be given morphine and other medications. I thought nothing of it all, only asked for more injections, as I found them most pleasant. After a few hours I was released. I was lucky, it had been a very small and very young spider. It did not do much damage.

Major Crawford was away, and Frances' parents were separated. Major Crawford had graduated from West Point and had served in the Philippines but at some point he had taken to drinking. In a moment when he had too much alcohol, he slapped a colonel. Major Crawford had been discharged. It was an honorable discharge which was the reason Mrs. Crawford lived in Carmel in close proximity to Fort Ord where the major and his wife still had access to the commissary and other military perks. I was told he traveled and would return from time to time. Actually, he would be away for long periods, drinking increasing amounts until his health would give in. The military would then pick him up and put him in an Army hospital where Mrs. Crawford would fetch him as soon as he had dried up sufficiently. He would stay a little while in Carmel and go away again, hence the little empty room behind the garage

—

since he was away that summer. He would do this several times and in 1956 Frances, her mother and I drove to Southern California to bring him from an Army hospital back to Carmel. His drinking finally destroyed his body and he died in 1957. He was buried in the National Cemetery of San Francisco with full military honors.

Those two months in Carmel were very seductive. It was not only the beauty of the site. Mrs. Crawford cooked wonderful meals. We went to good restaurants. That helped a lot. Frances's sister was there with Milton and Jane Mayer from Chicago. Milton was a well known left leaning writer. They had many friends in town. We attended a party for Haakon Chevalier, a professor of French at the University of California at Berkeley who had been a close friend of Robert Openheimer, and had somehow become involved in accusations of spying for the Soviet Union. Every left wing person in the Monterey peninsula was there and it was a lively group. It was a good bye party for Chevalier who was returning to Paris. There were many more parties, we met Eric Berne the psychiatrist, and I met painters including Ephraim Doner who made tiles and knew Henry Miller. In short we made more friends in two months than we had acquired together until then. Carmel was great, we were going to be married, we were in love, every one smiled at us and not studying for exams was exhilarating.

In September we boarded the train in Gilroy to go to Los Angeles and from there a train to Mexico City. We had with us quite a few trunks with all our belongings — kitchenware, clothes, and many books. We went to El Paso and then down to Mexico City. The scenery was impressive — valleys, mountains, long sunsets — a golden light. We were on that train for several days. Mrs. Crawford was to fly down later that month bringing two

—

Siamese cats, Ming and Ch'ing belonging to Frances. The idea was that we would find an apartment, move in so as to be able to receive the cats. Lucy did not want cats in her house. The marriage was set for around the 20th of September.

First days in Mexico City were very busy, finding an apartment and arranging for the marriage. We immediately hit a snag — Frances' divorce papers had to be translated into Spanish and certified by a Mexican Consul in the United States. Elizabeth was immediately asked to arrange this. She would have to go to Fresno to find the closest consulate. Luckily she was still on vacation in Carmel at the time.

We found a flat at Calle Nebraska 25, about 5 – 6 blocks from my parents place at Oklahoma 27. It was a nondescript modern building. We were on the second floor — it had a living room, two bedrooms, and kitchen. We moved in with a few chairs and a table lent by Lucy and a bed we bought. We also obtained a sofa bed for Mrs. Crawford's arrival. But time passed and the translation of the divorce papers did not arrive. Mrs. Crawford arrived mid September with cats and waited from day to day on the sofa not knowing when we might schedule the marriage. This in cramped quarters, in a foreign country, in a new apartment was demanding. Arranging the marriage ceremony was not difficult per se, as we had agreed that it would be a minimal affair. We would only have parents, the four witnesses required by Mexican law, a representative of the American Embassy, to legalize the marriage in the U.S.A., and the Juez de Paz. The judge would come to my parent's house for a fee. It would be in the afternoon and we would drink champagne, and have a few things to munch.

—

At some point, I went to see the judge to plead my case. Could he not marry us now so that my mother-in-law could return home? I explained the situation in our small apartment: the cats, the sofa, the mother-in-law waiting day after day. The judge listened. I pointed out that the paper work could be done when the certified and translated divorce decree were received. I delicately mentioned a bigger fee, and he agreed: mothers-in-law could be a problem.

We were married on October 2, 1950. Three days later, I started working as an assistant engineer on the construction of a new thermoelectric power plant at Lechería, located north of Cautitlán in the State of Mexico, as contrasted to the Federal District where Mexico City is located, about one hour drive north of our apartment.

Mrs. Crawford was able to return home in good spirits. Her daughter was married and no longer living in sin.

—

VI

MEXICO: WORK AND MARRIAGE

Mexico City College hired Frances and, as a result, we made friends with a large number of American expatriates — some were attending Mexico City College on the GI bill of rights. As life was cheaper in Mexico City than in the US, Mexico City College was able to grow rapidly and it found many prospective students. Usually young, married ex GI's who were happy to settle in Mexico and be able to rent a flat and hire a maid with their GI bill money. The college had no trouble finding professors — some were Mexican intellectuals or artists — others, like Frances, wanted to live in Mexico and were happy to accept a small salary. Increasingly, there were also refugees from the anticommunist scare in the U.S.A. These Americans preferred to move to Mexico City to evade Senator McCarthy and his accusations of communist spies in high places. This large, mostly left wing intellectual community of American expatriates living in Mexico was very different from the business oriented Americans whose children I had known while attending high school. This new community had many ties with Mexican intellectuals, mostly left leaning intellectuals and many who had served with the Republicans during the Spanish civil war. Old members of the Lincoln Brigade had also moved to Mexico, so we immediately made many friends in these circles, although neither Frances nor I were especially

—

politicized. At best I still thought vaguely that I could be interested in socialism but I was working for a foreign company in Mexico, and I had joined the Harvard Club of Mexico City none of which were real socialist hot beds.

Lechería was at least a one hour drive. We had bought a second hand two-door Ford sedan from Monsieur Maryssael and I drove this car back and forth. I would leave at 6:45 am arriving at Lechería before 8 a.m., where I was, among other tasks, to supervise giving blue overalls to our workers. We ate lunch at the Good Year tire plant down the road from our construction site and I usually left work around 6 P.M. arriving back in the flat late — around 7 to 7:30 p.m. depending on weather and traffic. During the rainy season the road between Cautitlán and Lechería was often flooded and I learned to drive in deep water, not so deep as to reach the engine, but enough to cover the tail pipe. You had to run the motor full blast with the clutch in, so as to make sure the water did not enter the motor through the tail pipe. In this way you could move a car even with water inside the driving compartment. This knowledge turned out to be most useful when I was flooded out of our house on Greer Road in Palo Alto several years later.

At Lechería, I distributed overalls to the workers. I had to see if the old one was decrepit enough and sign a chit. So anywhere I would go I would always be pursued by workers "Ingeniero, Ingeniero, por favor, mire ud, necessito mis overalls..." please look at my overalls, I need new ones, and as a good socialist, I would sign.

I was assigned to work with the American "erector" to assemble a set of pre-cut cooling towers made of West Coast redwood. The "erector" is sent by the manufacturer to direct the construction. As the Mexican engineer, it is my role to transmit his instructions to some 200 carpenters under my command. This "erector" was a calm, dull, Nebraskan who had very little to say about anything except how we had to sort the myriads of wood parts and get them gradually nailed together. I guess I had never met anyone more devoid of any spark of life. He would sit for hours in a little cubicle and chew gum, looking blankly ahead and from time to time he would spit the gum and call me — "got to get the H-25 pieces now" — and then he'd go on staring ahead. Now, as it turned out, the latrines at Lechería were few and at the other end of the construction site. Both the "erector" and I wanted to finish the job fast so, since the piles of wood to be nailed were quite high and well disposed, we encouraged our carpenters, as long as feasible, to urinate "en sitio." Unfortunately my Mexican engineer colleagues and superiors were against such loose behavior — "no es decente" they claimed. So I had to argue with them anytime they caught one of my workers in this act of "indecencia".

They thought it was great "decencia" to have a worker spend the entire day polishing their cars, or having several mechanics repair them. In fact none of the Mexican engineers would have any contact with the workers — outside of giving orders — there was a sharp social cleavage between the "educated" class and the laboring one. No Mexican engineer, with one exception the head surveyor who did all his own physical work, ever touched anything like a wrench or ever had dirty hands. I was evidently crazy because I had the carpenters teach me how to hammer a nail with only one stroke, something I could do very well at the end of a few weeks. As the cooling towers went up, I had to learn the art of walking on planks way above ground. Here there was democracy. Everyone in the construction world, engineers, foremen, workers walked on narrow planks spanning great voids. It was the elegant thing to do, and once used to it one hardly paid attention — except when a worker got too sure and fell from the main structure where the generators were to be housed. We heard a cry and everyone ran where he had fallen. Our doctor (we had a doctor and a nurse in residence since we had close to a thousand workers there) — our doctor reached him, opened his cranium — it was split in two — and said "está bien muerto." He sure is good and dead. I was some distance away — luckily I could not see too clearly — although I did see him open the head.

After the cooling towers, my next task was to install the electric controls of the main crane. All that work took place way up the main structure above the generators. I spent everyday having to think at all times where I was walking and how I was walking. The work was fairly complex since we had to connect all the wiring of the crane. It did not last long. The cooling towers had taken many months — the crane took one or two; but it was exhausting. By the time I reached Nebraska 25, I did not have much energy left. After the crane, I was in charge of calculating how much we were spending and writing construction reports. At one point, I was asked to calculate how thick the crane cable should be to lift the generator so as to set it in place. I did all the calculations, we installed the cable and I was present when the crane began to lift the generator. There was the oddest length of time when the crane operator had been told "lift" but nothing happened. I could see the cable was straight and tight and even seemed to stretch. I thought — Oh God, I miscalculated, it is going to break — and just then, suddenly, the generator lifted and was placed on its base.

In the summer of 1951, Frances became pregnant. Since she was 30 years old when we married, we had decided to have children immediately, and Frances had

—

stopped using birth control. I was elated with the news, since several months had elapsed before she became pregnant. But early in September, Frances had a miscarriage. This unforeseen event was quite a shock to both of us. I had no idea that there was such a thing as miscarriage. When the doctor explained that it was highly probable that the baby was defective, it dawned on me that babies did not come automatically as perfect dolls. Frances told me she felt ill, that I had to find help, I rushed to the home of Betty Gold, whose husband was a student at Mexico City College while she was a nurse with the Hospital de los Niños Lesiados — the Shriner's hospital for maimed children. Betty came to the flat, only to find that our doctor had come and had already disposed of the unborn fetus.

In January of 1952 a Monsieur Durostu, a Frenchman, who worked in the office of Monsieur Maryssael accepted another job. At that time, Mexlight was setting up a research group in the General Manager's office to undertake long term economic and financial studies necessary to obtaining a World Bank loan. A Belgian engineer, Monsieur George van Campenhout was coming from SOFINA's headquarters in Brussels, and an American, David Goldstein, was coming from AMITAS, the New York office of SOFINA. With Durostu gone, Maryssael wanted a permanent replacement, he needed someone who spoke French, English, and Spanish, who could understand figures and forecasts. He remembered meeting me and asked me to come see him. On 16 January I was appointed Special Assistant to the General Manager. It all happened very suddenly and my life was completely altered. I was no longer trudging all the way to Lechería. I was no longer a member of the Sindicato Méxicano de Electrecistas — the workers and engineers union. I was now joining twenty or thirty "empleados de confiancia"

—

who worked directly as managers or for management. I would report to Calle Gants #20 where Mexlight occupied an entire city block. The building had a vast hall downstairs with payment windows where customers would come pay their bills. I would be a block and a half from Sanborns on Calle Madero. I would also be doing studies and learning how to use adding machines! More importantly, I would be paid more — no longer by the day, but for the month, something like 3,500 pésos a month which was a little more than 400 dollars.

Frances was pregnant again and the baby was expected for July 1952. This time we were more fortunate and she was in good health. We decided to look for a bigger place to live in. We could now afford a small house and Frances wanted a little garden if possible. The Gold's were renting a small house in San Ángel in the southern part of Mexico City. It is a quaint old village that has been taken over by the spread of Mexico City. It has the village atmosphere of Coyoacán — with cobbled narrow streets and in a newer section, little houses designed by a Mexican architect named Manuel Parra. This newer development surrounds the San Ángel Inn, which had been an old hacienda and was now converted into a restaurant — much too expensive for us. All this is not too far from the old town of Villa Obregón (San Ángel) where there is the lovely Plaza del Carmen with the convent and church of the Carmelites. We looked in the area and found a house just behind the garden of the San Ángel Inn at 61 Calle Aida and moved there in early June 1952 when Frances was eight months pregnant. The rent for this Manuel Parra house was 600 pesos a month, about $70 dollars.

On February 4, 1952 there was a major strike of Mexlight workers. Mexico City was dark. Earlier the Labor Ministry had allowed a 15% rise in salaries, pending

—

confirmation from an independent fiscal review that Mexlight's earnings would be sufficient to cover this increase. The independent review found the company not able to sustain the pay increase but the Government still refused to allow Mexlight to raise electric rates. Mexlight was told to reduce salaries again — never a popular move — thus, the strike. All hospitals were given emergency services except the Anglo American Hospital where Frances was planning to have our first child.

The General Manager's offices were on the first floor. We, employees of "confianza" had been drafted and were busily reducing the paychecks by hand as the payroll department refused to perform this ugly operation. I was a socialist hard at work reducing the salary of the workers. I had been a good socialist at Lechería — good enough to be invited by the workers to join them at a barbacoa. I was the only engineer invited — where I drank pulque and got quite drunk — but I could see no issue. It was a fact that the government was amusing itself with Mexlight, they had allowed the pay raise but not increased electric rates — so what was to be done? Mexlight had not been paying dividends for several years, there was no fat to trim.

Monsieur Gustave Maryssael was tall, always impeccably dressed, and spoke excellent Spanish. He would often argue phraseology with the head of the legal department who was Mexican. He was also courageous. When the workers broke down the door at the end of our corridor, he came out, with us behind and he faced the workers. He told them that beating us or tearing the place down would not increase their pay, we had to find a way to increase our rates, that is what we were doing, they should go for the moment and let us try to solve the problem — The workers stood , the doors broken. It was tense before they left. I realized that it was not only a matter of

—

socialism or capitalism, it was the problem of having ends meet.

Frances taught at Mexico City College where she met Hans Hoffman, a graduate from the Psychology Department of the University of California at Berkeley — another PhD who had come to Mexico City because he had been a member of the communist party during his undergraduate years. Together they had begun a small psychological counseling center and they were quite involved with a number of Mexican psychologists in starting a Mexican Psychological Society with a code of ethics and standards of professional achievement. There was also an Englishman and his wife — Robin Bond who was a marvelous teacher of art and the three of them were concocting some vast project to study the Mexican personality —a project that would be financed by American foundations —   we had many parties to plan all this, wonderful parties with Mexican art students, psychologists and others, we would dance or have guitar music and sad Mexican songs and drink tequila or whiskey and there would be old hands from the Lincoln Brigade to sing their 1936 songs from the Spanish Civil War. We knew George Oppen the poet and well known left wing personality. George may have once been a communist but he lived very comfortably in San Ángel with his two maids and he also employed two or three workers who made furniture he designed and sold. Later, George would make a cradle, a heavy solid rocking cradle that required two people to lift, for our second child and new daughter Anne. Madame Oppen would hire a model and I did sketches at their house. We also knew and saw the cultural attaché at the American Embassy and went on horse back trips around Mexico City, ate tamales at a little stand, listened to a few Mariachi singers walking in a forest. At that time we loved living in Mexico.

—

On July 6, the day of the presidential election when trouble was expected in the streets, Frances began her labor pains. We reached the hospital before 8 a.m., before any possible demonstration This was the election of President Ruiz Cortinez who had promised mechanized agriculture for everyone: agricultura mecánizada para todos!. Labor was very slow, Betty Gold came. I was not allowed anywhere near the to-be mother. Mike tried hard to be born on the 7th —but he was born at 11:20 pm. I was finally shown a tiny baby around midnight, called my parents and went home to bed — I hardly saw Frances. In those days men were left to pace in the waiting room. The baby was shown for a few minutes behind glass — I only saw the doctor the next day. Mike was very small, he was kept with oxygen in an incubator for 24 hours before we could take him home, taking a portable incubator with us.

We went back to Carmel on vacation in September '52. This was my first vacation since starting to work. I had from September 8th to the 25th — taking advantage of various Mexican holidays around the 16th. We went by airplane with Michael Francis who was then three months old — he was a good traveler. As soon as we arrived in Carmel, Mexico devalued the peso from 8.65 to 12.50 to the dollar. My salary of near $400 a month had fallen below $300 — this did not help make me feel good about working in Mexico. More than ever, Carmel seemed wonderful. The weather, the ocean — of course the fact I was not working helped a lot — also the food — Mrs. Crawford cooked delicious meals. I kept thinking I should try to move to California. I liked California, especially being at sea level. Mexico City's altitude did not suit me.

I had brought several paintings I had done in Mexico with me. I thought I might give them to family or

—

friends. They were "portraits" of young women, still influenced by Picasso's earlier work, but also starting to look like my own. The women had blank eyes and they were painted with a single color background. We met a local painter at a party. Richard (Dick) Lofton invited me to bring my paintings to his studio as he wanted to see them. He had a little studio in a small building away from the main house of a rich woman on Santa Lucia Rd. The studio overlooked the San Carlos Borromeo Mission. He said he liked what I was doing; I was clearly influenced by Soutine. I had never heard of Soutine but I was pleased someone who knew how to paint thought I might be able to do so. To my surprise Dick invited me to paint in his studio during the remainder of our stay in Carmel. There was a small wood stove to ward off the Carmel fog and a huge unfinished painting of bathers hiding behind a protective curtain. He lent me an easel and I did two or three paintings there. By then I was sold on California. I was impressed one could be a painter and not have to work in offices adding figures. But I was only an amateur. I had not gone to art school. My father would never have allowed that, and I was in no way passionate enough to plunge into bohemian life. Not to mention I had a wife and a very young child. At the end of our vacation we returned to Mexico City.

Mexlight had obtained some foreign financing to build a third hydroelectric plant below the Necaxa installation. Now the water coming out of the Patla plant below Necaxa would detour through a new tunnel and come from thousands of feet above the site of the third plant at Tepexic, way down in the tropical rain forest. Work on the tunnel had nearly been completed, but the French contractor had run into serious unforeseen problems and was stopping construction in the hope Mexlight — and the foreign financial agency would pick up some of the unforeseen costs. Early in 1953, Sofina had sent an

—

engineer to review the situation. Monsieur LePage was in his sixties and I was detailed to be his assistant. He was a small delicate man, very considerate, well read, an interesting companion to visit and travel with. I was impressed by the huge difference between this thoughtful, educated European engineer and the few American engineers I had met or worked with at Lechería. We had him for lunch at the house, he sent large bouquets of flowers and we spent several weeks in Necaxa going down traveling the length of the Tepexic tunnel, observing how the rock formation had managed not to be what it was supposed to be. I therefore spent several months working with Monsieur Lepage until we could reach an accommodation with the French contractors.

We made several trips to Necaxa. During one of these, I noticed that Mexlight had established a construction camp at the bottom in the rain forest and that they had horses there. I knew the chief construction engineer as he was from my old department when I worked at Lechería. He invited me to come down for a weekend and to bring my wife. We did this later that month. We rode horses for a day in the rain forest. I had never been in a deep tropical rain forest. One could hear the marvelous sound of birds and see strange huge trees; covered hiding places. One sensed moving hidden animals. There was the river. Everywhere vines reaching up; we saw small monkeys— and mostly birds, green, purple, blue, white, brown and all of them talking without stopping. By then Mike was five months old and he would stay with Eladia our maid and her son Pepito. Betty Gold would keep an eye to be sure everything was okay.

This trip gave me the idea to organize other visits to Mexlight facilities. At the time Mexlight still operated in the central plateau at 50 cycles as do several European countries — instead of 60 cycles as in the USA. But there was a very small enclave in the Mexlight service area that was at 60 cycles. This was an old mining town called Temascaltepec east of Toluca and south of Valle de Bravo. It was about four hours out of Mexico City. One had to leave the main road to Zihuatanejo just before another town also called Temascaltepec de Gonzalez. It required a jeep, as the side dirt road that reached the isolated mining town of Temascaltepec went through a difficult mountain pass.

In April 1953, I arranged to visit this plant. A company jeep was obtained and we left with Frances and Mike Gold — Betty could not leave her work. On the way we passed a village specializing in making sarapes — the blanket with a hole peasants wore in winter — and we bought several. The road was terribly dusty so that we generated a huge cloud of dust. As long as we moved, the dust stayed behind, but each time we had to slow or stop, our dust cloud would catch up and engulf us. We arrived in the mining town completely covered with dust — sand, earth, all the way inside our clothes, all over the new sarapes, way down the ear, the eyes, the hair — long showers took care of us. The old mining town had cobbled streets, old street lights, and was marvelously silent at night. The engineer in charge had arranged a hunt for the next day. We left on horses, were given rifles, and had a falcon in our party. We rode for several hours, reached a remote area where there was water and a large population of water fowl. Suddenly these birds came over us, we all shot — birds were hit and one fell nearly on Frances, splattering her with blood. It was early in the afternoon, we continued for a while shooting again. We had the horses, the falcon, the abandoned mining town, the hunting party, the dead birds — we were back 300 years. No socialism at this time. We were gentry with our falcons hunting on our lands.

—

Work in the office went well. George van Campenhout taught us how to make long term forecasts. We simply assumed electricity demand would continue to increase at seven per cent a year — doubling every ten years. We calculated the costs of building the necessary facilities — hydroelectric or steam plants like Lechería calculated the revenues of the company, how much Mexlight might borrow from the World Bank and to what extent the electric rates would have to be raised to allow us to service the debt and even pay a small dividend to the shareholders. We became good friends with the van Campenhout's. They were in their late forties with high school age children, a boy and a girl — the Goldstein's, my other new colleague from New York, had no children. Madame Goldstein was a Jewish princess who did not entertain much. In addition, she was always sick. She did not adapt to Mexico City and managed to go from one sickness to another, but David, who was about my age was fun and very clever with forecasts. We did all our estimates with Marchand mechanical adding and multiplying machines that we cranked manually. The office was therefore noisy — later we obtained electric machines that still made quite a bit of noise but we no longer cranked.

I became skilled in inventing and organizing expeditions. Later in 1953, I arranged for an expedition to the river Apulco. Part of the problem was that the Mexican government wanted to take over the electric industry just like it had nationalized the oil industry. The government had created the Commission Federal de Electricidad which operated some hydro plants and sold us the electricity they generated. There was this idea that hydro plants should be built by the government — an idea Mexlight did not accept as it meant the beginning of nationalization. Even if

—

electricity could not generate the income oil could, it could generate many jobs all through the country and the PRI, the Partido Révolutionario Institutional, was keen on the political aspect of the gifts and favors — vote for us, we will give you electricity — or we will give you jobs — and the ideological aspect: electricity is no longer in the hands of foreigners, electricity in Mexico is Mexican. But there was the issue of foreign loans and Mexlight had hired an ex-United States Ambassador, George Messersmith to chair its board, and later, General William H. Draper Jr., another well-connected United States financier and military personality to fill that post. The idea was to pressure the Mexican government to relent on nationalizing electricity by facilitating foreign loans for Mexlight, hence our office, my job, the forecasts, and so on.

My thought was that we should run an expedition to the Rio Apulco so as to have in-house data on its potential hydro possibilities. I somehow convinced George Messersmith and General Draper of this scheme. Maryssael who realized it would take more than a brief expedition to obtain useful data, gave in if only for the symbolic value of being able to mention that Mexlight had established a toe head on the Apulco. This river is south of the Necaxa river, and runs east from the mountains to the Gulf of Mexico. It is the only important river with the exception of the Papaloapan River, which also runs east but was already controlled by the Federal Commission of Electricity.

My idea was to measure river flows, something I had learned to do in my classes at Harvard, by going to a site where the river is close to where it cascades down at Zacapoaxtla — and where hydro facilities might eventually be built. This was a site in the State of Puebla that would require one day on horseback to reach the river, measure

—

and return to the closest village plus one day to reach it —
so three days on horseback, plus two days to go to Puebla
and return. Five days of holiday paid by Mexlight. Thus,
Frances and I left on our expedition. We had breakfast on a
cold morning in a small town in the State of Puebla called
Tezuitlàn. We had lamb grilled on a fire, beer and coffee
with bread and rode horses to the next isolated village. We
met some Indians on the path, our guide was an engineer
who operated Mexlight facilities in the first town. He rode
ahead and kept repeating "algo es algo, dijo la monja" —
something is something said the nun — at first he knew the
Indians — but later he did not and some would hide from
us. We were some ten or twelve riders. At a village close
to the Apulco called San Juan Acateno, there was a road —
a dirt road — but we had come by horse traveling through
shorter trails so as to have the horses for the next day
journey. There was also some kind of inn with a restaurant
and a very loud jukebox. The next day we left at 5am. We
had lamb again for breakfast. We rode on trails following
maps to the Apulco and found the river. It was by then
warm enough to allow us to go in so as to be able to
precisely map a slice — that is draw a straight line across
the banks and map the exact depth across the river. Then
once you have the area, the water goes through, you
measure the velocity of the flow by measuring how far a
very light object on the surface — or in the water, travels in
a minute. That gives you the volume of water flowing per
minute, hour, and based on other data, say our records of
flows of the Necaxa River, we would be able to estimate
the potential of the Apulco. We had lunch with us: more
lamb, beans and tortillas. In the afternoon, we returned to
our inn. By the time we arrived, we had had a full day.
The inn of San Juan Acateno was in full regalia — a
wedding was underway. An orchestra was blaring away.
They were playing 1920 tunes: The Sheik of Arabia by Art
Tatum! We changed and joined the party — drank beer,

—

ate more lamb and danced into the morning hours. Mexlight was in some ways, a fun employer.

This is when I started collecting Mexican pre-Columbian artifacts. The engineer had shown me some and I found them interesting. When I returned to the city I bought a piece from the Misrachi Gallery just in front of the Bellas Artes Opera House. We had heard that some pieces were being found somewhere around the "Basurero", the garbage dump north of Mexico City. So one day I went to the garbage dump. It was like a village with lots of people working the garbage, salvaging objects. I asked about "idolos" but no one knew until I found the local shoe shine boy who told me that right behind the hill they were excavating large pits to make bricks and were finding idolos. So I drove around the hill, found the brick ovens. It was a vast excavated pit dotted here and there with small ovens where clay bricks were fired. As the clay was dug up, idolos would appear. I had arrived at Tlaltilco, a site of very early pre-Columbian settlements dating to about 1000 B. C. Frances and I became quite active, going to Tlaltilco every Sunday morning and buying a few pieces that had been found. We would drive the car and park near the pit. Nothing would happen for a while. Then gradually, we would see in the distance men or women coming our way. They brought little bundles of "idolos". We paid "toston" for small heads — about 25 centavos — say two American cents. When we had a bit more money, we would go to the "Dealer", a man who bought from the brick makers and obtained the better, larger pieces — but he charged ten to a hundred pesos and that was a lot for us in those days. Once we went with the van Campenhouts, and they took pictures of our buying spree.

We also went to the Cuicuilco Pyramid in the Pedregal, the larva bed south of Mexico City, close to San

—

Ángel— we were with an American friend. We saw some workers on their way to the pyramid — there was a small museum there. They had been working on road repairs in the area and were carrying a bag full of small pieces they had found. We bought the entire lot, but they were only small fragments. Finally, we were given the name of Mrs. Sanchez, this was an American woman in her sixties married to a Mexican who over the years had acquired a reputation as the best purveyor of pre-Columbian pieces — Diego Rivera bought from her. She was well known, and middle men — or finders from everywhere in the country came to her with finds to sell. She was very friendly; we explained we did not have much to spend, so she sold us a set of cara sonrientes, smiling faces and a small statue of an Indian priest all from the Mexican East Coast around Vera Cruz. She gave us the lot at a very low price. From then on we were collecting.

When we married, Frances and I agreed to have an open marriage. This may sound strange but fitted the concept of marriage we shared. We wanted the relationship to be flexible, adaptive. We did not want to fall in a rigid arrangement where one lies to one's partner. The rules were simple — one might have affairs outside the marriage as long as: 1) the other partner was informed so that he or she would not learn about it from someone else, 2) the affair was discrete — preferably someone the partner did not know or did not see often, 3) the affair did not last long, the idea was to satisfy curiosity but not create custom, and 4) the affair did not affect in any way our married life — in other words, the affair should be ended if the other partner felt it was a problem. My idea, when we made this agreement was that this would take care of separations — that is periods of time when for one reason or another, we were not together and met someone else. I had had no occasion to use this agreement when Frances informed me

—

that she was having an affair with her Mexico City College colleague Hans Hoffman. This was sometime after Mike's birth in 1952. This did not please me since we were seeing the Hoffmans socially, and by the time Frances told me about it, the affair had been going on for some time. Anne Hoffman knew nothing about all this. Hans, it seemed was annoyed to be told that I had been told. I thought this affair did not meet our rules — first, because it was lasting, second, because I found it embarrassing since I knew the Hoffmans and we saw both of them socially.

Frances and I went to Necaxa in late March 1953,for a weekend vacation. Frances had forgotten to bring her birth control, but we decided nevertheless to risk a pregnancy. We had thought we would wait two years between children — but this would make it six months less. As it turned out, Anne was conceived that weekend in Necaxa.

Meanwhile her affair with Hans Hoffman continued. It was a repetition of the problem I had had in Chicago with the well known columnist Sydney Harris — but in Chicago Frances had not responded to the advances he made. I was still much younger in experience, in presence and self-assurance than Frances, Sydney Harris, or Hans Hoffman. I did not know how to deal with the problem, and this is one additional reason I began to think seriously of leaving Mexico.

As it turned out, Hans Hoffman would die soon after. He and Anne Hoffman returned to Los Angeles in the late fifties. He was to die in a car accident — he was driving another woman with whom he was also having an affair. Anne Hoffman moved to Berkeley.

—

A Proto Hippie

That year in Mexico we met Guido Tennissen. He rented a little house in Betty Bachrach's backyard. Betty Bachrach and her husband were also living on the GI Bill, and Guido made sandals. I liked Betty Bachrach very much and even had her pose nude for a painting. The painting was a failure and my liking her never went anywhere — she did not like me at all that way. I painted a double portrait of her on top of the nude failure. Guido, a Dutchman, had been drafted in the Dutch army, was sent to the U.S. to train, had deserted because he did not like the army and had come to Mexico. Betty liked Guido and had rented the little studio to Guido against her husband's better judgment. Guido had deserted his US Army training camp by going to a beach on the US east coast. He had carefully left clothes at another beach — left one set at the first beach with his military identity papers, swam out to the other beach and hitch-hiked down to Mexico City where he was now living, making sandals.

Guido was a pro-to-hippie — the hippie movement did not yet exist in the early fifties, but Guido was an early version. He had even acquired a reputation as such. For example he had received a telegram from Chiapas from an American inviting him to live a "natural" life in the jungle. Guido had been non-committal — and the man was coming for dinner at the Bachrachs — we were invited. This was another pro-to-hippie. This man had left on foot from Connecticut for Mexico with his wife and child. He had sold his farm, taken all his money and was determined to grow banana trees in the south of Mexico because the banana tree was the only existing non-aggressive tree. Its roots do not attempt to push the roots of other growing plants. After a few days on the road, wife and child had

—

abandoned him, but he had continued walking for months had arrived on foot in Chiapas and there had heard about Guido — would Guido want to join him? Guido as it turned out was having an affair with Betty Bachrach, so he did not go south. The man was very serious, quite convincing and certainly well informed about plants — he left the next morning for Chiapas. This time he took a bus both ways. He did not walk for Guido.

Guido was to reappear twice in our life — first, in the late fifties when he lived in Big Sur in California with a German girl and he made sandals there too. He made two pairs for me: one in Mexico and one in Big Sur. He left Big Sur when he attempted to steal a neighbor's sheep and was shot at. Second, he reappeared in Paris in the early sixties when Frances and I were sitting at the Deux Magots cafe on Blvd St Germain, and who is walking in front of our table? Guido, the German girl and Betty Bachrach — now divorced. The three of them are living together with a monk — a French monk on a farm in Normandy — a very primitive farm with no running water. They had come to Paris for a weeks stay. They were sleeping in a maid's room with a single large bed and sink and nothing else. But they seemed happy together. They came several times to our apartment to bathe. I saw Betty Bachrach once more, much later in the seventies in Berkeley when she was visiting Anne Hoffman. She told me that Guido was near death somewhere in Europe, still with the German girl. After that I had no more news, Betty Bachrach disappeared also. At some point in this long story, Guido had returned to Holland to face a court martial for his escape from the Dutch army. He had served a brief prison term —Betty explained that he did not want to die a fugitive from the Dutch army.

—

Departure From Mexico

It became clear to me after Anne's birth in January 1954 that Mexlight was not going to make it. I had been detailed by Monsieur Maryssael to work with an English engineer/economist from the staff of the World Bank to prepare an overall study of the future needs for electricity in the Central Mexican Plateau. We had a small office downtown where other World Bank staff visiting Mexico would stop and use our phones. A group of these had come to Mexico to negotiate downward the government graft percentage that high government officials took from all new projects. The Bank had to include the percentage of graft in their cost estimates; otherwise the projects would never be finished. They were of the opinion the government did not want Mexlight to expand. All the new projects would be built by the Commission Federal de Electricidad, and sooner or later when the CFE had expanded sufficiently, the government would nationalize Mexlight. As it turned out, their predictions were correct. The government never allowed Mexlight's rates to be increased so as to allow any dividend to be paid to share holders. The values of the shares on the Toronto stock market went down. The government secretly bought these undervalued shares until they acquired a controlling interest in the company. At which point they paid Sofina a very small amount for their shares and thus bought Mexlight out right at a bargain price. This was a much better deal than the 1938 expropriation of the foreign oil companies under President Cárdenas. There was no political outcry, no demands for restitution, no impact on continued international flow of investments. All this happened several years after our departure.

We either stayed in Mexico which meant moving to

—

a bigger house or we should return to the United States. There were only two bedrooms on Calle Aida. Anne slept in her immense cradle in our bedroom, but Frances felt that each child should have a separate room. The alternative was to leave, to take the plunge, for me to immigrate to the United States. I would have to find employment. I consulted both Ambassador George Messersmith and General William H. Draper, Jr., both on the board of Mexlight —both Americans and well disposed toward me — as our little group of van Campenhout, Goldstein and myself were the only staff who could concoct figures, provide data and estimates — something they were always needing.

Maryssael believed in the old European employment tradition, where one spent an entire career in one company. He had trained me, and just as I was becoming more useful to him, I was talking of leaving — and without an offer or anything. That did not make sense. But Messersmith and Draper were more flexible, in the American tradition. One should take risks and face challenges. Draper had contacts in the financial world of San Francisco, he would be pleased to write to his good friend Mr. Blyth who was one of the financiers (Blyth and Company) in that city. Mr. Messersmith an ex-Ambassador called the U. S. Embassy and asked them to help me obtain an immigration visa. It would not be a big problem since I was married to an American citizen and could therefore apply out of quota. But Maryssael was increasingly unhappy with my leaving. One day he called me in his office and lectured me — I was not a leader, I did not have the qualities of a leader, I would never succeed in the United States.

We were back in Carmel on vacation on April 19 1954. We had our picture taken by a photographer — Cain

— who lived in an adobe house he had built two blocks from Madame Crawford. This time I went to San Francisco and contacted the Harvard Club. I was an officer of the Harvard Club of Mexico City. I obtained the names of potential employment leads. The weather was magnificent, the beach beautiful. I had decided to leave Mexico. Mrs. Crawford was delighted to have us return, we could stay with her until I could find employment. Frances wanted to return to the States — she thought it would be better for the children. When we returned to Mexico City in early May, we had made a final decision: I would apply for a no quota visa and immigrate. I would actively look for employment in and around Carmel and San Francisco. I went back to work on Calle Gante on May 9, 1954. To place these dates in historical perspective, on May 7, 1954 the French garrison at Diên Biên Phû in French Indo China surrendered, but at the time, we hardly paid attention.

Unknown to me, the work I was doing for Mexlight or for the World Bank was something relatively new. Making forecasts of future indicators to examine how different government policies affect the economy or society was not generally done. What was later called policy research was still in infancy. There was a tradition of Town Planning and analytical studies had been done especially in war time but, at that time, there were no Schools of Public Policy. I had been very lucky that Monsieur Durostu had decided to leave the employ of Monsieur Maryssael. Otherwise, I would have remained in the Construction Department and my ability to immigrate might have been quite different. But somehow, by chance, I had found myself doing forecasts, cranking data on the Marchand calculators — and as it turned out, few had any experience in that type of analysis. Much later, when reading an account of World Bank activities, I found out

—

that the 1953 study of the future demand for electricity in the Mexican Central Plateau, in which I participated, was the first policy research and technical assistance project the World Bank ever undertook.

I was much too young, only four years out of school in 1954, to be able to negotiate offers of employment before going to San Francisco. A risk had to be taken, if worse came to worse, if for some reason I was unable to find any work, we would always be able to come back — not that Monsieur Maryssael would hire me back. I was aware that he was too furious with my going but by then I knew enough people in Mexico City to think that I could easily find work.

At Mexlight General William H. Draper, Jr., the Chairman of the Board let me think that if I ever had to come back, he might need an assistant. I never came back. During the Kennedy administration, General Draper who was by then no longer chairman of Mexlight was asked by President Kennedy to head a task force on the world population problem — to design a new U.S. policy regarding birth control in developing countries. I met him quite often at that time and assisted him to obtain many previous studies on that topic. Draper would continue this work under President Johnson and was instrumental in increasing funding for US support of birth control programs.

Nevertheless, being cautious, we decided to leave in Mexico a good deal of the furniture and equipment we were not taking — notably a couch, some chairs — beds and so on. These were left with my parents or stored in the shed of the cabinet maker on Oklahoma Street for about a year — when they were sold or given away. We did take with us most of my paintings, small furniture including the

—

record player and our idolos. These were packed by Mudanzas Gou and shipped via Laredo while we took the plane. By then, it was October of 1954.

Leaving Mexico also meant leaving my parents. During those four years my relationship with them had changed. Marriage and employment had meant I was no longer the child having to report morning and evening what I was about to do. But it did not end the reporting. It would continue, in one form or another, throughout my life as long as they lived. We would maintain through the years a long correspondence. Later, the telephone was added and in the late years of my mother's life, I would continue to call her once a week at precisely the same time on Sundays. This was never an easy logistical problem. Much later when I had settled in the USA and my mother had returned to France all my vacation travel was centered on her. I did pay attention to filial duties.

My parent's relationships with the women of my life were never easy. This is not a simple topic. But it can be summarized briely. My father tended to like the women I liked. He did not seem to mind the fact they were not Jewish. But he did not have too much time to share with them. Bridge and his own friends were far more important to him. My mother was far more complicated. She wanted to like them but also, deep down, hated them. No one was good enough for her son. Frances quickly took her distances from her. We would invite them to dinner and went to Oklahoma 27 for dinners. But Frances was always very cautious. Later as I will recount for you, Karen would encounter her own set of problems although she achieved a closer relationship. But all this was yet to pass. We are still in 1954.

—

VII

IMMIGRATION TO CALIFORNIA

I immigrated to the United States on a non-quota immigrant visa on October 6, 1954. My children, Michael and Anne, who were born in Mexico had to leave that country with their Mexican passports. They entered the United States as U. S. citizens and were included on their mother's passport. Anne was only a few months old, her "profession" on that Mexican passport was listed as "Niña lactante", a suckling baby.

We flew to Los Angeles, then on to Monterey, California. Meanwhile, Mudanzas Gou moved our household goods including Frances' piano by rail and truck. Frances' mother lived on 15th Avenue in Carmel, near a school and the mouth of the Carmel River. It was an easy walk to the lagoon and Stewart Beach.

I had two letters of introduction written by General William H. Draper, Jr., who had previously been associated with the investment banking firm of Dillon Read. One was addressed to Charles Blyth of the leading investment banking firm in San Francisco. The other, was for Mr. Black, the Chief Executive Officer of Pacific Gas and Electric (PGE). I also had been in contact with the Harvard Club of San Francisco.

—

Betty, Frances' sister lived, at that time, in San Francisco where she was a Psychiatric Social Worker. Once we had settled on 15th Avenue in Carmel, I made phone calls, obtaining appointments with Mr. Blyth, Mr. Black and the head of the Harvard Club. I took what was then a convenient daily train from Monterey to San Francisco where Betty housed me for several days. I saw Mr. Blyth who received me for a good half hour. I explained the kind of economic and financial forecasting I had been doing for Mexlight, and he suggested that instead of working for PGE, I should contact the Stanford Research Institute. I had never heard of SRI — but he explained how they, meaning leading business people in Northern California, had created it with Stanford University to have an applied research facility on the West Coast that would help develop the economy. It was a "think tank" working for clients including governments, corporations and philanthropies. He would call "Hoot" Gibson, the head of economics at SRI and have Hoot interview me. Charles Blyth had been or was still on the Board of SRI. I thanked him but told him that my hope was to work for PGE, since I had the experience of Mexlight and was in hope that Mr. Black, the CEO would take me on his staff.

Meanwhile, Mr. Black was out of town and I had lunch with the Harvard Club man who took me to the Bohemian club for lunch but did not have much to offer. He was in the wood industry and he thought that between Mr. Blyth and Mr. Black, I was already in good hands. I enjoyed the Bohemian Club, a 19th century San Francisco institution.

Mr. Black finally received me. He did not think he needed me on his staff but assured me that PGE would offer me a job and he had someone in personnel interview

—

me. I also saw "Hoot" Gibson in Menlo Park (the train again served me well). Hoot was very desirous to please Charley Blyth and Charley was such a good friend and if I knew Charley, then surely I was already a good friend of SRI and would I meet Bill Platt and see what he thought. So I met Bill Platt who said how wonderful, they had just made a bid on a contract in Chicago to do a long term economic study of the demand for electricity in that area, they would need someone with my experience, they surely could use me at SRI. They would make me an offer.

I returned to Carmel and within the next week I had two offers: one from SRI and one from PGE. Both were offering about the same salary — $450 per month. PGE was offering to place me in their distribution department — or was it their transmission department — as an engineer — they would train me for some weeks or months. SRI was offering to have me work in their Economics Department. They expected to have a project contract for me and, at the time, I did not realize that it would mean spending most of the winter in Chicago. Finding SRI more romantic — or at least more diversified or maybe closer to the kind of analysis I had been doing at Mexlight — anyhow, in total ignorance of what SRI did, I accepted their offer. This was the end of October.

Palo Alto And Stanford

At this time, school was starting, but this was of no consequence since Mike was only two; we began looking for housing in Palo Alto. We would leave the children with Mrs. Crawford in Carmel and drive her green Chevrolet to Palo Alto to look for a house. In 1954 it was possible to buy a recently built house in the 10 to 15,000 dollar range. It was easier to buy a house than renting one. We found such a house for $13,000. It was an Eichler tract home

—

built in the late forties a simple modern design three bedrooms, two baths with the kitchen giving directly into the living room with an area to eat in. There was a nice backyard. The house was not too far from Highway 101 surrounded by similar tract houses. There was a G. I. (World War II veteran financing) loan we could assume. After a down payment of about $3,000 the monthly payments for interest, principal and taxes was $85 per month. Since I was to earn $450, I was to spend less than one-fourth of my salary on housing. The house was at 2826 Greer Road in Palo Alto. I did not realize at the time that the house was located in a flat area with limited drainage to the bay as Highway 101 served as a dam. We were to find out soon enough that no drainage can mean flooding when it rains too much.

While we were buying a house, Mudanzas Gou had been on their way from Mexico City. The shipment had arrived and was in storage in Monterey, California. Bekins moved us from there to Palo Alto. By early fall we were settled. Frances' piano had been set up, we had bought a few pieces of furniture, Danish modern, and the record player and cabinet from Mexico City worked. The short wave radio, the ever present Hallicrafter, was installed in the bedroom and an antenna strung across the roof.

Stanford Research Institute was located in several buildings. The scientific work was mostly in facilities in World War II temporary buildings at a site in Menlo Park. But the Economics Division was on the other side of Highway 101 in rented space in East Palo Alto. This was a set of large rooms broken up into a maze of eye level partitions in which one or two persons worked. There was quite a bit of crowding and additional rooms were rented around the main buildings in private homes. I was given an office to share with a tall young woman also just hired.

—

She was American, her name was Marian Crites. She had just returned to the West Coast from Paris. She had lived for many years in China. She had been hired because she had some librarian training and was expected to help prepare bibliographies for various research projects. Marian's French lover soon appeared on a motorcycle and Marian seemed genuinely pleased "he followed me all the way here" she would say but it was not clear whether she liked Monsieur Alexandre Frutschi or not. Yet he was young, good looking and kept coming around making a huge racket with his motorcycle under our "office" window. He had found a job as a waiter in the only good French restaurant on El Camino Real south of Palo Alto, called L'Omelette. This was a big place, always a bit dark, as restaurants tended to be in the fifties. There was so much cycling around our office that Marian finally gave up and became Madame Frutschi.

Meanwhile Stanford Research Institute had not obtained the contract for the study in Chicago, so they had very little for me to do. Places such as SRI depend on contracts to keep their staff and it rapidly becomes a problem to remain on overhead. Each week you'd be asked "on what project do we charge you?" and if you keep saying the overhead — sooner or later it will be adios amigo. Well, it was more formal. They ask you to see Hoot or Bill and the conversation is very genial. "We are thinking of your future, we are concerned about your doing well, maybe another organization would be better suited to you." You are not fired but you are expected to make professional arrangements and depart.

Obviously I was far too ignorant of the applied research world to be able to generate contracts and anyhow I was not too concerned since I knew that the P.G.E offer was still standing. I had declined it "for the moment." So,

—

since I could not work on research proposals and since there was little to do, I would check in, in the morning, see Marian, listen to motorcycle woes and given the distance to the main office, I would leave, return home and paint the exterior of the house before winter set in. This way Frances could go shopping without the kids and we could settle in. We only had one car at that time. A two-door Ford bought in Monterey. I needed the car to get to East Palo Alto as there were no practical direct public links. Bill Platt did not seem too concerned about my idle days and he may not have been aware I was painting the house. This way Frances had some mobility.

First Solar Energy Conference

The director of SRI was Jessie Hobson and Jessie was a man filled with ideas. I certainly did not know at the time that he might be gay but I liked him and as it turned out, he had some sympathy for me. Jessie was interested in solar energy and we had met at one of these endless SRI meetings where self-congratulations were the order of the day. At SRI, institutional survival meant large contracts. Each time someone went to Washington and came back with a large project, there had to be a celebration. The clan was gathered and Hoot would tell us how Dick Foster had gone and obtained one million dollars from the Air Force. The clan would applaud and we would rejoice since more than half that money went into the overhead and that was what kept us idle hands alive. Jessie had met me and he decided I should undertake a study of the economics of solar energy. This would be an internal study, financed by SRI which would provide the core of a presentation that Jessie intended to make at a World Symposium on Solar Energy, which SRI was in the process of arranging in collaboration with the University of Arizona at Tucson. This was financed in part by the American and Foreign

—

Power Company which operated utilities in Arizona. Henry B. Sargent, the President of American and Foreign Power was behind the project In short, Jessie found me a permanent niche on the SRI overhead which saved me from being guided out "for your own good" — Charley Blyth not withstanding.

The bad consequence was that I was transferred from Bill Platt who never cared if I painted houses to Herr Burda a German-American scientist who was to head the collective SRI undertaking in Solar Energy. Herr Burda was the very serious kind of manager. Rules were very important. He was a stickler for details, penny-pinching, myopic, heavy, slow, ponderous and quite arrogant. Hours mattered now. Eight sharp in the morning, and all that jazz. I was an engineer who passed as an economist. He was a scientist who did not like economists. As you can see I obviously did not like him and I assume he reciprocated these feelings. This did not facilitate life at all. But I embarked on an economic study of the costs of various forms of solar energy and obtained data from a series of potential areas of the world so as to be able to compare the costs of solar against the costs of conventional fuels in Africa, Latin America, and other parts of the world. Herr Burda wanted his name on the study and he constantly wanted to see what I had done. Meanwhile the plans for the Solar Energy Conference were taking shape and my language abilities were to save me from the clutches of my German colleague. While Burda was in charge of the solid scientific work, Merritt Kastens, a nice engaging administrator was in charge of the organizational arrangements for the Conference. He had initiated a correspondence with relevant scientists in Europe, Asia and Latin America. There was much work in France where Félix Trombe had built the first large solar furnace at Mont Louis in the Pyrenées. So while Kastens could read German

—

— thus not needing Burda — he needed me to read French and Spanish. I was transferred from Burda to Kastens.

We were now at the beginning of 1955. My new role was social. I contacted scientists the world over and helped Kastens receive many visitors in Menlo Park. We had luncheons on the expense account. This was a new experience. We had dark luncheon restaurants in the 1950's, no outside windows, you walked in blinded from the outside light. The waitresses wore scanty skirts and bare midriffs. The customers were all males, all on expense accounts. Martinis were ordered, after that one ate steak, potatoes — maybe with beer or wine. The meal would be completed with pies and watery coffee — and then, one was back out in the blinding sun. It was amazing we did not have more car accidents after lunch. Anyhow that period was my initiation to management and organizational life. I learned to use the telephone — that is long distance telephone — something I simply thought as an extravagant luxury. It was so nice to talk with Washington, D.C. and ask them "what is the weather there like?" — as if one had all the time in the world to talk long distance. They would say that it was very hot or it was snowing and the smug Californians would say that it was so pleasant in Menlo Park.

After leaving Burda and company I had moved to the main SRI facilities which at that time were in Menlo Park, where SRI is located now, but in temporary army buildings from World War II. These were quite pleasant. There was a central corridor with offices on either side. Windows in each office, a fair amount of space, no one above or below, not too hot in summer, heated in winter. Merritt was a pleasant boss — I could go home for lunch if there were no visitors. I would take time to do some shopping to help Frances, help with the children, stay

—

longer around the house at lunch time and make up the time after five. So I could still come home in time for reading stories, set the table and have dinner with them. By then Mike was 3 years old and Anne going on two. It was not easy for Frances but her mother would come up from time to time to visit and help with babysitting and we often went to Carmel for weekends.

There was a neighbor who also helped. This was a young childless couple living next door in a similar house. The husband was often away. I should explain that this neighbor began something new in my life. In Mexico I had had no occasion to use our open marriage arrangement. Frances had had that affair in Mexico that annoyed me. I did not care much for the neighbor; I thought she had not much of a brain although she had conventional good looks.

Frances had gone down to Carmel with the children leaving me in Palo Alto. It was during the week and the husband of the neighbor was away but she had a girl friend visiting her in the afternoon. They had both come to the house after I had returned from work "to see if I was okay", she knew Frances was gone. I offered drinks we sat in the living room and began a long discussion of married life — of affairs. I do not know how we got into that subject but I explained how Frances and I had an open marriage, how I thought it was so important not to lie to one's partner and so on. They left — the friend to go home — the neighbor to have her dinner. But later that night the neighbor called. Would I please come to her house, she needed help for something. She came to the door in a negligée. Then she invited me to her bedroom where she posed. I thought that the costume and the whole presentation was terribly artificial, but being an "homme sensuel moyen", I did go into her bed and made love but told her it would be one time only. I promptly told Frances when she returned and

Frances talked to the neighbor and everyone agreed we had too many drinks that it was a mistake and in fact there was no re-occurrence, I really liked her as a babysitter not as a bed mate.

So this neighbor was helpful with the children since she had a lot of time on her hands. Her husband was often away on jobs for weeks. The houses were adjoining and identical. She could just as well come into our house, listen to the radio and read a book or do her sewing, when we wanted to go out as if she was at home. There was also a drive-in movie house at the corner of our housing track and the Bay Shore Highway. We would put Anne and Mike to sleep in the back seat — Anne in a portable crib between the seat and the front seats, Mike on the back seat, we would watch the movie and drive home. The drive-in was very convenient. We rarely hired babysitters. Cost was a factor but I think there were very few teenagers in our tract. Most of the couples were young, recently married — many with GI loans and with children under ten.

The World Symposium on Applied Solar Energy took place in Phoenix and Tucson Arizona on November 1-5, 1955. There were 900 registrants and a Solar Engineering Exhibit which was attended by nearly 30,000 curious visitors. The meeting was chaired by Lewis W. Douglas who had once resigned from the Roosevelt Administration finding it too communist but had served as Ambassador to England. Many scientists were present at that meeting. Coverage in the press helped for the first time to bring solar energy to the attention of the general public. At the exhibit we had a large solar pump sent by the Somor firm in Lecco Italy. There were also solar cookers, a Novoid solar engine, a Bell solar battery for communication equipment, solar space heaters and other displays. At the Conference there were papers on solar

—

machines, cooling with the sun, solar water heaters, algae as an energy converter and many more. There were panels and plenary sessions. We had experts from the US, Japan, Europe and the Soviet Union. Jesse Hobson delivered my paper on the economics of solar energy and I had my picture taken at the concluding plenary while translating the remarks of Gaston Dupouy, Director of the French Centre National de la Recherche Scientifique.

A Flood In The House

In December 1955 the rains were heavy. It was raining everyday, heavy rains that soaked the earth. Our new tract or subdivision had been built by the Eichler people south of the San Francisquito creek that runs through Palo Alto. That creek went under Highway 101, the Bay Shore Highway, and the highway was built up, forming a dam between the housing track and the bay. All this of course was unknown to us. In addition, there was another dam. Right by our neighbor's house was an embankment and an open ditch going west to east, draining into the bay. We were in a bowl: to the north we had the creek, east and south we had embankments and west the terrain rose toward the hills.

As the rain got heavier, the creek went up and in late December just before Christmas I returned home to find water standing in the street. The police were around and we were told there were problems at the highway bridge above the San Francisquito creek. Frances and I were not worried presumably the water was not draining well from our subdivision because the creek was high, but nothing much more Being cautious and "prévoyant" I said we should lift the carpets and roll them so that if a little water should seep into the house, there would be no problem. We did take care of the rugs and went to sleep.

—

At some point early in the night I heard some strange marine sounds — like water noises. I turned in the bed, put my hand on the side and — surprise — there was water on the floor. We got up, woke the children and I decided to evacuate immediately. I opened the front door and a small wave gushed in. We had about a half inch in the house. The street was about a foot lower, maybe more — so the street was under water but the street lights were on. We opened the garage, the car was in about an inch of water, we moved the children in, rushed to gather a few clothes. I called the Kastens, woke them up, asked if we could go to them. They had a large house in Portola Valley — high and away from any creek. They told us to come right over. We started the car, closed the doors and backed into the street.

Meanwhile, the police had finally arrived and they were using a loudspeaker to wake people up — urging them to leave. Tree trunks and debris at the highway bridge over the San Francisquito was sending creek waters into the adjacent flat lands. Neighbors were walking out of their houses, walking in about 18 inches of water. I knew from my days in Lechería how to drive in deep water. I kept the accelerator at full blast, moved the car slowly by using the clutch. The car had water inside, but the children were in the back seat. Mike was delighted — "the car is a boat, the car is a boat" he kept chanting.

The house was flooded for two days and we were only able to return when crews dislodged the pile of tree trunks that blocked the creek at the highway's bridge. Water damage reached 16 inches inside. Luckily the house had a cement slab floor which was unaffected. The biggest problem was books and records including the old 78 rpm in albums. About ten people from SRI came in to help. The books were laid to dry outside, the records were saved but the albums had disintegrated. The mud was swept out. The beds were also lost but a local bed company offered beds at wholesale prices to help out. We moved back three days later. But we had already decided that sooner or later we would move to higher ground.

Frances, who had worked during our entire stay in Mexico City, decided not to attempt to do so in California . For one thing we no longer had the two maids and more importantly there did not seem to be work for her at Stanford. She had visited several of her professors, and several years later, when we returned from France, she would find work again. But during my years at SRI, Frances spent her time with the children. She did do some testing for a local psychologist as she was an expert at giving and scoring the Rorschach test.

I learned valuable skills at SRI. First and foremost to do applied economics research. That is gathering facts and writing in tight time limitations. The Solar Energy 1955 Conference took place both in Phoenix and Tucson, Arizona. I published three articles on solar energy, alone or co-authored, in professional journals. I helped with the creation of an International Solar Energy Association and for a while we edited a new journal called *The Sun at Work*. I also worked on a series of economic studies totally unrelated to solar energy. I learned how to take on a topic one knew nothing about. For instance, the demand for paint products in the United States — or the future of Japanese exports to Latin America or the probable demand for coal in Western Europe — and within a very tight time frame — gather relevant information, analyze it and write a report for a client.

There is a discipline here that requires a sense of timing. You have to understand that what matters is the

—

report. And the report has to be delivered on time. One cannot be a perfectionist. The task consists in gathering as much information as possible in the time available and writing the results of the analysis before the due date. Clients do not want delays and do not want to go over budget. SRI had professional editors who came into the scene very early. One learned to search only for the necessary. This was quite different from my first experience on the economics of solar energy when I had plenty of time to gather information. Here one had to elaborate a strategy. What will the report say — how do we get the data to permit us to say it? Call Washington. There was this marvelous young man, Skip Lea at the SRI Washington, D. C. office. You would call Skip — ask how the weather was — commiserate on the differences in temperature between the two coasts and ask Skip — can you find any studies on paint products or on Japanese exports or on coal demand? Skip knew all the relevant report producers in many government agencies — commerce, agriculture, and so on. In a few days all the federal stuff was on hand. Relevant projections of demand or supply were found. We might have some in-house studies — work done for other clients that could be used — we would do some projections of our own. I had no sophisticated mathematical skills — and keep in mind we had no computers. This is still the Marchand addition, multiplication machine and cranking numbers was just that — although by now the machines were electric and you no longer had to crank to get results. You pressed "add" or "multiply" or "divide" and then read the results on the top of the machine. So we did linear work, by and large — straight line projections. But there were mathematicians on the staff who did much more sophisticated analysis. I was not part of that group. Our work consisted in bringing together disparate sources of information, making some sense out of it, and packaging it.

—

SRI International

Hoot Gibson was an ambitious man. He wanted to move into the international scene. I have found over the years, that many Americans like the international scene not so much for the problems or prestige it provides, but for the opportunity it offers for long distance travel. He wanted to start an international division within the economics group. He had been impressed by the visibility of the Solar Energy Conference and more importantly there was money for international research: the emerging US foreign aid programs, the development activities of the few large foundations, particularly the Ford Foundation in New York, and International organizations such as the World Bank. Hoot hired Ed Prentice, a man who had worked for the US Aid program in Asia to head a new International Division. Ed came to Palo Alto and since I spoke French and Spanish, and knew Mexico, I was named Assistant Manager of the International Division.

We began looking for contracts Ed did most of the traveling to Washington and New York, while I ran the office. This is where I learned how to write proposals, how to maintain contact with distant colleagues and how to manage contract research. A number of economists joined our group. Eugene Staley who was a respected author of a book on the newly emerging developing countries, Bill Bredo, Morgan Sibbett, Bill Moran, and many others. We obtained many contracts including large contracts from the Ford Foundation to help modernize the small industries of developing countries. Staley went to India; Sibbett went to newly independent East Pakistan which is now the totally independent Bangladesh. We published a short treatise on how governments in developing countries can attract foreign investments. We became known, so well known in

—

fact, that the CIA arranged to have one of their agents on our staff as a cover for work abroad.

The art of proposal writing at that time consisted in asking large scale questions, the important problems and issues — so large that we had no real hope of having answers. But it showed what we considered important. The proposal then detailed the scale of effort that would be mounted, the number of people who would be involved — where and when the work would take place. The budget completed the picture. If you did not answer the large questions, at least you could demonstrate you had gone through the motions.

Since my position at SRI was well consolidated, I was writing proposals, bringing in money and Hoot was gong ho for the International Division. Frances and I began to look for a place to build in Portola Valley. Some time had elapsed since the flood, and it was already a memory. We had heard that some houses in the tract had sold at reasonable market prices. Presumably Palo Alto was improving the creek channel to avoid a re-occurrence. We found a lot overlooking Portola Road. The lot had three-fourths of an acre and in those days Portola Road was a sleepy silent country road. In front, on the other side of the road, there was a Jesuit School —surrounded by mostly green playing fields so there was little risk that many houses would spoil the view. Corte Madera Rd., still unpaved at the time, led to our lot. My parents, always happy to further investments, would help and we hoped we could build a three-bedroom house for about $15,000 — so that with the lot we would pay about $20,000. A Mr. Okermann had been highly recommended. He was an aging, but still very solid and large Finn who did contracting and building. We hired a draftsman and designed a three-bedroom and living room house with a

—

space for a painting studio and open kitchen giving into the activity room. There were to be two fireplaces back-to-back and brick walls in our bedroom and fireplace walls — to remind us of adobe bricks we could not afford. Okermann did build solid. Masses of concrete were poured for the garage below the living room, and we did pay — at the end — $26,000 for the house instead of $15,000. But there was no doubt our bunker would withstand an earthquake. The house had radiant heating. The major problem seemed that we could never get rid of the poison oak on the lot behind us.

We placed 2826 Greer Road on the market and it sold rapidly for about two thousand more than we had paid and we moved to Portola Valley in September 1957. I thought I would never move again. The site was rural. Between our lot and Corte Madera Road there was a large ditch, a kind of romantic moat, we had a septic tank and few neighbors to worry about. Every evening there was the fog right behind the hills overflowing towards us. I thought I loved living in the country like that. We had rabbits for the children in the small backyard, plus the two Siamese cats, Ch'ing and Ming who had returned from Mexico with us. At some point we also had a number of small rodents who spent time running in their cages, when they were not caught by the cats. Frances and the children decided to buy a pet skunk while I was away on a trip to Washington. This pet skunk could not spray and was presumably harmless — but not so. This was a wild thing in our house. There is no genetic background for pet skunks as there is for dogs, cats, horses and so on. Skunks are not normal pets and this skunk was no pet at all. This is my memory of my relationship with this newcomer in the household. It would attack me while I was walking in the house and try to bite. It did just that at a cocktail party when I was carrying a tray of glasses and drinks. But Frances, Mike, Anne and my

—

third child Marc loved him. I was stuck with him until we left for Washington, DC.

When I started work for SRI on November 8, 1954 , I immediately met with the security people. SRI had many classified contracts and the entire staff had to go through clearance procedures. Moreover, I was told that I should immediately apply for US citizenship. The security people kept insisting that in the long run they did not want me to remain French they wanted to be able to clear me to secret level and that meant naturalization. I did not mind at all, on the contrary. I was anxious to become American. My mother had lost her American citizenship when she married and as a result, I had been very impressed by the importance of American passports in 1940. To me, in 1954, an American passport was the final guarantee of safety and I therefore immediately began the process of naturalization. Not that I worked on classified projects, in fact Frances and I were very clearly politically on the non-military side of things. My work at SRI was never classified. The process of obtaining American citizenship would take several years. I would finally become an American citizen in 1958.

Time-Life Conference On Foreign Investment

Hoot Gibson and Ed Prentice had met with some Time-Life people in New York. Impressed by the visibility of the October 1955 Conference on Solar Energy, they had come up with the idea of a conference on economic development in third world countries that would bring together leading bankers, industrialists and government people to discuss the importance of private investment. The conference would take place in San Francisco in the fall of 1957. Meanwhile I would be sent on a tour of Latin America to try to interest leading industrialists and bankers

—

to attend. Thus, in the summer of 1956, I left for a trip to a half dozen countries including Argentina and Brazil. But I wanted a chance to go to Paris, I had not returned to France since leaving in 1942. So, with Kasten's help I arranged to undertake a study of the Solar Furnace at Mont Louis in the Pyrenées. In exchange, I would lecture on solar energy in Latin America. So we added Bolivia and Peru to my trip since there is plenty of sunshine on the altiplano and I would go to Venezuela and Chile and ultimately fly via Dakar from Rio to Paris on Air France's south Atlantic route.

In July of 1956, I flew to Mexico to briefly see my parents, then on to Venezuela via La Habana. It felt good to me to change planes in Cuba since I had stopped there while on the SS Serpa Pinto in 1942. But as it turned out, my suitcases went from Mexico to Madrid while I changed and took a different plane to Caracas. La Habana Airport was teeming with people — it was night and confusion was everywhere. The white shirts of 1942 were everywhere in evidence. Cubans were far more expansive than Mexicans. The crowd was so thick that I just managed to find my way in time for the Caracas plane. But we flew away and in the early hours of the morning I could see the coast of South America. I was reminded of seeing the Orizaba Mountain over the ocean in 1942. In Caracas I was to see Joe Slater who then headed an oil company philanthropic foundation: the Creole Foundation. Joe and his wife took pity on my suitcase problem and invited me to stay at their house. It was a Saturday, they were going to take a trip to the rain forest the next day and I would go with them. My suitcase had been located in Madrid and would reappear on that following Monday. So we went in their car and unknown to me, I sat on chewing gum the Slater's children had left on the back seat. As I was walking in a public park with them, this very polite young Venezuelan approaches me

—

and tells me — "sabe ud" — do you know, he says with great sadness on his face — that you have Chicklet on the back of your pants? It seemed as bad as if my fly had been open or I had a hole in the back of my pants: "sabe usted que tiene Chicklet en su pantalon?" I thanked him and he left in great sadness knowing how hard it is to get rid of well-pressed Chicklet. The Venezuelan rain forest was a disappointment. It did not match the sounds and colors of the birds, monkeys and hidden animals in the trees around the Patla hydroelectric plant in Mexico.

In Peru, I felt well but in Bolivia I stood stupidly in the La Paz airport — with no oxygen in the brain and therefore a very slow and limited thinking process. "Don't you need to get to a hotel?" I was asked — as I stood around waiting with my suitcases. I just stood there, looking blank, shuffling from one foot to the other. In due time I made it to the hotel and further down in altitude to the home of the director of the U. S. Technical Assistance Mission who had me lie down and breath oxygen. But Bolivia in 1956 was fantastic. Indians were everywhere and there was the music of the Altiplano I had heard in 1949 at Rex Crawford's house in Philadelphia when a German musicologist had brought his own early recordings for us to hear. But even in 1956 recordings of Altiplano music were rare. Without oxygen, walking in La Paz was difficult and I was constantly out of breath. I had a cold in addition — and keep in mind, it was winter there. But I searched and searched until I was able to buy four or five 45 rpm small vinyl pressings of Indian groups playing Altiplano music. The music gods smiled on me. The day I left La Paz, I saw and heard right on the side of the tarmac, a group of Indians dancing to a small native orchestra. As the doors of the plane were closing, I could hear the deep lamentations of the long Andean flutes. Upon my return to California, I contacted the new listener supported radio

—

station KPFA in Berkeley, I lent them my Bolivian 45 rpm records and this rare music was played on the air.

Santiago and Chile reminded me of France. There were little carts drawn by tired horses on rural roads and everything looked sad under the rain the way the French country side can look damp, dark and ill lighted in the winter. Since I was in Latin America and not France, I was invited to an Argentine cook out — a barbacoa where lamb's intestines were cooked — these were a revelation. Keep in mind it was winter and cold but somehow I had joined a group from the University of Chile where I was to lecture on solar energy and there were women and men — and guitars — and here I was finding a different Latin American musical expression reminiscent of the best of Mexico's old songs. The chinchulincs (i.e., the intestines) were wonderful but young women did not seem to be available. I had been on the road for more than two weeks and desire was back — or in the front of my mind. I was staying in each place for four or five days and by the time I had found my way around, I had to leave. I kept hoping that a beautiful tourist would be alone in the room next door and that we would meet in the hotel elevator. After a deep look into each others eyes, with full understanding of the precarious nature of life and relationships, she would invite me to her room. But the elevators were unresponsive to my dreams.

In Buenos Aires I stayed with my Harvard Conant Hall roommate, Claude Enrique Luis Pablo Dechamps — already successful in business. I also saw Francis Cahn and lectured about Solar Energy at the University. I had my picture in the local paper. Claude was still at his parent's house — there were butlers with white gloves serving baby beef. During my visits in town promoting the next conference, I met many industrialists — all seemed to have

—

gomina on their hair — slick and shiny and they spoke endlessly about Peron, how he had ruined the country. Again, I found no willing lover in elevators.

I left Argentina and went to São-Paulo where I now had a language barrier — again, meeting after meeting with gregarious Paulistas. Then on to Rio on a plane that nearly collided with another Brazilian airliner, but managed a safe evasive maneuver that made me even more aware of the precarious nature of life and the stupidity of unshared beds. Rio was warm — the beaches were not empty — by then it was a painful realization that female sexuality could be so visible so near and yet so distant.

The big scandal that week in Rio was the sudden departure of the French Ambassador's secretary who had left her job and her family to go live in a favela, a shanty town around Rio, with one of those handsome life guards on the beach. But I was not tall and dark and the young nubile dark women in the smallest bikinis on the sea front belonged to another world. I met several Frenchmen at the hotel and it was decided we would visit a brothel — later after dinner. These compatriots were careful, not very adventurous. Once we had entered the brothel, we were unimpressed by the dreariness of the staff — these were not the elegant slim dark young women of the beach. One of the French mentioned venereal diseases and a cold front hit us. We left — each for our rooms and distant sleep

From Rio, I flew via Recife and Dakar to Paris. This was my return after 14 years abroad. In those days business travel was often first class, and first class on the Rio-Paris Air France super constellation was a large cabin with a bar and only two rows facing each other of comfortable chairs that swiveled to face in any direction: a club like atmosphere. We would fly all night, refuel in

—

Recife and arrive the next morning in Dakar where we would land, have a shower and continue to Paris where we would arrive in the late afternoon having gone from winter to summer.

The Russian Ambassador to Uruguay was on that flight. It was also the solo inauguration of the pilot. The clubroom had a few empty seats and the stewardess was in high spirits. It was dark and the night was long. The motors, this was before the jet aircraft, were noisy. We drank champagne, and more champagne. We tasted Iranian caviar and some food and more champagne.

The stewardess called the pilot to join for a toast: his solo of the south Atlantic route required plenty of champagne. He joined and sat on an empty seat. We had several more toasts and more caviar. Then the stewardess decided to end the cold war, at least in that cabin, that night. We would have a Russian toast and, as is done in Russia, we would smash our glasses on the floor, they were glass not plastic. So we did, all in high spirit over the dark South Atlantic. The pilot finally went back to the cockpit taking several glasses for the rest of the crew and we flew into Dakar where it was dripping hot. We took a few steps in the airport and had a shower. Unfortunately, we left the stewardess there. She was French and accustomed to looking one in the eye. She knew about the precarious nature of life but her bed that night was in Dakar while mine was going to be at my uncle's house in Paris.

We arrived over Paris in the late afternoon. We had changed into a smaller plane in Dakar and now I was sitting next to a Frenchman flying from Dakar to Paris. His wife was sitting right behind us. They were very impressed that I was returning after a 14 years' absence. As the plane made a long loop over Paris, they showed me the sites, in

—

case I had forgotten: the Eiffel Tower, the Louvre, Notre Dame, the Sacré Coeur. This was August 5, 1956.

My uncle Maurice (Momo) and Aunt Alice (Tante Lo) were waiting at Orly, together with several of my cousins. It was an official family reception. My parents had already returned — but I had not. We went to Neuilly where Tante Lo's cook Marcelle had prepared a grand dinner. I was very shaken by this return. I felt very French, and it was easy to feel French when the food was so good and the reception so warm.

Now I waited for Frances and Mike who were to arrive several days later. Maurice had lent me a car and I went to fetch them at Orly. When Mike saw me, before going through passport control, he left his mother and ran to me. But the police intervened and separated us until his mother's passport had been stamped. At that point, I opened a bottle of champagne and toasted their first visit to France.

Betty Crawford, Frances' sister, was to join us and we were to drive to Mont Louis and spend a week there while I visited the Solar Furnace and gathered information for an article. Betty arrived but not alone. She was with a male friend from New York, a psychiatrist who had recently broken off with his girlfriend. As we left Paris it rained, and it rained everyday during the trip south. The friend wore a raincoat and he was tightly wrapped in it, ensconced in the back seat of the car. Apparently, he had not slept well on the plane, for he slept all the time. We would try to point sites to him. He would open his eyes, peer out of the rain, or through the rain and go quickly back to sleep. When we tried to take him with us to visit a Romanesque church or a chateau, he would refuse. "What's the name of this church?" he'd ask — we would

—

give it to him — "check, seen it" and he would fall back in his corner. He became too much for Betty — or maybe it was true and he had to return to New York and his patients. We had come down through Limoges so we took him to the airport in Toulouse where he would catch a plane back to Paris and New York.

Mont Louis in the Pyrenées was sunny as it should be to sustain a solar furnace. Professor Félix Trombe was charming — he invited the four of us to a splendid meal in a local restaurant, but the hotel, the only one in town, was a disaster. It was a small hotel for British tourists — for lower middle class British tourists, who came on packaged deals for one week before returning somewhere in the midlands. The food was abominable, as if the French had decided that the only way to please the English was to make them feel at home. The atmosphere in the dining room was deathly — low voices murmuring sadly about the number of days left, the walking excursions left to tackle, and then the food was enough to depress everyone including the French staff that clearly was not enjoying any of it. Betty and Frances said they could not stay. They would leave with Mike and explore the environs. I could stay on since I had to write a report on the Solar Furnace. They would take the car and go down to Perpignan and the seashore. I could walk from the hotel to the Solar Furnace, and if I was unhappy — too bad — they certainly would not stay another day in this English enclave.

They left the next day with my uncle's car, leaving me on foot, in the charming hotel. By the time they came back, I was in a foul mood — they even took an extra day for some reason or other and refused to stay in Mont Louis. We slept that night in Font Romeu, very close to Mont Louis. Frances and I had a bad argument which ended with her punching me and my falling backward in a closet. This

—

was the same splendid immense hotel I used to stay at, when I went skiing in the winter with the McJanet School. Now the hotel was vast and empty, it was 1956 and summer.

We had come down through Limoges, Brive, Cahors, Mont Auban, Toulouse, and the Col de Puymorens (where we had nearly crashed into a cow on the road). We returned via Perpignan where we did not stop since "they" had already been there, Sète, Montpellier, Nimes, and Valence. We had a fantastic meal in Vienne, south of Lyon; good food soothed all the unhappiness. Vienne was the home of several three star restaurants including the summit of French cooking: the Restaurant de la Pyramide of Madame Point — we ate at a lesser known place but the Quenelles de Brochet were out of our own experience. By the time we reached Paris, we were again in good spirits.

I had learned that traveling with family is not easy. Frances and Betty had also had a fight — we had detoured from Montpellier to Arles and Betty wanted to stay longer in Arles. I think we must have slept there at least one night. Frances wanted to move on. It reached an impasse, they would not talk to each other, I was trying to negotiate. Betty was on one side of the square where St. Trophime — the great Romanesque church is located. Frances in front of the church, and I was running from one side of the square to the other seeking appeasement. Anyhow, without good food, there is no way to succeed when traveling with family. Mike during all this time was a wonderful companion. He was four, quite willing to visit churches, he did not like French milk, but with the three adults, he kept up very well. No one as far as I remember had a fight with him. We returned to California on September 29, 1956.

France, in 1956 was just coming out of the

—

economic and psychological devastation of war. There were no super highways on our route south, the hotels were old fashioned with bathrooms at the far end of the building, there were few people on the road, we did not need to make reservations to find space, the dollar went a very long way. Salaries were very low. Trombe had an assistant at Mont Louis who did all the work of running the laboratory, in fact did all the work period. This man was twice my age, had a high rank in the CNRS (Centre National de la Recherche Scientifique) but he was earning less than half of what I was paid at SRI. In short, France was very attractive to me, but it was also evident that I could not return to France unless I found a way to be sent there with a dollar salary. Meanwhile, I would stay at SRI, become an American and wait and see if I could somehow return to France as an American.

The Time-Life World Conference on Foreign Investment took place in San Francisco on October 14-18, 1957. Two or three men from Henry Luce's staff worked with us, visiting us periodically in Menlo Park. This was a new crowd for me, people from publishing with contacts everywhere, used to constant traveling, arranging, negotiating. They seemed much less interested in substance and much more in appearance. What mattered was how things looked, what one would think of it, not how useful it would be. As far as the conference was concerned, the point was to bring together big names from all over the world. We would have world class speakers make impressive speeches. We would have knowhow, talent, things to watch and hear, we would have Time Magazine cover these events, and we would make history.

Every time these new New York friends would arrive, they would rush to the phone with their little black notebooks "Who do we call for tonight? Vanessa? Let's

—

see — there is also Olga remember her? Let's see if she can get us two more girls — they had names and phone numbers for every town in the country and probably in the world. They certainly gave a sophisticated New York macho appearance. Nevertheless, the Conference was a success, as far as what was said about it. A lot of VIP's came. Vice President Nixon came. Henry Luce came. Big names from industry and governments the world over, except of course from the communist world. We had Nelson Rockefeller, Eugene R. Black the President of the World Bank, David Sarnoff from the Radio Corporation of America, Marcus Wallenberg, a leading Swedish banker, we had Stephen Bechtel, George Meany from the AFLO, Count Ahlefeldf from Fried Krupp, Abdol Hassan Ebjetaj of the Seven Year Plan Organization of Iran, Giovanni Agnelli from FIAT, the Director of the Bank of Japan, the President of Mitsubishi Sekiyu... Even Gustave Maryssael came from Mexico. I will not bore you further with the list. It is in the book that James Daniel of Time-Life, published in 1958 under the somewhat optimistic title: *Private Investment: The Key to International Industrial Development.*

In the spring of 1958, I took a course on citizenship. I learned about the Constitution, the three branches of government and a little American history. I passed an exam. Then on July 25, 1958, together with a lot of other foreigners I went to a ceremony in the courthouse of San Mateo County where I was naturalized. Frances was there, I think the children and our neighbor Beverly. I tend to dislike ceremonies and I am not taken by sugary rhetoric. It is not the rhetoric that moves one at naturalization ceremonies. It is the people who are there each holding a little American flag and such a variety of languages and appearances. There were few, if any French, but some Italians, Greeks, Germans, there were many Asians already

—

in 1958, there were some Latin Americans, some Mexicans. They all looked earnest, happy, they had found a universal home bridging across all their backgrounds. Thus, I became a citizen of the United States.

A Futuristic Study

In 1959 Eugene Staley and I undertook a study for the Foreign Relations Committee of the United States Senate. This study had a $10,000 dollar budget. It was a small but adequate budget in 1959. We were to analyze possible future scientific developments and discuss their impact on U. S. foreign policy. Again, I did some traveling. I went to New York and Boston. My task was to interview scientists —in both hard and social sciences to obtain their judgments of what might "matter" to the United States in the future. For example, I spoke to Henry Kissinger — then a professor at Harvard — and he impressed me as being very impressed with himself. I do not think he helped us at all but maybe he kept his ideas away from others who might use them. I met with many scientists concerned with the cold war and the arms race who thought our study should emphasize arms disarmament research — a concept new at that time. I met with psychologists and sociologists, with chemists who said synthetic coffee was a possibility — and what would this do to Latin America or Africa? I met with birth control people, with weather modification people, with thought control experts. Between New York and Boston, I spent four or five weeks doing interviews, gathering materials.

SRI New York office helped arrange many of these meetings. The secretary who handled all this for me was a young Jewish woman who lived with a girlfriend. I took her out to dinner one night in New York and we went back to her place where we made love. This was my first serious

—

affair since my marriage with Frances. The Jewish secretary liked me and I liked her. She was younger than I, interested in ideas, in the study we were undertaking, the people I was meeting. I saw her on two trips to New York and I think we corresponded for a time. We were more like friends than lovers; maybe it was the Jewish thing. We went one weekend to the seashore — it was summer and quite warm. The roommate had a convertible and we drove out of New York to a beach on the north shore. It was one of these beaches with thousands of people and little umbrellas in the breeze. My friend and her girlfriend wore bikinis. For some reason I never understood, Frances refused to wear bikinis. She claimed she was older than the bikini that the bikini had come after her time. Here I was in New York with two young women wearing bikinis, while I drove the convertible, returning to the big city at dusk, making love to one of them.

Somehow, this relationship made me feel buoyant, and much younger. I was no longer under the control of Frances. It felt different; I was no longer "the junior partner". But when I returned to California, I told Frances about it.

The Study for the Foreign Relations Committee was my first real writing experience. It required bringing together a huge amount of data and making it relevant to top policy makers. Staley was a guiding hand, a very kind and sweet guiding hand. But I did most of the work and wrote most of the initial drafts. Finley Carter became the new director of SRI after Jessie Hobson's departure. The study led him, Staley and me to travel to Washington and to the Senate to testify in front of Senator Fulbright and members of the committee.

Most of the time of that briefing was spent with

—

Finley, who had been the CEO of a large American light bulb manufacturer before his retirement and his appointment at SRI, answering questions about light bulbs. Instead of focusing on our study, several committee members wanted him to admit that the light bulb manufacturers had purposely designed short duration light bulbs. Finley kept pointing out we were there to testify on the study about the future. But the future did not seem to interest the committee. They wanted something more tangible and politically useful: did electric companies swindle the American people with bulbs that need constant replacement? What may happen in 1975 or 1995 was too far away. I learned a lesson: politics is the here and now. The distant future is for poets and statesmen. Fulbright may have been a statesman, but not so most of the members of his committee. The study was published by the US government and caused considerable attention in the press. Even the Brazilian Government was upset by the thought that synthetic coffee could some day replace the coffee bean. Looking back at that study, I can see the limitations of our ability to predict. We say near nothing about computers, we completely miss global warming, we do not even imagine OPEC and its impact on energy policy. Obviously we lack the supernatural faculty of divination, what the Ancient Greeks called "mantike". But I became interested in futuristic research.

Eugene Staley was a gentle person. He was not a cold war warrior. Years later, during the Vietnam War, he was denounced by the left because of his role in Vietnam. Out of his mission to that country, came the fortified village concept the United States attempted to implement in the South. Staley was more naïve than sophisticated politically. His heart was in the right place but I am afraid others used him. In '59 Staley was friendly with Gunnar Myrdal and we met with him in Menlo Park on several

—

occasions. Our joint research interests were centered on the use of new technologies to assist the economies of developing countries. Joe Stepanek had joined us and I worked with him and others on a project having to do with the use of technologies suited to the economics and levels of education in developing countries. In a way, this was an offshoot of the solar energy work. Now we were talking about other problems such as: financing for small firms, other energy sources, new small industries, pumps, brick manufacturing, small hydro plants, health, education and sanitation installations and also, new birth control programs. We also began with the assistance of the Ford Foundation a series of projects in India and elsewhere to help small industries develop around new industrial parks where financing and marketing assistance could be facilitated.

Return to France with Congolese Help

The naturalized citizen was still attempting to return to France. My chance appeared in 1960. Belgium was going through the motions of giving independence to the Belgium Congo. At the Time-Life Conference we had made new Belgian friends. A contract was negotiated with the Société Générale de Belgique, a vast holding company with many assets in the Belgian Congo. SRI would undertake a study of the future of trade, investment and foreign aid to the newly independent countries south of the Sahara. The Société Générale was thinking in terms of a blueprint for international cooperation to replace the too visible Belgian presence in the Congo. The thinking in the board room must have been: "We want to help these brave, but not really capable Africans. Once they obtain independence we will still have to run things for them. We need to set up an international consortium to accomplish this."

–

Bill Moran, who had come to SRI, directly from the FBI in Washington but had some expertise in Africa and I would undertake the study. I would go to Paris and not Brussels and gather data from there. The fast train between Paris and Brussels took three hours then. Moran would head an international mission including representatives of diverse Belgian interests, to the Congo. I would commute from Paris to Brussels.

Thus, from April 7, 1960 to September, 11 of the same year, Frances, the three children including the newborn Marc Alain and I spent a spring and summer in a furnished flat at 8, Avenue Charles Floquet, near the Champs de Mars, very close to my last apartment in Paris at the corner of Avenue du Général Détrie and Avenue de Suffren. Marc was born in January 1959. Either Frances decided to have a third child or there may have been a birth control failure. She informed me that she was pregnant some time after she knew it. I thought we would have two children and stop. This was an unexpected change but I rapidly adjusted. My father was happy, a third child is not a great burden after two but a second son is twice as many boys when you have only one.

The stay in Paris was not without logistical problems. Marc was only one year old, Michael was eight, Anne, six. The older two children were already attending school in Portola Valley — they were taken out of school early and Frances was given materials to work with them in Paris. Someone was hired to help with Marc. Meanwhile, my parents, who knew we would be in France, had been traveling in France. This trip was interrupted when my father had a stroke, a stroke that left him unconscious with constant epileptic fits. My mother and the four relevant aunts were taking care of him in a rented apartment in the sixteenth arrondissement. I had to travel to Brussels, deal with establishing my own family in Paris and deal with my mother, who in times of real difficulty, tended to be fully dedicated to the task and impossible to satisfy. She would fire nurse after nurse, hire "docteur" after "docteur" and run a highly dramatic clinic with the help of her sisters-in-law. Frances could not help at all — except to the extent she liked my father and was sorry to see him in that condition. But she avoided my mother like the plague and for good reasons. The aunts did yeowomen service, relaying guard every night, trying to calm my mother and keeping doctors and nurses from leaving slamming the door.

The Société Générale was seeking other corporate partners to fund our SRI study and I had to go with them to Frankfurt to meet potential German partners. These efforts did not succeed. We would have to limit the study to the budget provided by the Société Générale.

In Paris, Frances was learning to live in France, but she was not the only one. I had forgotten. The previous trip had been easy. We had stayed at my uncle's Neuilly house. Marcelle had cooked. Marc was not yet born. Anne had stayed with her grandmother. Hotels might be primitive but it was easy to adapt. Now we were setting up a household in a foreign country: where does one buy soap and other products to clean with? — The "marchand de couleurs" — there were no supermarkets. We had to learn to go shopping in the neighborhood stores, learn the language, the customs. Frances was doing most of the cooking. I was slowly learning to do a few dishes such as Boeuf À La Bourguignonne and could help at entertaining time. But she had to deal with a small French stove and with the vexing hours of the opening and closing time of our numerous small local food merchants. The tiny ice box meant one was continually rushing down to Avenue de

—

Suffren to obtain necessary ingredients. French food shopping in 1960 had nothing to do with our American experience. You went from store to store. Milk was found at the crémerie, vegetables at the fruits et légumes, meat at the boucherie. In each there would be a line waiting to be served. It was all very pleasant but terribly time consuming. I liked the sing song when you entered the shop:"M'sieur Dames" and the repeated one upon leaving: "V'oir M'sieur Dames". But Frances and I did not enjoy these "courses", these buying expeditions, when it rained and it rained often. It was a challenge and we were not prepared for it.

We bought a new Simca car in Paris. This was a two door sedan with what was new then, a sun roof. There was no indoor parking and already then, it was not always easy to park on Avenue Charles Floquet. Meanwhile, SRI had asked me to also work on a study of the future demand for coal in Europe. I had to go to London to gather data while Bill Moran; my co-project manager was in and out, trying to organize the Belgian mission to the Congo. The various Belgian groups were fighting among themselves as to who would go or not go and who would do what or see or think or agree or not agree. It was a constant hassle with endless phone calls from the apartment to Brussels or with Bill still on the American West Coast.

I think that the 1960 trip was my maturing experience. It was terribly messy, stressful and difficult. Michael was taken to see a French psychologist because he had been having some difficulties in school and it was thought this might help. The psychologist thought he had been minimally brain damaged at birth and would have some difficulties learning, but these minor problems would evaporate with time. Yet this also took me by surprise, I did not know one could have learning disorders — it was all new to me. I did not know one could have endless epileptic fits where my father had to be held to avoid hitting or biting something. I was learning about living.

We managed one vacation by train to Florence. We took the old Orient Express, we had adjoining compartments done with beautiful wood and cabinets, we left Marc in Paris with one of my aunts and for a few days this was an art discovery experience with a capital A on the word Art. In Florence Mike and Anne began their "museum visit training" they would find useful during our next stay in Europe. We were tourists again, eating in restaurants, having coffee in front of the Palazzo Vecchio and getting lost in the Uffizi.

A doctor decided to place my father in complete silence and darkness. He was moved to a clinic in Ville d'Avray. By the end of our stay he had acquired consciousness again and was able to walk. It had taken me and my aunts, days to persuade my mother to let go and allow the move to the clinic. When I went to Ville d'Avray before leaving France my father said simply "I've come from very far away." But he was far from normality. He and my mother could no longer return to Mexico. They took an apartment at 53, Promenade des Anglais in Nice, where my father was to live the last two years of his life.

While my father recuperated, Bill Moran had gone to the Congo. The mission had been a disaster. The various Belgian groups in the delegation had fought among themselves. They had met with Patrice Lumumba, the African leader, and as Bill reported: the Belgians fought among themselves while the black insurgents were making fools of them. Moran was not optimistic about international cooperation in foreign aid, trade and investments when it was not even possible for the Belgians to come to some accommodation. He predicted plenty of

—

unrest. All this turmoil did not stop us. We wrote our report and it was published as a handbook which it was not, but the publisher saw a niche in the book market and we came out as the co-authors of my first book: *Handbook of African Economic Development*. The book had a mild success as there were few books on African economic development at that time. In it we explained how aid, trade and other economic policies of the western countries should be coordinated to facilitate African growth. Of course, we had near nothing to say on how such coordination might be achieved.

We were to return to lovely California. In many ways I loved California, the marvelous climate, the fantastic scenery. Sitting in the rain in Paris, I tended to want to be in California, I liked Paris. I kept thinking of Henry Miller whom I had met in September 1959 at the bar of Nepenthe, the restaurant high over the ocean in Big Sur. The reason I had found Henry Miller at the bar of Nepenthe was that he was waiting for a new girlfriend of his who was working there at the time. We had gone (Frances, Bill Dale and his wife) to Nepenthe to show Bill who was from our SRI Washington staff, the marvels of California. I had seen Henry Miller at the bar and gone to speak to him. We had spoken for a half hour in French about California and France. We had returned that summer from our first trip when we had visited the Dordogne. Henry Miller was nostalgic for France and very nostalgic for the Dordogne as we spoke in Big Sur — but now, being in France, I was remembering Nepenthe and I was nostalgic.

As soon as we were back in California, I was determined to find a way to go back to Europe, but it had to be, I realized, with an American salary. It was not clear to me how I would be able to find a sponsor who would want me in Europe. SRI of course might, if we expanded

—

sufficiently to justify an office abroad. But then SRI would locate in London, and in London I had no particular advantage against many colleagues who would be delighted to move to that city. I was aware that France or Spain were not markets for SRI, the demand for US applied research was simply not there. The difficulties we had had finding additional sponsors for the African study confirmed my reasoning. I had not thought of international agencies. I knew nothing about UNESCO and no one ever suggested I might apply to the secretariat for a job. I saw myself as an economist who knew how to do forecasts, market research and other applied work for industry. I knew something about the economics of energy — or about economic development in third world countries — but I felt insecure about my training. I had no PhD. — I was not a real economist, and the idea never crossed my mind I could simply knock at UNESCO's door. Bill Moran, my co-author had come to SRI from government service in Washington. He thought I should go to Washington — that was where the action was taking place — that was my next step he kept insisting. But I did not quite see what I might do in Washington or New York. Yet I realized I would have to move out of California and obtain a more reliable way of earning my living if I ever wanted to return to France.

During my years at SRI, I continued with my "hidden" career. I painted when I could find the time. We often would visit Mrs. Crawford in Carmel and I had met other local painters. Sam Colburn, a water colorist, among others. They provided an encouraging environment for me to continue. I also had many talks on Stewart Beach with the psychiatrist Eric Berne, the author of *Games People Play,* and *I'm OK, You're OK.* He swam there, in the freezing water. We had our own game. We would set up a firm to sell pyramids. This entailed many detailed ways to

—

present and promote our somewhat heavy merchandise. Eric was helpful. He seemed to think painting was important. As for success in life, he had no idea how to achieve it. As far as he was concerned he did not fathom why his books had turned out to be so popular. In his view one did what one found one did. If I wanted to paint I should paint. Later he would die just after swimming in the freezing water at that same beach..

The head of Public Relations at SRI, a sweet gay man, heard about my painting. He had contacts in San Francisco. He had me get in touch with the Lucien Labaudt Gallery. I met Marcelle Labaudt, the widow of the painter Lucien who had one of the few galleries in San Francisco that took unknown artists. She invited me to participate in a show. That was my début. I had a three person show there in 1957. The next year a show was held for me at the SRI Headquarters in Menlo Park. Both shows were reviewed in local newspapers and the reviews were like most reviews, they were words, pleasant or infuriating.

—

VIII

JOINING THE KENNEDY
ADMINISTRATION

I was naturalized in July 1958; SRI obtained a clearance at "Secret Level" for me on August 29 of the same year. The clearance was issued by the Air Research and Development Command. The security officer at SRI who had become friendly over the years, told me that there was a huge file about my mother and that was why the clearance had not been "easy". Of course, the huge file had to do with the fact she had lost her United States citizenship when she had married my father, given a Nazi sympathizer as a reference, had gone illegally to Washington from Mexico where she met people in the Passport Division of State to give them a piece of her mind. On the other hand by 1958 the cold war was in full swing and Nazi supporters were no longer a national threat.

After our return from France in September 1960 I began to actively seek contacts in Washington. I met a gay man who had taken a fancy to me. He was the head of an investment mutual fund, who was a client of SRI. He had invited me to New York suggesting that with my scientific and engineering knowledge and my economist experience — I could become a stock analyst on his staff. This plan did not go far because I interviewed in New York but declined dinner with him since I had already made a date

—

with my New York Jewish bikini friend. The experience propelled me into looking for something new to do.

Frances had dutifully reported that during one of my many absences, she had had an affair with our gardener. He was a very handsome, young American Italian, a gentle man I liked. The affair seemed to continue and again, I thought that was not our agreement. As had been the case in Mexico, once Frances had affairs outside the marriage, these tended not to end. The gardener, like her previous one, was convenient; he came around to our house when I was at work. I thought this affair was lasting too long. In contrast to my Jewish friend in New York who was faraway and whom I saw on rare trips to that city, the gardener was known to me, and I resented having to see him. I hoped that by going to Washington Frances would be able to forget her new friend. While she wanted to stay in California since both her mother and sister were near by, she was also fascinated with the thought of being in Washington at the beginning of the new Kennedy administration. She wanted to give it a try, we would keep the Portola Valley house and rent it, and thus keep an escape hatch.

Job Offers

Kennedy was inaugurated in January 1961. I had been in touch with Joe Slater, the man I had met in Venezuela — the head of the Creole Foundation. He had returned to the United States and was in Washington. He had given my name to Henry R. Labouisse who was then involved with United States foreign aid in the Department of State. It was then called the International Cooperation Administration, ICA. He had also given my name to other agencies as he knew I was looking for a job. He had put me in touch with the head of the Development Loan Fund,

—

another arm of our foreign aid. Out of these contacts I was appointed from April to June 1961 on the President's Task Force for the Reorganization of the United States Aid Program under Mr. Labouisse. At the same time, I was also appointed to serve with the President's Science Advisor on a task force elaborating a plan for U. S. assistance for scientific developments in Latin America. These were task forces, not permanent appointments. Washington was borrowing people right and left to elaborate new programs, SRI was agreeable, to lend me to the new national effort. During those months I went back and forth from California to Washington. My cousin, Roger was living in Washington at that time. He had joined the legal staff of the International Bank for Reconstruction and Development, the World Bank, but I had many other friends, particularly Bill Dalc of our SRI Washington Office and Ted Geiger of the National Planning Association at whose houses I often stayed. Before the task force ended its work, I got to know Mr. Labouisse who had also once been in charge of Palestinian refugees for the United Nations and was a consultant to the World Bank. He recommended me to them for employment.

The World Bank, with contributions from member governments had established a fund to finance projects at low interest. As a result the Bank began to consider investing in education since it was increasingly clear that investments in education and training were necessary for economic development. The concept of human capital was in vogue. At SRI we had written about and been involved in projects of "human capital formation". Since the Bank was considering investments in education projects, it made sense to send my name as a potential staff recruit.

As I made contacts and took the Civil Service

—

Exam, I was concerned whether I could be appointed in Washington — given my inheritance of my mother's "file" but there was no harm in trying. At first nothing seemed to work. No appointment offers came my way. A friend from Portola Valley, Ken Cooper and his wife Sally, who had worked with us at SRI, had been appointed in the Cultural Unit of the State Department. He wrote providing advice how to buy houses in the "restricted" real estate market of the Capital of the United States, but I had no offers.

Finally, in November there was a break through. The World Bank wired me on November 29, 1961, offering me an appointment in their new Education Division. Just a day or so before, I was invited by Joe Slater who had gone to work for Phillip H. Coombs at the Department of State to join him on the staff of the first American Assistant Secretary of State for Educational and Cultural Affairs. I accepted the State Department offer. I did so because Joe was very persuasive. This was an opportunity to participate in the transformation of American foreign policy making. Until then economic or military interests dominated at State. With Coombs appointment under the new Kennedy administration, the United States was to use education and culture as a third policy dimension at State. This sounded fascinating.

In May 1961, the Civil Service Commission had classified me at GS 15 level and although I reported for duty in Washington on January 1, 1962, I was appointed on December 1, 1961 and worked with Phil Coombs at a conference in San Francisco.

Mrs. Crawford decided to offer us a house in Carmel. Mrs. Crawford was getting older and she wanted to leave her affairs in order. She wanted to write her will so that her elder daughter Betty could inherit her house. I

—

should explain that Mrs. Crawford lived in part on the military pension of her husband; in part on income from an undeveloped lot in Seattle — the only remnant with a portion of the Washington Athletic Club property of the substantial holdings the Crawfords had had in Seattle prior to World War I; and in part finally on buying houses, moving into them, remodeling them and selling them. Thus, she had moved several times since the days on 15th Ave near the Carmel lagoon and was living on Casanova and then on Guadalupe, each time the house was a bit smaller, a bit less attractive because Mrs. Crawford had less and less money. But she knew the area well and kept an interested eye on the real estate market. Thus, she found a house on San Juan Road, bought it for us furnished for $16,000 of which $3,000 was for the furniture. At the time it was number 631 San Juan, later to become a complicated 24314. Mrs. Crawford made the down payment of $1000, and we assumed both the first and second mortgage. Since it was furnished, we promptly rented it, using the rent to pay the loans and taxes.

Washington DC

Frances gave me a set of specifications, I went alone to Washington, took a real estate agent, found a house at 2853 Allendale Place, N.W. just off Connecticut Avenue near Rock Creek Park and bought it in one weekend. I think it was the sixth or seventh house I had seen. My parents helped finance the minimum required as down payment and I obtained a loan to pay for the rest. We packed our furniture plus the Simca car in a Bekins moving van that left for Washington. Frances and the children went to Carmel — this was over Christmas and the New Year. I went to Washington, Bekins arrived, Bekins unloaded into Allendale Place, I set up the house ready to receive Frances, the three children and two cats. When everything

—

was ready, they flew in from the West Coast directly into a house they had never seen before. We did not lose any time.

I never worked so hard and for so long hours — never before — never after. I was a Special Assistant to Philip H. Coombs, the first American Assistant Secretary of State for Educational and Cultural Affairs. The idea was to diversify American foreign policy, to go beyond economic and military considerations or actions and to enhance the cultural and educational dimensions of policy thought and programs. C.U. as our end of the State bureaucracy was called, had until Coombs appointment been a "bureau" — now it was elevated to the same level as the other important units of State — the Assistant Secretary level. Thus, just like there was an Assistant Secretary for European Affairs or for Economic Affairs, now there was an Assistant Secretary for Educational and Cultural Affairs. It was our task to design new programs, to go to Congress and ask for the money and to implement them. We were inheriting many activities including the Fulbright program that had been C.U.'s responsibilities in the past plus new ones. To complicate matters further, Coombs had been at a White House meeting with the President and had somehow become involved in helping redesign the US foreign aid educational activities, especially in Latin America. This work involved the Organization of American States (OAS) headed at that time by a Colombian businessman and ex Minister of Education, Gabriel Betancourt Mejía (the father of Ingrid Betancourt), assisted by a Spaniard borrowed from UNESCO named Ricardo Diez Hochleitner. I continued to attend the meetings on the reorganization of the US Aid program, but on behalf of State instead of as a member of the Labouisse Task Force.

My days were busy, going to State early in the

—

morning, coming back late in the evening, having a stiff drink, eating and immediately going to sleep. I was still involved in some of the remnants of the task force work I had done the previous year. In addition my first assignment was to prepare the United States position for an international conference sponsored by UNESCO, the OAS and ECLA — the Economic Commission for Latin America, to take place in Santiago, Chile in March and April 1962. This was a conference on the future of education in Latin America. The task of preparing a United States position for an international conference has more to do with the creation of new United States initiatives than just attending the conference and presenting a "position". But the creation of new initiatives in the United States government does not take place spontaneously. Agencies and their representatives do not get together and say: "what's the problem how can we solve it?" There are always many interests to satisfy. For example many American private and government agencies, corporations, or universities are interested in education and science in Latin America. The Weather Bureau, educational test manufacturers, or the military that have schools in the region will have something to say. There will be many more. Before State can prepare a "new position" or start a new initiative, there has to be lots of consulting across units of government and consulting with Congress where citizen's interests are also expressed. As a first step inter-agency committees are set up for that purpose. After a week on the job, I was chairing such a committee. I had no idea who the participants were or what their purpose was because everyone on the list was identified with the initials of their bureau — things like HEW/IE which meant someone from the International Education Bureau in the Health Education Welfare Department but I did not know that. Not to mention, most of these people were there for one reason only — to make certain that whatever State

—

proposes to do, does not in any way affect their own activities or their ability to obtain continued congressional funding for their agencies. This is turf protection.

Much had to be learned, and this is why I worked from 8 to 9 pm. on many days and sometimes later when other assignments were added. When I could only catch Phil Coombs at foreign embassy receptions to get instructions I would reach home later at night even if we only stayed for a required courtesy half hour at each embassy. These cocktails with the Diplomatic Corps became the only time available for briefing Phil and deciding what to do.

Once at State, I had thought I would be on the ground floor of American policy. I discovered I was isolated in a little area surrounded by lots of very savvy and experienced bureaucrats who were not very impressed by new upstarts, by political appointments of the Kennedy administration who thought naively they could "change things." All these bureaus had direct links to Congress, they were not easily swayed by directives from the top. I had to learn to navigate the shoals of Washington politics. The situation was further complicated because Coombs had come from the Ford Foundation under the wing of Chester Bowles. But Governor Bowles, who was now Under Secretary of State, was identified with the left of the Democratic Party. While President Kennedy had appointed him to State, he was not in a strong position — the President was more to the right and so was the Secretary of State Dean Rusk.

My contact with the "big picture" was very limited. I once took the elevator with Governor Adlai Stevenson who had been appointed by President Kennedy to represent the United States at the United Nations, and Governor

—

Averell Harriman who was then the Assistant Secretary of State for Far Eastern Affairs. He had the responsibility for the Vietnam desk at State. I am in the elevator alone with these two men. They are both very tall, maybe they hardly see me. I will hear important matters. Here is what I hear: Harriman "Have you seen the last cable from Saigon?" Stevenson "yes." The elevator stops. Harriman "We get off here." Stevenson "good." They leave the elevator.

UNESCO Conference In Santiago

I went to Santiago, Chile on 8 March 1962. Coombs was supposed to attend but was delayed. The conference had already started. I arrived and went directly, in Coombs place, to a small "major policy" dinner offered by M. René Maheu, the Director General of UNESCO where he was trying to persuade the "donor" countries — namely the United States and Europeans to agree to a target figure for overall foreign aid for education in Latin America which would set the aid each donor country would provide. The lead man from the United States at the dinner was the Assistant Administrator for Latin America of our International Cooperation Administration ICA, a very kind somewhat portly Puerto Rican named Jose Teodoro Moscoso. He was supposed to assist Coombs in negotiations with representatives of the Latin American governments — the ministers of education of all or most of the countries of Latin America, including Jaime Torres Bodet of Mexico, the man who built the Mexico City Museo de Anthropología.

Maheu was convincing everyone, including our Assistant Administrator for Latin America at ICA until I said that I thought the U. S. would not agree. During our long preparation for the U. S. position, and as a result of my participation in the Foreign Aid Reorganization Task

—

Force, I knew that the U. S. foreign aid program, was now going to be based on "integrated national planning" This meant it could not earmark a percentage of U. S. aid for education, particularly since education does not require much foreign currency. I pointed out that a Santiago resolution earmarking a percentage for education was going to run against an aid philosophy based on national plans where foreign aid is set for priority sectors which could vary from country to country. That was a conversation stopper. I knew from our preparations that this would not work. Until then, US Foreign Aid had been allotted mostly on political grounds. Under Kennedy Foreign Aid was to move away from budget support to foreign governments to allocations based on local or national planning to establish priorities for both government and outside help. The Assistant Administrator Teodoro Moscoso, who had not been party to the Task Force work and not been sufficiently briefed, was embarrassed but René Maheu was furious.

What UNESCO wanted is simple: set targets for the development of education in Latin America. For example, achieve 100% primary education by 1975 — calculate cost, determine how much the Latin American governments can provide, namely a reasonable percentage of their budget and the difference is foreign aid. Once you know the total in foreign aid for education, earmark a percentage of each donor country's contribution and have UNESCO send missions to each country to spell out how the money of the donors is to be spent. Of course, that was a good plan for UNESCO. They would be the "conscience of the world" on education. But I could see this would not wash in Washington. The Congress or the U. S. Aid Agency, as it would soon be renamed, would never agree to such an approach. It did not fit the new "integrated planning" rhetoric and it transferred to UNESCO decisions about US aid paid by American tax payers, a no-no in Congress. The

—

dinner ended in confusion.

Next day, Coombs arrived and we went in the evening to the Mexican Embassy in Santiago for a reception. Meanwhile, I had made peace with Teodoro Moscoso who realized I had saved him from a lot of trouble back home. In the main reception room at the Embassy there was a trap door open in the floor leading to a basement library. The room was full of ambassadors, ministers and important people. Everyone had gone that same afternoon to hear the Cuban Minister of Education who had made a three-hour speech. "When the heroes of our Revolution came down from the Sierra, when they entered La Habana and the crowds were cheering them, when these heroes came and the people were clamoring for them to sign their names on paper souvenirs of this moment in history . . . a long silence . . . these heroes did not know how to write, they could not sign their names...". At the reception, the talk was all about how the speech had been so long and how everyone stayed in their seats. But now in the evening there was wine, champagne — and then a cry, a thump — the US Assistant Administrator for Latin America had backed into the trap door, fallen to the bottom and had a broken leg. Help was obtained, but Coombs had lost his link to Latin American delegations. Since I spoke Spanish, he appointed me.

I learned fast about negotiations. We did not have an easy time because we had a large number of Ministers of Education who were very cheered by Maheu's approach. They liked the idea of having a Santiago Resolution that would earmark a percentage of foreign aid for education. Plus, the fact that UNESCO had made such a neat calculation of the exact amount needed. This would solve their having to negotiate with their own Ministers of Finance, UNESCO was offering the cake and they wanted

—

to eat it. The U. S. delegation kept meeting trying to decide how to handle the dilemma. There were six or eight of us, including Professor Rashi Fein now at Harvard, then with the President's Council of Economic Advisors, and Professor Fred Harbisson who was a recognized expert on educational planning. Rashi Fein discovered that UNESCO's calculation of the possible contribution of Latin American governments to education was based on the best known and accepted projections of Latin American economies made by Paul Rosenstein-Rodan an American economist. So, as these countries grew in the next ten years and they contributed a percentage of their growing budgets to education — you could calculate how much they could provide for their own education investments and the difference was the needed help. But Fein pointed out that Rosenstein-Rodan's projections were conservative, they were considerably lower than the economic growth targets the Latin American governments had set for themselves at Punta del Este only a few months before, when Kennedy's Alliance for Progress had been created. Faster economic growth translates into larger government budgets and therefore more money for education. The next day at a dramatic plenary session, Coombs pointed out that the Santiago Conference could not use targets for economic growth lower than those set for the Alliance for Progress. And if you use the Alliance for Progress economic growth targets instead of the Rosenstein-Rodan estimates and apply the same percentages of government budgets to go to education, it turns out there is no need for foreign aid. The UNESCO plan was falling apart. There was a problem; the Latin American delegations realized a compromise had to be found.

Being so keen to do well in my new role, I decided to try to have a direct link to Maheu. He had come to the conference with a very good looking young Brazilian

—

woman. Maybe she knew something about what Maheu was thinking and might tell me. I invited her to dinner the next night when I knew Maheu was to have dinner with the heads of all the delegations. We went to a small restaurant away from the Conference, she spoke French, and she was very anxious to speak to me because she assumed I knew Maheu well. I did not learn any secret plans for the Santiago Resolution. I learned instead about her plight: how Maheu flew into Rio, how she met him, how he swept her off her feet, how she joined him in Santiago, how she loved him, how she wanted to go to Paris with him. I did not have the courage to tell her he was married. This ended my detective work.

A compromise was reached. The "Declaration of Santiago" called for countries to elaborate national economic plans including education. But the "Declaration" also urged the signatories of the "Alliance for Progress" to target no less than 15% of public foreign aid to education. We could accept the word "urged" as it did not commit us.

We returned to Washington on March 19, 1962. On the dark tarmarc at the airport in Santiago awaiting boarding, I talked with Ricardo Diez Hochleitner about the fiasco of Santiago. He said: "When one fails, look for what's good in it, ask: what can be learned?"

Contact With Spanish Elites

Ricardo decided that I should go to Spain. Franco was still in power but the U.S. should establish contacts with the emerging Spanish elites. We convinced Coombs and Coombs convinced the Spanish desk at State. On April 15, 1962, I left on a secret mission to Spain. I was to establish contact with potential future political leaders of a future democratic Spain who might be invited to the United

States under our various exchange programs. At that time, I was also appointed to a Spain planning committee within State since the matter of post Franco Spain was a concern and an opportunity.

Just before departure, I was also sent to an interagency meeting on Cuba. When in Santiago, I had met and talked to some of the Cubans on their delegation. I thought we should de-escalate our relationship with Cuba. The Bay of Pigs fiasco had taken place in April 1961. I and several Latin American hands at State tended to think that less pressure on Cuba would result in less confrontation and in a possible accommodation with Fidel Castro — thus reducing Cuba's dependence on the Soviet Union. But the interagency meeting included private sector representatives. We few never got to say a word. The entire atmosphere was on the "absolute need to rid the American continent of the communist infestation in Cuba." This taught me that one does not easily turn around the ship of state.

In Spain, I visited with university students and met two or three "future leaders." Ricardo had come to Madrid to organize the meetings. The Minister of Education was my official host. They opened a small church, so that I could see the Goya paintings there. I was taken to Avila where we were received by the local aristocrat, I attended a luncheon at the American Embassy and I briefed the Ambassador on my mission. Everyone was hopeful about the idea of creating an intensive program to expose leading Spaniards to U. S. political realities.

Phil Coombs unexpectedly sent me a telegram: he informed me that he had resigned; he told me that I should not worry. I was dumbfounded. I had no idea why he would resign. I asked a contact at the Embassy to wire Washington and try to find out what happened. He called

—

back to say that Phil resigned because he was asked to resign. I was in a quandary. What was I supposed to do? I was a political appointee and I assumed I had to resign with him. My contact at the Embassy concurred, I should return to Washington. My mission was to last to May 5, but I returned on April 28. In Washington, I arranged to have lunch with Arthur M. Schlesinger, Jr., who worked in the White House and was a friend of Coombs. Schlesinger explained: Phil had been going to the hill (to Congress) to testify on our budget. He was asking for a very large increase. Congressman John J. Rooney, a Democrat from Brooklyn, supervised State appropriations in the House of Representatives. Congressman Rooney had been around for a long, long time and he did not like this upstart from the Ford Foundation lecturing him about the importance of a cultural dimension to American foreign policy. Anyhow, Congress was restive with President Kennedy. The early "romance" was over; there was a feeling in the White House that some gesture needed to be done. When Rooney came to complain about Coombs, the President decided to sacrifice him. I was told that Coombs successor, Lucius Battle would keep me if I wanted to. I met Lucius and he was very polite, very cold, very nice and very uninteresting. I called the World Bank. Yes, they were still interested. In fact they had just hired Ricardo Diez Hochleitner away from UNESCO and the OAS to create a new education division. I attended the swearing in ceremony of Lucius Battle and I informed him. My service with State was extended to end on July 17, 1962 as it would take me a month to clean up my activities.

Before leaving, we had a request to send an expert to Paris to attend a UNESCO meeting about the creation of an International Institute for Education Planning. This request had landed on the desk of another Coombs assistant named Robert H.B. Wade with whom I shared an office. He

—

had asked me to suggest an American expert to attend. Time was very short, I suggested he send me. I was an expert on educational planning. I had attended the Santiago Conference. We had elaborated a 30-year plan for Latin American education. What better expertise could he find? We went together to see Battle, our new boss agreed.

The State Department sent me to Paris on June 22, 1962. By then I was already on the Bank payroll and still on State's. But I attended the UNESCO meeting as an "American expert". The Bank had their Paris office send a representative. Before going I consulted in New York with the Ford Foundation, I spoke to Phil on the telephone as he was in Essex Connecticut; I spoke to the Bank people. The UNESCO idea was to create an institute that would be sponsored by the Bank and UNESCO. This institute would be responsible for missions to developing countries, thus giving the Bank general guidelines for investments in education. UNESCO was worried that if the Bank went into financing education projects, the Bank would tend to displace UNESCO in the field. Hence, an institute sponsored by both would serve as a conduit between them. I thought Phil should head this institute. But Phil was in no condition to discuss anything, he was home in Essex, Connecticut not far from Chester Bowles' house. I called him, but it was too early to talk to him. I thought that if we could involve the Ford Foundation, everyone would be happy at the Bank and UNESCO, and if we did involve the Foundation, there would be more pressure to hire Phil. Behind all this, there was the thought that if Phil went to Paris, I would go to Paris also.

In Paris, I arrived at the meeting, it was chaired by Malcolm Adiseshiah, the Indian Deputy Director General. I met the German expert, Helmüt Becker who knew Phil well. Becker suggested I become the raporteur of the meeting. This is the person who writes the drafts of the recommendations. Since I had consulted with various people at the World Bank and at the Ford Foundation before coming to Paris, I had no trouble designing an Institute that would be acceptable to these organizations. For example, it would be established within the framework of UNESCO but it would not be controlled by the General Conference of UNESCO, it would have its own independent board of directors on which the Director General of UNESCO would sit. Presumably, the Director General would then appoint the director of the Institute on the recommendation of this board. While in Paris, I met with René Maheu and told him about the Ford Foundation's interest and the possible availability of Phil Coombs. Maheu had had his nose rubbed in the sand by Coombs and me at the Santiago Conference, but Maheu was very much a political animal and more than that, he was a statesman. He liked the idea that Phil might head the Institute. I explained the circumstances of his firing by President Kennedy, and Maheu understood.

Upon return to Washington in July 1962, I was also to serve for two weeks as a consultant to the Organization of American States at a conference on Adult Education somewhere in the northeast. Frances and I drove out north, stopping on our way north in Essex, Connecticut where I briefed Phil on the Institute and the possibility of his becoming the first director. I was very pleased on that trip because I had somehow managed to be, for several days, on the payroll of three agencies: the State Department, the IBRD and the OAS. But it was the end of my US government service.

My principal memory of those days is the gray suits; State was only men in gray suits. But this is the time I began to be fascinated by bureaucratic life. SRI had not

—

taught me anything about bureaucracy. In those days, SRI was task oriented. We worked on projects and solving problems was what it was about. But the government was completely different. Bill Moran had warned me, but I was totally unprepared. I had arrived a virgin — or at least with lots of naivete. I simply thought that the various government agencies would do the task at hand. I thought we only had to explain the problem and everyone would work on it. I had no idea about the complex battles taking place in Washington — or if I thought there were battles; I expected ideological battles but not narrow sectarian turf interests or the visible prod of powerful interest groups. For example, I thought we should make clearer that the Alliance for Progress needed more funding, that we should go the Hill and make clear to the Congress that we had not measured the scope of the effort needed to transform Latin America. But the wiser hands at State would just say go and try if you feel so strongly about it. But you will not get very far. In a sense, they were right. Phil's experience explains something about vested interests.

While at State, I had great latitude, I consulted widely in Washington. I could call a car at any time and have a chauffeur take me to another agency or even to the White House, yet I had no latitude when communicating with individuals abroad. All telegrams including to our embassies had to be signed "Rusk", the Secretary of State. This required a clearance. So, one night I was trying to tell the US Embassy in Santiago my time of arrival and asking for a car at the airport to go directly to the Director General's dinner. That cable needed a desk clearance from the Chile desk, but the Chile desk had left for home. It took me one hour to find someone who could clear the request. I am not sure who I found and whether that person knew where Chile was, but the cable was sent, the car was at the airport and, as described above, I attended the Maheu

—

dinner.

One of my contacts in the White House was Richard Goodwin, an Assistant Special Counsel, who also seemed to have responsibility for Latin America. He was good with words, but I realized he did not know much about Latin America, yet he was quite willing to call people; "The President has asked me to tell you that..." and whatever he thought was relevant. I had a sense that in government there were tremendous opportunities for action. Nothing I had done before or after compares — but there is also a lot of ignorance. At best, it is the one-eyed leading the blind. There is no time to do better, no time to find greater wisdom. It is a roller coaster except we all wore gray suits. There was a man in the U. S. Aid Agency who talked about the need for "bureaucratic engineering," for knowing the right people in each agency so that one could contact them directly when decisions had to be made, and through such personal intervention one might achieve results. This man did not use the word "networking" to describe the core of his notion of bureaucratic engineering because that term was not yet in the public parlance. But he was networking and he taught me how to network — how to use the phone and other means of informal communication to give life to the rigid and sanitized official procedures. It was all a revelation to me. I kept learning that people mattered and that bureaucratic regulations were there to be used, not to be feared. I learned to look behind the appearances and the pious rhetoric; I also learned to believe what I knew and not what I read in the papers. The press, I realized, told stories that could be read, but the stories one could read were not necessarily identical to the stories which one knew about and was involved with.

—

IX

INTERNATIONAL SERVICE

I joined Ricardo Diez Hochleitner and Duncan Ballantine on June 8, 1962, to create a new Division of Education within the Department of Operations at the International Bank for Reconstruction and Development. Until then, the Bank had invested in more conventional projects such as ports, rail or road links, agriculture and the like. But starting in the late fifties there were many to argue that it was not enough to invest in physical things to achieve economic growth. It was also necessary to invest in people. Governments should make conscious investments in education and training and agencies such as the Bank should consider projects in education. The Bank had, early in 1962, sent two missions to Tunisia and Algeria to recommend training projects, but the Bank lacked a rationale for its involvement in this new area. What kind of projects would the Bank finance? When? Why? Our new Division of Education would define the procedures and philosophy of the involvement of the Bank in education. It had been decided that two new missions would go to Afghanistan and to Pakistan, and we would work out the way education projects would be processed within the Bank.

Our first task was to deal with a prevailing sense of dismay within the Bank about education investments. The IBRD borrows money on world financial markets, namely

—

it issues bonds that are bought by a wide public, and it then lends this money to governments who presumably repay it as their tax receipts go up as a consequence of these investments. The Bank, in September 1960, had established a new "soft loan" window — it obtained contributions from donor countries and these funds were lent at a much lower interest rate to governments too poor to borrow at the going international rates of interest. Early education projects would be financed out of the soft loan window. Many Bank officials were very concerned that if the Bank financed education projects, its image on the international bond market would be affected. The public might become reluctant to purchase IBRD bonds. We had to deal with this concern within the higher echelons of the Bank. I prepared an internal note that showed how the American banking community was quite used to school district bond issues and pointed out that there was little basis to assume that our bonds would be affected by our involvement in education. In 1962 the United States was still an important source of private financing for the Bank.

It was decided that Duncan Ballantine would go to Pakistan. I would go to Afghanistan. Ricardo would stay in Washington. The head of the Bank's Operation Department was an Englishman, Hugh Ripman who was a Buddhist, or at least a devotee of Madame Blavatsky. He had had a stroke but had managed to learn to speak again. He had a dry sense of humor and was quite willing to spend half an hour with me to explain how he could move pain by concentrating on "seeing it" move, say from his head to the tip of his fingers and then out of his body.

I quickly found out that the Bank was not the State Department. As my cousin Roger who was in the Legal Department pointed out, the Bank made a small profit between the rate at which it borrowed and at which it lent.

–

But the Bank had been very cautious. It had never made bad investments. For example, it had never lent to Cuba so that when Fidel Castro took over, the Bank had lost nothing. The result was that the Bank had plenty of resources for its operations. At that time we were more than 2,000 employees, mostly in Washington. But the Bank only made — say, 20 or 30 loans per year. Therefore, you had two thousand men or women a year for 20 or 30 loans, which translates into a bit less than 100 men/women a year per loan. This simply meant that for each loan there would be a tremendous amount of activity, research and discussion before any decision was made.

The international culture of banking was decidedly elegant. My colleagues were mostly Americans or Europeans. In 1962 the top staff of the Bank counted few people from the developing world. We had lunch in a very gracious dining room at the headquarters where most of the senior staff had access. This, in contrast to State where there was a wider hierarchy of dining rooms. At the Bank, there were private tables and collective tables if one was eating alone. They served cigars after lunch and I would try to puff and look relaxed. It was no longer gray, but good quality English striped blue suits. Moreover, the women employees recruited for jobs then mostly held by women, secretaries, receptionists and so on; had a distinct different hue. They, in contrast to the men, were mostly from Latin America or Asia. Many were distractingly beautiful and we were impressed how the Bank was able to recruit such good looking women, and curious to know if it was an accident or a deliberate policy. Roger assured me it was deliberate. In 1962 the Bank served men of power. There was even an individual, I was told, whose task was to arrange for providing women to visiting dignitaries from countries where such practices prevailed. This was not publicized.

—

In August, Frances received several phone calls from her first husband. Professor Sydney Miller, now teaching somewhere on the East Coast, and he wanted to see Frances again. She thought he wanted somehow to get back with her. She agreed to see him once, but asked me to join. We invited him to lunch at the Bank, and the Bank provided. Sydney was received by a gorgeous Asian woman, he was guided to our table, invited by a head waiter to select his menu, given a leisurely lunch, and while we chose cigars and cigarettes, he was told that Frances did not want to see him again. Frances always thanked the Bank for having taken care of Sydney. At that time Sydney was still an assistant professor, and the splendor of the Bank was too much for him.

Afghanistan

The mission left for Afghanistan the first week of September 1962. The head of this mission was Ahmed Tukan, a Palestinian from Nablus, who had just retired from UNESCO where he had, among other things, been in charge of education in the Gaza Strip. Later, in 1969 he would briefly become Foreign Minister of Jordan The mission also included a German school construction architect, Gunther Naleppa, an American university professor of vocational education Gordon Swanson, an American Swede from Minnesota. Tukan knew a good thing when it came his way and the Bank mission received all his worldly attention. This was to be the first World Bank mission to Afghanistan, the first loan to that country. Ahmed convinced Ripman that we should do all the necessary consulting. Obviously, before financing projects in education and training, the mission would have to consult the ILO, the International Labor Organization and UNESCO. These were in Geneva and Paris. So we would first go to Europe, then fly to Afghanistan. After that, we

—

should consult with the Ford Foundation and the relevant place for this was New Delhi. Since the Foundation was not active in Kabul we had to plant the seeds of their possible engagement in New Delhi where the Foundation ran a very large establishment. Then, we should consult with the Economic Commission for Asia — where? — in Bangkok and after that a few days of "recuperation" in Hong Kong and Tokyo before flying back to San Francisco and Washington. We would spend one month in Afghanistan and about three weeks more going and returning. We would be back in Washington around the 17th of October 1962. Tukan also found that it would be convenient for the mission to fly to Beirut where we would spend a three day weekend, while he attended to a few private matters.

Tukan had an apartment in Beirut and one in Washington. His other relatives were in Beirut. His wife and daughter were in Washington where everything was so dull: "In Beirut, she would say, we go to the balcony and see life — but here in Washington — there is nothing, nothing." We would fly from Beirut to Tehran and then take an Ariana plane, the Afghan Airline, to go to Kabul. I did not know at the time that Ariana in 1962 only flew DC 3's, the old work horse of World War II. I said that instead of Beirut, I was thinking of a few days in Rome — what about the Food and Agriculture Organization — they are in Rome. But Tukan said nonsense, one could always go to Rome, but Beirut was different and anyhow he would throw in a day trip to Baalbek, the Greek ruins — a magnificent site. I was convinced.

I met with my mother in Geneva, as my parents wanted me to have a power of attorney on their Crédit Suisse account. I went to the ILO, I saw the lake and the fountain. I rejoined the group in Beirut. Ahmed was

—

Cambridge educated, short, and a ladies man. Frances would say you only had to look at him to know that he loved women, would make them happy — something in his eyes she said. Ahmed was a good Moslem, but he liked his whiskey and always had a bottle around. In Beirut and Baalbek, we managed to find alcohol, but Ahmed was going to even find it in Kabul. We flew to Tehran, had very little time there and then on to Kabul, on the put-put DC3. I was never very happy about flying, but Ahmed pointed out that the DC3 was closer to the ground than the bigger planes and needed less space too land — so it was safer in its own way. In Beirut we did some of the night clubs, but nothing much. Ahmed had relatives there and everyone knows what everyone does in that town. In 1962, Beirut was the playground of the Arab world. There was lots of money and in consequence, we could not afford much — just a belly dance here and there. Baalbeck was well worth the detour and we had a true Lebanese meal on the road, when we ate endless small dishes of Mediterranean cooking, quite similar to the traditions of my Salonika family.

The airport in Kabul was a small shack with contingents of soldiers guarding it. It took some time to clear our Laissez-Passer, the United Nations passport, and the site was grim. We were driven to the Kabul Hotel, the only western hotel in town at the time. But from the airport on, it was clear we were somewhere different. Afghanistan, in 1962, had not yet been invaded by the hippies and the new road linking Kabul with the Russian frontier was still under construction. The U. S. was helping build the southern end while the Russians were working on it in the north. How helpful can one be? The Russian invasion was still to come. There were men riding horses, women covered from head to toe in the chador, antique trucks painted from one end to another, miles of dust and

—

something of the sixteenth century about gestures, expressions and behaviors. Maybe it was the falcon on the fist of the rider, or the way they rode the horse with that long cape draped on their shoulders. And also it was the dignity, the presence of the men, their immense beards, the sharp eyes, the hard profiles, the small steps of the horses, the mountains everywhere around the mud town. At the hotel we were given immense rooms inside the compound and a man in turban, shirt and western vest would sleep on the floor across my door, my night guard.

For food we went across the square in front of the hotel to the new American built cafeteria, the personal property of the Afghan Minister of Finance. The cafeteria played either American jazz or Chinese court music, alternating from Billie Holiday, to long sensuous musical interludes from the Ming Dynasty. It served the usual fare: rice, chicken cooked in rice, more rice, more tired and hard working chicken cooked in rice and sometimes a dark stew where lamb entrails could be seen floating in a bed of unknown vegetables. It was the only "clean" western style restaurant. Afghan eating places near markets looked interesting but we were assured by everyone that one bite would send us running to the bathroom. The cafeteria was filled with Russians, Chinese, Germans, a few French and American agency personnel working on contracts. The more permanent foreign embassy people ate in their compounds. The U. N. Representative, a very warm Scotsman invited us to eat several times at the U. N. Mission. In the western missions, usually in a large compound consisting of several houses and office facilities surrounded by large walls and guarded night and day, the fare tended to be imports. Tins and cans from the home country and here and there the beginnings of frozen foods. For example, frozen turkey and peas at the U. S. compound — but these lacked the strong flavor of our tough Afghan chickens, and the revelation of the Afghan melons. We preferred the cafeteria as we had our own private dinning room, where we were served ice cold beer courtesy of Ahmed. He explained he just told the manager of the cafeteria that he was allowed, as a good Moslem, to drink beer, he claimed he had a dispensation from a relevant religious leader and the matter had been easily resolved.

The mission met the Minister of Education and Ahmed said in his best Cambridge accent: "Sir, our mission wishes to visit the schools in the north of your country." He paused, "Sir, our mission wishes to visit the schools in the south of your country." Another pause, "Sir, our mission wishes to visit the schools in the east and the west of your country. Please sir, arrange for our mission to travel in your country." The Royal Afghan government had asked the Bank for a 15-million dollar loan. Before leaving Washington, we had been told "to design something around five million dollars." But in terms of local good will, we represented the hoped for 15-million, not to mention we were the first World Bank mission to Afghanistan. We met the Finance Minister, and we were entertained at the Royal Palace by a nephew of the King whom I had known as an undergraduate at Harvard. He introduced us to King Mohammad Zahir Shah. The Royal Afghan Government then organized a series of trips to the north, northwest, east and south of the country.

We flew from Kabul north to Baghlan. Since we had to fly over the Hindu Kush Mountains, the DC3 took a long time circling north of Kabul to gain enough altitude to go over a pass. By the time we were flying over the mountains we seemed to be in them. The plane followed a narrow pass surrounded by tall snow covered mountains on either side. Being very close to the ground, we could easily see sheep just below us, there was considerable turbulence.

–

There were a dozen or so Afghan passengers and they did not do well in turbulence — they were sick all around us, which in a way made me more courageous. I was not in as bad a state as they were.

We stayed in Baghlan, a small provincial town, with unpaved roads and much charm, for two days. We had enough time to visit two schools where Ahmed dutifully noted the size of classrooms and the location of the blackboard if there was one. We returned to the airport, or airstrip, I do not think there was much of a shack there, to catch the same plane coming again from Kabul, to fly on to Mazar-I-Sharif close to the Russian border. But the weather was not as good as on arrival, there was a wind storm which in Afghanistan means a dust storm: large twirling masses of dust above ground. The plane landed and out came a UN expert — English, I think, and his Turkish wife. We had met them in Kabul several days earlier. They were being stationed in Mazar-I-Sharif. The Turkish wife was disheveled as she came up to us waiting in the dust to board. "It is impossible," she shouted, "I am not continuing — the pilot cannot see anything, he has no instruments, he hangs out of the window trying to figure where we are — everyone is sick — do not go." The husband indicated they were getting off in Baghlan — his wife could not take it and I had the distinct impression, he was just as happy to stop until the weather cleared. Ahmed was not affected. I pointed out that there was no point taking unnecessary risks but Ahmed said that if Ariana was flying, we would fly. The dust was thick, one could hardly see the plane and I cannot say I felt good boarding that plane. I thought that was the way these things happen. One knows one should not go on, but one does, the plane crashes and that is the way it is. I felt terrible but followed our leader and I went on. The plane quickly climbed out of the dust and by the time we reached Mazar, the dust had abated.

We visited more schools. Ahmed took and wrote down measurements, looked for blackboards and pointed to the absence of glass on windows. In one school he asked to see the lavatories. They said next time. He insisted. Finally, they took us outside and we walked to a corner of the compound where we could see a mound in the distance. Ahmed said thank you. He had seen enough. We found time to visit the blue mosque of Mazar-I-Sharif. We removed our shoes, went in and were surrounded by grave bearded men saying their prayers. We went to Kunduz where we visited more schools, slept and returned to Mazar.

The Royal Afghan Government had lent us a fleet of Russian Volga cars. We were to tour out of Mazar to Balkh and go west to Akcha in Jozjian in the company of a group of Ministry of Education people and a few armed guards. At Balkh we visited the site — mostly unexcavated, on the old route from Europe to India. Balkh is the ancient Bactra of the Greeks; it was once under Buddhist influence, became a center of the Zoroastrian religion and was razed to the ground by Genghis Khan in 1220. As we stood where Greeks had stood centuries ago, we could see the empty countryside all around. Suddenly a cloud of dust and a small car appeared in the distance, it came closer and finally stopped at our site. It had English license plates and sure enough two English women stepped out. They had petrol cans in the back seat. They had left London, made their way to Iran, traveled from Mashhad to Herat and now they were in Balkh. They were going to India. They spoke of their trip like one speaks of a weekend visit in the country. They had been on the road for months, had had no problems. Here we were with several cars and armed escorts. Were they courageous or

—

simply unaware of risk? They left after a while rapidly becoming a diminishing dust cloud in the distance.

We left for Akcha, Jozjian where we would sleep and have dinner. In the village of Akcha, Jozjian we stopped to wash up as we were covered with dust. We then went through a reception of school children lined up around the road on both sides with flowers in their hands. As we approached they threw the flowers on the ground in front of us and started to clap their hands. We walked on a moving bed of flowers as the clapping grew louder and louder keeping up with our procession. The sound of clapping moved and rose with our progress, a strange experience.

At the end of the line up, the Volga's were waiting to take us up the hill above the village to a site near a very old stone tomb. We arrived in a few minutes. Afghan carpets had been laid on the ground overlooking the village and the tomb just below us. A contingent of armed soldiers closed the access to the carpeted terrace. We could see several hundred people from Jozjian behind the soldiers waiting for us to arrive. Around this natural terrace small tables had been set up in a long circular arc, so that each two chairs had three small tables in front of them. Thus, we sat in little clusters of two chairs and three tables facing the sunset. The soldiers took up a formation and on order sent a volley that echoed in the valley below. Several speeches were made and a banquet was served — the rice, the chickens, and many unknown sweet delicacies. I sat with Ahmed. When the night fell, the soldiers brought torches, musicians appeared, they sat on the carpet in the middle of the semi-circle and for a long time they played Afghan music while we talked and visited from cluster to cluster. Ahmed said that I would not forget that trip and he was right. When we left, the moon was shinning on the dark granite tomb. We drove back to the village where we

—

were to sleep in dormitories. We could finally use a bathroom.

We returned to Mazar to take the plane back to Kabul. The trip was an exact repetition of our trip out. The Afghans were sick, the sheep on the pass seemed to be ten feet below us, and the plane had to circle north of Kabul to come low enough to land. We were back in the massive hotel. My night guard slept across the door. But that night, there was an earthquake. The hotel shook and thousands of Afghan dogs howled in the silence that followed.

Ripman came to visit us to make certain we were obtaining the information needed for the loan. I told Tukan we did not need to bother him with the size of classrooms or the location of blackboards. But we did need some data on enrollments in various vocational streams since the Bank loan would not be for blackboards. We needed salary data since we were going to justify Bank investments in education on the basis of the additional income school graduates would receive. Ahmed delegated these tasks to me.

We took Ripman to Paghman and Istalif, two villages north of Kabul, closer to the Hindu Kush Mountains. Istalif was, in 1962, a proto tourist village with many crafts, lovely old houses and a little green valley. At the picnic I asked Ripman to throw me a tomato — they were in a basket in front of him. Ripman grabs it and throws it smack at my face. This is his way to make me "see", to understand the meaning of life.

Ripman undertook official visits with us: we went to see the Minister of Education, the Minister of Finance, the Chancellor of the University of Kabul. I was beginning to understand the differences in my World Bank role.

—

When we were in Washington, members of the staff like us had little influence. There, we wore short pants, we were the kids so to speak. Abroad, on mission, we became exalted VIP's. The Minister of Finance listened attentively to our presentation. In Kabul, we wore long pants.

The University of Kabul had been established in the early 30's by King Mohammad Zahir Shah. We were impressed by the fact several of its faculties conducted their teaching in different foreign languages depending on external sources of aid. For example the Faculty of Law operated in French while those of Science and Engineering were in English. A third one was in German. This certainly constrained participation in higher education to a miniscule elite.

Ripman left and we went on the trip to the "west of your country sir." We boarded two Volga's to go down to Jalalabad close to the Khyber Pass and Pakistan. This was only a three-day trip — one day down, one in Jalalabad and one to return. The road to Jalalabad, like most mountain Afghan roads, is full of holes, it is narrow, it is extremely steep and it twists down a narrow gorge. You can see way down below the small lories inching their way up or down and at every turn you hope a lorry will not suddenly appear smack in front, forcing the Volga into the precipice on our right. When we were in the north, in Bactria or in Jozjan, we were on trails, dust everywhere and from time to time, caravans moving slowly — the problem there was not to lose the trail and get lost in deserted valleys. The mountain road is a different challenge. Many lories are overloaded and to save gas, they coast when going down hill which places a lot of stress on brakes. There are animals on the road, sheep going here or there and there is the driver who believes that the way to impress the foreigners is to drive fast.

—

Jalalabad was much warmer than Kabul, being at much lower altitude. There were lots of melons and grapes. We stopped on the road and a man gave us a melon and then refused any money. We visited some schools. Ahmed did his measurements and the mission ate at a banquet, organized by local educators. I was glad on the return, that it was uphill instead of down. At least the driver went slower. But we passed an ugly accident that had happened the day we were in Jalalabad. Two lorries had collided and one was way down the gorge. We were told the lorry that had gone down was packed with people in addition to merchandise and many had died. This did not slow our driver, we raced on toward Kabul.

I decided not to go on the next trip — three or four days in Kandahar in the south of Afghanistan. I had too much to do in Kabul, gathering data and anyhow I do not know how many classrooms one can measure efficiently. I wanted to discuss with the Ministry some of the administrative problems I was finding. For example, when we had been in the north, this was in the town of Kunduz — we had asked to see the laboratory in a secondary school. They had a lab provided by the German Aid Program — but it was all locked up and never used. In fact, there was a huge lock on the door and on top of the lock, a paper glued to the lock with the signatures of some half dozen local school officials. We were told that was normal practice. The lab was on the inventory of the school. If anything was missing or broken, the school staff would have to pay. Since these were imports from Germany, it meant weeks or months of teacher salaries. There was no question of using the lab, it might cost too much if anything was amiss.

We could also see that there were very few, if any,

—

textbooks. Teachers taught on the basis of notes taken when they had been trained. Students took notes and they, in turn, taught from their notes. Swanson, who knew some chemistry, looked at their notes and found them all garbled, the formulas had been modified over the years, in short, in chemistry students learned an incantation. I had some good conversations at the Ministry — but not much result. The control of school property was not even their responsibility. I realized I was getting into a much larger problem I would not be able to solve, at least not in a short visit. So, I did some shopping. I bought two carpets and many other souvenirs.

In our group, Tukan was clearly a ladies man and at the receptions he was always able to surround himself with the prettiest western wives around. The King had decided one or two years previous, that the Afghan wives would be included at official receptions. But this change was so recent that there was, as yet, no culture of shared behavior. The Afghans at the ministries were nearly always educated abroad and were therefore familiar with western ways. Our principal contact at the Ministry of Education had been educated in Japan but he had traveled to England and France. His wife, in contrast, was attending these receptions for the first time. The Afghan women were therefore terribly shy, painfully so, and we were torn between attempting conversations as if they really were not visible or involving them and causing them great anguish. Naleppa and I kept hoping we would find some lone British traveler, but the two women of Balkh had not appeared in Kabul. They were supposed to go over the Chilbar Pass in the Hindu Kush and that road was, at that time, much worse and much longer than what we had experienced on our way to Jalalabad.

One day there were several French women at the

—

hotel who looked me up. Was I the famous Professor Émile Benveniste? Apparently there was an international meeting of linguists in town and they had seen my name on the register. Émile Benveniste was still alive then, and he was a world authority on Indo-European languages. They did spend time making certain that I understood that there were more than 200 different languages in Afghanistan and we should make every effort to preserve them. I warned them the Bank would probably not be of much use but suggested we discuss the matter further, that evening. Unfortunately they were leaving for Herat that same day.

Swanson was a family man and for him discussion of women or sex was a taboo subject. The women in the street were mostly hidden in the Chador — or as it was called in Afghanistan — the Shadri — with a little veil opening for the eyes. The only women one could "see" were Nomadic women, who wore colorful costumes, but they belonged to other worlds. Afghanistan was a man's country. By and large, we only saw and spoke to men. At the end of our stay, we were even attempting to discern the eyes or the forms beneath the Shadri's. Naleppa was discouraged. He had been told many women never washed since the Shadri covered everything. The notion of unwashed women shocked his German sensibilities.

After four weeks in Afghanistan we boarded the DC3 of Ariana and left for India. In 1962, Afghanistan and Pakistan had broken relations, as a consequence; Ariana could not land in Pakistan. We had to fly over all of Pakistan until we might refuel at Amritsar, in the north of India very close to Lahore and the border. The plane was loaded with as much fuel as possible and flown relatively slowly at low altitude to save energy and make the leap over Pakistan. We left early in the morning and flew for hours and hours over the plain of Northern Pakistan until

—

we reached Amritsar in the late afternoon. We refueled and reached Delhi at night. There, we spent two hours at the airport dealing with Indian bureaucracy before we could leave for our hotel.

We saw Delhi, but we were exhausted. The streets were so crowded we did not do much sightseeing. The Ford Foundation was interested to see us but cool to any idea of involvement in Kabul. Tempers within the mission were getting frail. Swanson was very unhappy with the food, Tukan was still reacting to the way he had been held back at the Delhi airport, Naleppa and I were not finding any release for our needs and everyone was plain annoyed. In addition, we did not seem to find the mail we expected at the Foundation and it was best to avoid all members of the group. In a way we had become accustomed to Afghanistan and Delhi was a let down. We had come from the top of the world to a swarming mass of humanity.

We left Delhi in a larger plane, went way up along the mountains of Nepal, we could clearly see Annapurna, flew over Burma and landed in Bangkok. Our spirits came back. Finally, we had left the worlds of men and again found women, in a city with a lively spirit. We met with the UN Economic Commission for Asia and that night Naleppa and I went our way, Tukan went to see a friend and Swanson was left to his own devices. Naleppa had been in Bangkok before, in fact he had lived there for three years and knew it well. "Follow me," he said as we entered a taxi bar. It did not take long to find two attractive women to dance with. We took them to dinner; they took each one of us to their rooms. Naleppa, and I walked back to the hotel, we were in a joyous mood. We found Swanson looking dejected.

Hong Kong followed. We had messages and mail

—

in Hong Kong which helped. Ahmed had the genial idea to rent a junk on the water in Aberdeen for the afternoon. Thus, the mission floated for some five hours in the middle of thousands of other junks while listening to Chinese opera on a small radio. It was raining lightly and we could watch normal Chinese life on other junks. There were people cleaning, washing, grooming or working — women, men, children, and animals — thousands of them. The junk took us to a floating restaurant at nightfall. We packed and left the next morning and slept in Tokyo.

In Tokyo we were booked at the old Imperial Hotel: Frank Lloyd Wright's masterpiece. It was an aesthetic experience; we ate, visited the gardens of the Emperor's Palace and left the next day for Hawaii and San Francisco. At the airport in San Francisco, we could not find Ahmed. We were tired, went to sleep. The next day Ahmed appeared all smiles. He took Naleppa and me aside and asked if we had noticed the stewardess, indeed we had — how could we not notice her? Well, he told us, she lives in South San Francisco and he winked happily. Do not tell Swanson, he whispered. We left the hotel, flew again and reached Washington late at night on the 17th of October 1962.

Frances and the children were happy to see me. I was happy to see them. I was also glad to be back intact. I opened the suitcases and out came all the treasures of distant lands. In time, I reported my infidelity to Frances, and she reported that in my absence, she had met a young Norwegian who apparently was very infatuated with her, and she said she liked him a lot.

At the Bank I now had two tasks. The first was the loan for Afghanistan. In 1962 the three main centers of power in the Bank were: the President and other top

—

management, the Legal Department, the various region departments (i.e., Europe, Africa, etc.) and Operations, that was us. Our first task was to get support in the appropriate region unit, the Afghan desk so to speak, get the lawyers in line and see what the good pleasure of management might be. Management, of course, answered to an array of government representatives, where each country vote was related to contribution to the budget, so that in 1962 the United States dominated the Bank. There were many meetings, much paper work, a second mission would be sent to Kabul to work out the details of the agreement. Loans took a long time, this credit was no different: we returned in October 1962 and a $3.5 million credit to Afghanistan was not announced until November 23, 1964.

The second task consisted in getting UNESCO to establish an International Institute for Educational Planning in Paris with support of the Bank and of the Ford Foundation. Ricardo Hochleitner and I worked on that undertaking. We drafted all the correspondence from the Bank and at the same time, thanks to Ricardo's Paris contacts, we drafted in Washington, all the correspondence of UNESCO to the Bank and to the Ford Foundation that we transmitted to Paris through an assistant to René Maheu, for the signature of the Director General. This was my first and only experience being at both ends of a correspondence.

I had returned on October 17th. I was in my office at the Bank on Monday, October 21 when President Kennedy announced that the USSR had been building missile sites on Cuba and that unless they were removed, the U. S. would be obliged to intervene. The U. S. Fleet would stop any ships carrying military hardware from Russia to Cuba. We were confronting the USSR and for the first time it seemed as if the unthinkable was possible:

—

an atomic exchange between our two countries. These were grim days. I remember clearly looking out of my window at the buildings surrounding the Bank — we were not very far from the White House — and thinking — we are a prime target, all this could be dust tomorrow. I had had that same feeling in Afghanistan before boarding the plane in the dust storm. Radios were on in most offices and people would report, have you heard that... We also watched for signs of evacuation from the White House or from other agencies. It was a very tense period. One boat was boarded and allowed to continue and the next day, finally, it appeared that some ships were turning back. Later, we would learn how the U. S. had agreed to remove some missile sites in Europe and promised not to invade Cuba if the missiles were removed. It felt very uncomfortable during those days, but there were those who argued that Washington was the safest place to be: the Soviets would want to maintain an American government capable of surrendering.

My life in Washington was much less hectic now. I could keep normal 8 to 5 hours — more like 8:30 to 4:45, and take a bus back home. My status had gone down somewhat as I no longer had a parking place at the Bank nor did I have access to a black limo with chauffeur. But my salary had done well. I had gone from about $14,000 a year at SRI, to roughly the same at State — $15,000 a year, except now at the Bank this salary was tax free. U. S. citizens on the Bank staff had to pay taxes, but the Bank reimbursed them. The Bank was a generous employer. I was told no one had ever been fired. There was a man — I do not know his nationality, but he was pointed out to me. He had not been fired, but the bank had done the equivalent. They did not give him any work. He still had an office — with no window or telephone, and to be paid, he had to come in everyday. He must have been a moody

—

European to start with. He just sat there, hour after hour, reading the paper or looking at the blank wall. He looked depressed, and he was depressing to look at. It reminded me that the French used to place car wrecks at dangerous intersections in hope to slow traffic. That man was a bureaucratic human wreck to slow inept work.

Frances and I had an active social life. We had friends from SRI/Washington office days, friends from State and others we had met. Mrs. Crawford came, several times from California to see her grandchildren, we took weekend trips, did picnics. Anne and Mike were in a private school, outside the district, that they seemed to like. Marc attended a nursery school.

A Death

In March 1963, while Mrs. Crawford was in Washington, Frances and I arranged to take four or five days vacation in New York. On our second evening at the hotel, we received a call from Phil Coombs. Apparently, my mother had called from Nice that day, she had called the State Department, and they had called Phil to tell me my father had just died. He had died from a third massive stroke. We immediately returned to Washington so that I might pick up my passport. I was able to get a flight to Paris that same night.

I flew from Paris to Nice and arrived in Nice about two or three hours before the end of the ceremony during which the body of the dead is kept and family sit with it before the burial. I was taken to the Pompe Funèbre where my father's body was covered with a sheet, and the aunts and my mother stood vigil. They had been there for some hours, and I sat with them for an hour or so. After that, we went to eat and I slept at the apartment at 53, Promenade

—

des Anglais.

The next day we took the train to Paris for the burial. My father died on March 26, 1963. His burial took place on the 29th, in the Cimetière de Pantin near Paris, where the family had purchased a plot with space for eight, including my grandfather and grandmother. The Rabbi of the Buffault synagogue where Raffo had been married was there. This, you may recall, was the synagogue attended by the Paris Jews from Salonika. There was also a Cantor, and most of the family and old friends of my parents. The Rabbi spoke, but instead of speaking about my father, he spoke about my uncle Maurice who was quite uncomfortable in the circumstance. He, the Rabbi, accused Maurice of having left the synagogue. Maurice had become Protestant during the war and had not been giving to Jewish charities. The Rabbi went on and on what a disgrace this was for someone with such a prestigious Jewish name, such a prestigious family history. I thought the Rabbi was truly embarrassing. It was my father's burial; my father had been baptized in 1941, but in contrast to his brother, had kept going to synagogue in Mexico and had asked to be buried according to Jewish rites with his father and mother. There was no reason to go on and on about Maurice. The problem of course was that Maurice was wealthy and the Rabbi knew it.

The cantor made up for all the failures of the Rabbi. He sang beautifully, old Ladino hymns and the music put me in tears. After that, everyone shook hands with Lucy and me, the aunts, my uncle, the cousins, their husbands, wives and friends. Madame Akchoté, the old friend of my parents, came up to us, and when I saw her face — I had not seen her since 1940 or 1941 — I suddenly realized that when I was a child, I had been in "love" with her. But at the time as a child, I did not know I was in love. I knew it

—

suddenly there, in the receiving line. After the burial, we returned to my uncle's house in Neuilly, ate and I left the next day for Washington.

My father had spent the last two years of his life in Nice, where his sister, Marie and her husband had come to retire. My mother had rented the flat at 53, Promenade des Anglais, with full view of the beaches, the palm trees and the water. My father went everyday to a café near by, where his friends from Salonika or Mexico who had retired in Nice, would gather and discuss old times or gossip, while the ladies took care of shopping and cooking. In the afternoon they played bridge after their naps and at night they even went out from time to time. As soon as he died my mother packed up and returned to Mexico. Her house at 27 Calle Oklahoma had been taken care of by the two maids who had been waiting for her return since 1960.

My father had died in a port city, in the sunshine, looking on to the Promenade des Anglais. Nice was not Salonika, but his last days replicated in many ways the traditions he had known, He had gone to Nice in 1940 when he feared the Germans. He had gone again to Nice to live the few years remaining in his life. Nice was as close as he could be to what had been his home, his roots, his past.

—

—

X

PARIS AGAIN: UNESCO

In May 1963, arrangements for an International Institute of Educational Planning were finally in place. The General Conference of UNESCO had approved it. The French Government had offered to supply a building to house it in Paris. Coombs had attended the General Conference invited by Maheu. There he had found a Russian with whom he had negotiated a new cultural treaty when he was still at State. As a result the Russians had supported the creation of the Institute removing a major obstacle. Coombs then accepted to become the first Director, and the Bank agreed to transfer me to their Paris office so I could help Coombs, in the initial phase, until I could be transferred on to the payroll of the Institute. That month, I flew to Paris with Coombs for a ten-day initial visit to arrange temporary housing, hire a secretary and an administrator, and to get a sense where we might live. UNESCO lent us a car, and we did some driving around. My mother had returned to Paris from Mexico to ship some effects left behind. We went with her to St. Cloud as Coombs wanted to see what a typical outskirt area of Paris looked like. On the way back, we had a flat tire and Coombs and I went to work to change it. My mother was very impressed: "A French director would never change a tire."

UNESCO arranged for Madeleine Alpert to be our

first staff member and secretary; later Charles Berkovich became our administrator. Both were seasoned UNESCO staffers who knew the intricacies of the Secretariat. An office for Phil with space for the secretary was provided in the main headquarters on Place Fontenoy. A second office was to be provided for me, but it never materialized. Meanwhile we returned to Washington.

To Europe In Splendor

In Mexico, when we left, Frances lost Hans Hoffman, in Portola Valley she lost the gardener, and now she was losing the Norwegian. Maybe she had not minded leaving Hans or the gardener. But the Norwegian was something else. He had become very important in her life. I do not know or think she contemplated divorcing me. In 1963 divorce was not what it was to become ten years later, people like us did not divorce easily. One thought of the children and anyhow our relationship was still very close. I think she truly loved both of us and did not want to lose either. But going to France meant a painful separation for her.

Once again we moved in splendor. The piano and some furniture were sent to storage in Palo Alto. The rest was picked up and shipped to Paris by the Bank. An Opel car that was bought in Washington was sold, the empty house was placed on the market, and we left in the Simca for New York. On June 7, 1963 we sailed out of New York on the SS Cristofero Colombo of the Italian lines in first class, courtesy of the Bank. On June 15 the SS Cristofero stopped outside the Port of Gibraltar while the Simca, the five of us, and the few suitcases we had were delicately lowered on a barge that took us to the port. The SS Cristofero continued towards Genoa, its home port. We slept in Gibraltar that night, the children admired the

—

monkeys, and the next day we left by road along the coast of Spain for Tarragona near Barcelona. There my cousin Roland, his Mexican wife Geraldine and their three children had rented with us a villa for the months of July and August. The villa was in Torredembara just north of Tarragona. There was the old town, the rail tracks of RENFE, the proud Spanish railroads, and on the other side of the track all the way to the Mediterranean, there was a totally new complex built for the new tourists flocking to the Costa Brava of Spain. In 1963, this complex was just beginning. My cousin Roland returned ten years later to say it was difficult to find our villa among the high rises hugging the beaches. We were in a set of villas about 200 feet from the beach. We had a restaurant and night club right on the beach where we would spend a lot of time.

Frances settled in with Geraldine and an American au pair they had hired for the summer and who would be shared by the six children. I remained in Torredembara for several days In Paris, I would be staying at Roland's flat and we would alternate every other weekend going to Spain and the villa. There really was, in that villa, only one large bedroom with a double bed. The villa of course had all sorts of other problems, it leaked, the toilet flooded, there hardly was any furniture. But it came with a sturdy Catalan maid with fists on her hips who could be relied to get workers for repairs and knew where to buy Vin Fresc Blanc, oil and fresh fish. I left for Paris on RENFE, changed in Barcelona, and returned to France via the same border post, Port Bou, I had crossed in 1942.

In Paris, I found that Roland still housed a charming Dutch au pair who had been living with them during the last year. The American au pair had only been hired for the summer in Spain so that his children could practice English with mine. The Dutch au pair was blond, slight, and

—

pleased to make love. My stay alone in Paris would not be unpleasant.

I looked for apartments, both for us and for the Coombs. I looked for an office but could not get one at UNESCO headquarters. So I installed myself in the main room used by the General Conference of UNESCO. In that large room, each member government has two or three seats along circular tables that ring an amphitheater. There happens to be two seats at a table in the back, close to the aisle, for representatives of the World Bank. This desk became my office, from there I helped Coombs interview future staff members, prepared the budget and initial plan of activities for our first board meeting and kept pestering the Director General and French representatives at UNESCO to deliver the promised "building" the French Government was supposed to provide.

On September 30 1962, the first man in space, Yuri Gagarin, was honored at UNESCO. When Gagarin finished his speech, in the General Conference room where I was busy preparing our plan of activities, he came up the aisle followed by René Maheu. Gagarin saw me writing, maybe he thought I was an important newspaper reporter, everyone was applauding, he stopped and we shook hands, the applauding increased, Maheu looked puzzled: I still believe the Director General decided to help us obtain a building after this little scene.

At the end of July the furniture arrived from the United States. Since I could not find a suitable empty apartment, I rented instead, for $500 a month, a furnished flat at 24 Ave. Charles Floquet — the same building where my cousin Renée had lived in the late thirties — near the Champs de Mars. I had them store their furniture so I could use ours; we installed bookcases in the salon. The

—

huge American refrigerator and washing machine were squeezed in the kitchen. I moved in early in August.

In Spain, Frances and Geraldine have made friends with Paco, a Spanish gypsy who played the flamenco guitar at our little night club. Geraldine is strikingly beautiful and she appeals to the Spaniards. There is something of Spain in her — she is dark — but there is something else the men cannot quite discern. When I walk with her along the edge of the water going from one end of the beach to the other I can sense how hundreds of masculine stares focus on her as she advances, it is silent and yet there is this movement of eyes one feels without seeing it. Geraldine is a good wife, good mother and very devoted to Roland. But she enjoys Paco's pursuit. In fact, she is mesmerized by him — he represents everything that is crazy, wild, unknown. After the show at the club, he often comes to the villa where he prepares a sopa de ajo (garlic soup), plays the guitar, sings and romances Geraldine. Often his cantaor, the man who sings with him, joins us. We play and listen to music till late. When it is Roland who comes down for the weekend, Paco gives him flamenco lessons and visits until the morning hours. When I come, he often plays until 5 a.m. — after that, the tourists go for a swim and stay talking as the morning creeps in. Paco was a wonderful man because he was a nomad, he was not burdened by anything, he carried what he needed and kept nothing. He kept playing flamenco until we all collapsed.

This is a very happy period for Frances and me. Frances enjoys the vacation, she likes being a tourist, the healthy life at the beach, the cook who buys and prepares simple meals, Paco who plays wonderful flamenco music at 3 a.m., our love making after a quick dip in the salty sea. The six children get along well and the American au pair handles them without much trouble since they are at the

—

beach most of the time. Paco's cantaor who sings with him has a club foot, a wife in Valencia and is making love to a Belgian lady with the encouragement of her husband, a Belgian psychiatrist. The Belgian lady is often at the night club and she speaks of the sun, the sea, the excitement of life, her fulfillment while the husband nods and smiles. One night, we are at a little open air bar on a road near town. This is after the night club closes and Geraldine and Pacco are having a drink with us. The cantaor appears in great disarray. He is shuffling on the road pushing his bicycle. His wife has come from Valencia, she has a gun, and she has heard about the Belgian lady. She is looking for him, he is running away. "What can I do?" he moans, "She has a gun and I only have my bicycle…"

Paco explains how one sells a horse. You have to make sure his teeth look good — white, so they should be painted, then you stand him with the front feet higher than the rear — that makes him look bigger, then you feed him some grasses that contract the stomach so that the sagging belly is not visible, then you add to the tail if it is not adequate, and so on. It turns out that Paco has two wives he has not seen in ages — he has been married twice and never divorced. One wife is in Argentina where he once lived. One is somewhere in Spain.

Paco decides to invite us to go to a wedding in Manresa. We have the car and Manresa is on the other side of Barcelona. We leave with Michael, Frances and me on the front seats, Paco, the gypsy singer, and Geraldine in the back. The Simca feels heavy — it is not a big car. In Manresa we drive along cruising until Paco and the singer ask to stop, they have identified someone who is gypsy. The man walking looks like everyone else to us, but they ask him "eres Cálo?" are you gypsy? Yes indeed and the wedding is taking place behind the main square in a rented

—

hall. We arrive. It is a big room with chairs lined all around. People are mostly sitting around the room talking. Men, women, children, old, young — there are some two hundred people there. Men go around serving wine out of the Spanish gourd, something none of us seem to be able to do, you have to keep your mouth open and swallow the jet of wine directly. We are given glasses. We meet the bride and groom. Paco has brought his guitar and he joins other gypsies in a corner. In due time one of them strokes his guitar, another joins, a young man begins stamping his feet and clapping his hands. The conversations continue, more wine is consumed, some food appears, more people are now stomping or dancing, children join in, more gypsies play their guitars, the old ladies are getting up and they dance, moving their arms, the children imitate, there are singers and they begin and suddenly the entire room is on its feet dancing, clapping, stomping, singers follow singers, guitars follow guitars and we are all somehow part of it. Late in the night Geraldine is able to convince Paco that we must leave. Paco is singing and dancing on the back seat, the cantaor is singing and moving up and down with him, somehow we make it back from Manresa to Torredembara on the tortuous mountain roads, the Simca vibrating all the way back.

In Paris we interview potential staff members, draft documents and look for a building for the Institute. Since the French Government cannot seem to decide which one to give us, Coombs and I decide to go find one. There is a government Ministry created to repatriate French citizens from Algeria. It will close down in a few months. Coombs and I go and see the Minister who happens to be located very conveniently for me on Charles Floquet where we live but closer to the Eiffel Tower, on the park side of the street. The minister is charming and we explain our problem. We ask him to inform the French national agency

—

in charge of all public buildings that we have decided we want his ministry. This is the Administration des Domaines an ancient but weak agency. Apparently he transmits the message and the Domaines becomes concerned that UNESCO via the Foreign Ministry might dislodge this wonderful, elegant building which is promised to someone else. Within a week we are offered two old villas on a site rue Eugène Delacroix, property of the Ministry of Education. We finally have a home for the Institute. We will be on the other side of the Seine in the 16th arrondissement just off rue de la Pompe.

I have many meetings in the personnel department of UNESCO and I meet Rose van Vleet, a Canadian married to a Dutchman who has served with UNESCO in Latin America. We meet often to have lunch together, she speaks Spanish and English, and she has lost her French-Canadian accent after years in Paris. She is separated from her husband, and we keep meeting for coffee or lunch. She tells me about UNESCO; the intrigues of the palace, about Madame Maheu and about René Maheu's many mistresses including the official headquarter mistress who is invited to some functions when the wife is not. She tells me about the Latin American network about the Russians, about her life, her husband. I tell her about Washington, my life, and in no time we are like high school dates and behaving that way: holding hands furtively in the UNESCO cafeteria, looking at each other in the eye for long significant periods. She knows I am married.

Every other weekend I am in Spain, but on my Paris weekend I see her, we walk and talk and endlessly hold hands. On the last weekend before my final trip to Spain, Rose decides and she joins me for dinner. After we make love, I realize Rose van Vleet is very important in my life. There is something magical about how she feels, how she

—

moves. I realize that one can sleep with many women, but one rarely loves all of them. I loved Frances, and I loved Rose. Rose takes me to the train, it is a sad goodbye, and she waves from the quay. She has decided not to see me again, although she loves me: "I do not want to destroy your marriage." She will do as she says. We only made love once.

I look back on a ritual. Our relationship is that of a high school romance. We keep meeting inside the UNESCO building, either because I am walking from the large auditorium of the General Conference where my World Bank desk is, to Coombs little office, or she is walking from her department, Personnel, to interview someone in the building. We go and have coffee together, hold hands, it is all very dreamy. I like Rose because she is from both continents like me. Canadian, but has lived in Europe for many years. She has also lived in Latin America, working for UNESCO. While she is separated from her husband, Monsieur van Vleet who also works for UNESCO, they still share the same apartment because apartments are so expensive, it is easier that way she says, I meet her husband who is Dutch — and friendly.

She remained a friend and after Frances' arrival, Rose went and had lunch with Frances. She told her what she had told me; she was very elegant about it. We then saw her socially on a few occasions. She came to dinner or we would see her at some UNESCO function. Charles Berkovich, our new administrator, who knew her well, they had both started their UNESCO careers together in Latin America, would keep me informed about her when I no longer saw her.

She finally moved out from the joint apartment but never remarried. We did not correspond after I left in

—

1965. But when I went to Paris in 1970, I called her and we spoke on the phone. She invited me to join her for a weekend in the country at the home of a friend. But I could not join her. In 1971, Charles Berkovich told me she had died very suddenly from a tumor in her brain. She was in her living room talking, and suddenly fell, she was dead.

Return To Paris

On 17 August 1963, I left Paris and Rose, went to Spain to gather the family. On 29 August the Simca crossed into France at Puigcerdà-Bourg Madame. I meant to sleep again at the Grand Hôtel of Font Romeu — but when we arrived it was closed for major repairs. I did not have much time and we went to Paris by the most direct route: Toulouse, Brive, Limoges, Vierzon, and Orleans. Four or five days later we were all settled at 24, Ave. Charles Floquet. I had hired a Spanish femme de ménage who came for several hours daily and Nicolas, the wine people, would maintain, via weekly home delivery, our wine stores in a small cabinet with whites and reds of varying quality. In contrast the daily milk had to be purchased at the crémerie on Avenue de Suffren. This time we knew where to go.

The apartment had three bedrooms — one on the street, and two in the back, giving on a court where the sun, when it shone, penetrated for about ten minutes per day. The street, Avenue Charles Floquet, was noisy. There was an intersection with considerable traffic and more often than one would suppose or expect, there were accidents: a screeching noise of tires on the pavement, a thump, followed by crunching noises, followed by the delicate stream of broken glass hitting the pavement; then a brief silence soon broken by angry voices: "Alors? Espèce de…."and many other insults. The back rooms were more

—

silent although every household fight seemed to reverberate in that small courtyard. Frances hired an Italian au pair — a lovely looking woman girl from Bologna. She slept in the maid's room on the 7th floor. We were on the second floor and we therefore had a balcony. At night, from the living room, which was a corner room on Charles Floquet, we faced the illuminated Eiffel Tower.

I had returned home. I was practically in the same block as my parents' apartment at the corner of the Avenue de Suffren and Général Détrie. One could run a diagonal from 24 Charles Floquet through the rue Champfleury directly into 6 Ave du Général Détrie. We were at the Champs de Mars where I had played as a child. I had a salary in dollars, tax free. I was in Paris, I thought I was in Paris for good.

There were some difficulties at UNESCO. The French Government refused to stamp my American Passport as a permanent member of the UNESCO staff, since for the French; I was still a French citizen. Finally, the Foreign Office, the Quai d'Orsay agreed to stamp my UN Laissez Passer. The paper work took time and on October 14, 1963, I was transferred from the World Bank to the International Institute for Educational Planning with a salary of $18,000, tax free. I was a senior staff member at the IIEP, but the salary corresponded to the UNESCO rank of director (not "le Directeur Général", but a plain directeur, still a high level in the UN system. Madeleine Alpert, our secretary, would call the restaurant at headquarters to reserve a table for me and they would say they were full, "mais monsieur, il a le rang de directeur" she would shout in the phone, and the table would be reserved.

When we were still housed in the headquarters on

—

Place de Fontenoy, I would walk to the Avenue de Suffren past the École Militaire directly to UNESCO. I had taken that same route from Général Détrie to my Lycée on the Boulevard Pasteur or earlier when I played on the Champs de Mars and returned to my parents' first apartment on rue Léon Vaudoyer. But now I had the rank of directeur and with that I obtained a set of CD plates (diplomatic license plates) for the Simca. The CD plates were not only prestige but also gave the right to park most anywhere with diplomatic immunity. What I really liked about the CD plates was the opportunity to put down the window of the car when some French drivers would shout some disobliging remark about these stupid foreign drivers and give it to them in my best French high school slang.

The au pair took Marc to the park, Mike and Anne were enrolled at a new American School in St. Cloud and they were picked up by a school bus everyday. I worked on our move to rue Eugène Delacroix that took place late in the fall. Meanwhile, we were getting used to our Paris life. As mentioned the milk had to be brought daily from the crémerie, but at least the wine was delivered. We shopped on Avenue de Suffren, practically for every meal, even with our large American refrigerator. It was the way one lived in Paris. In any case one had to buy the baguette for every meal. It made sense to buy fresh all the time. The Spanish femme de ménage did some of it but her choices were hazardous. Shopping for food was not in the job description of the Italian au pair, yet we were feeding 6 people daily.

I kept official hours although Phil was prone to want to work late at night. I also refused to work on weekends. We had found a large apartment on the rue Edmond Valentin for the Coombs and I had gone to LeHavre, in a huge UNESCO Mercedes, to bring Helen

—

and him back to Paris. We were very close, walking distance from each other and Frances and I would often take Helen with us on visits to flea markets or on small trips when Phil insisted on working on weekends. Most weekends were spent going out of Paris, often for a picnic in a forest and we visited many small towns in the Région Parisienne: Provins, Melun, Vaux Le Vicomte, Moret-sur-Loing, Nemours, and Barbizon and, of course, the Fôret of Fontainebleau where we had most of our picnics. At the time, the auto route did not go very far south and sooner or later we were on Nationale 7, but more often on little "D" roads through the fields.

In November, we learned that Mrs. Crawford was terminally ill with cancer, and Frances decided to return to California while she was still in relatively good health so that they would be able to spend some time with her and the children. She and the children left for a month in California on November 22, 1963. I took them to Orly. With my UN Laisser Passer, I was able to stay with them all the way to boarding. That evening, I went to the movies with Roland and Geraldine; the Ranelagh movie house in their neighborhood. Coming out, someone said that President Kennedy had been killed, but we did not believe the man. We were speaking in English, and we thought it might have been a joke. Frances had a worse time. She was still on the plane to California. The pilot came on: "I have very bad news for you." She thought — a motor or fire? "The President has been shot in Dallas." She recuperated from her fright to understand the gravity of the news.

The Italian au pair was staying around the apartment, and for reasons unclear to me, kept walking around clad in tights and a sweater. In 1963, leggings had not yet been invented. Tights were an undergarment. Maybe she thought of me as a father figure — she was

probably half my age — around 18 or 20, and there she was
every evening curled up on the sofa in her tights and naked
below her sweater. All this annoyed me because I really
did not like her in that sense of things, yet she was young
and attractive. When after some days I made the mildest of
suggestions; she became surprised and offended. How
could I think of such a thing — me so old, married, father
of three children. She clearly had no intentions of one kind
or another. She liked to be in tights and wearing a simple
sweater. She did not seem to realize that I was not her
father, or maybe she did and enjoyed teasing me. She left
after 10 days for a vacation home and did not return until
Frances and the children arrived just before Christmas.

We had hired Jane King, the daughter of Alex King
who headed the Social Science Division of the
Organization for Economic Cooperation and Development
(OECD). I had become quite friendly with the Kings. I
went to her parents' apartment for tea ceremonies — the
Kings senior were very much into Japanese culture and
philosophy. We had become friends and I went with Jane
and her mother on a weekend trip to a small beach town
north of Rouen called Veulettes-sur-mer, where I had once
gone as a child. It was in early December, it was cold and
there was a chilling low fog hovering. Veulettes, even in
the sunshine is a stark resort: cliffs and below the cliffs,
round flat stones and the bones of animals who ran too fast
without looking. In winter, the row of hotels was closed
down with one exception and we settled there since there
was a fire. The English ladies immediately readied
themselves for a brisk walk in the moors above the
beaches. I went trailing behind as mother and daughter
walked for hours in the wind. We had dinner at the hotel
and Jane's mother retired early. I thought of Jane as a
friend more than anything else. But going to bed together
seemed like the right thing to do because of the cold, the

—

wind and the abandoned resort. She left me in the early morning to save appearances when her mother awoke. Jane and her parents remained my friends during those years in Paris.

Albert Baez was the Director of Science Education since 1962; he was a dedicated pacifist who had joined UNESCO to do good works. He had a PhD from Stanford and was very helpful to us in those beginning months. He was also the father of Joan Baez and Mimi Farina the folk singers. Joan came to sing at headquarters and I recall being in an elevator with Albert. I had one of Joan's recent releases, a 33rpm album with a large profile of her on the cover. I held it up right by Albert's profile. The profiles were identical. Albert retired some years after my departure and settled in Carmel Valley where Karen and I visited him in the 1970's. He had built a mini UNESCO facility where he could still hold small International conferences. The booths for simultaneous translation, the trade mark of the UN, were right there in Carmel Valley

We hired Raymond Lyons, an Englishman from the OECD, George Skorov, a Russian already at UNESCO, and Raymond Poignant, a Frenchman, who had been the permanent rapporteur of the French Planning Commission for Education and was a member of the Conseil d'État, an institution dating from the 14th century that handles litigation against or within the French Government. Charles Berkowitch hired a series of secretaries. Charles always admitted that looks mattered. We hired Jane King because she had had educational planning experience in Africa. Coombs and staff moved into one of the villas on Eugène Delacroix, and the other villa was converted into a conference building with simultaneous translation equipment.

—

The winter and spring of 1964 was cold and Frances became depressed. Cold winters in Paris or London can be very depressing. It is cold, humid and dank. As a result we tended to drink more, just to warm up. Part of it may also have been the Norwegian. He had gone from Washington to California to visit her while she was with her mother. Whereas Rose had left me, it appeared that the Norwegian had not left Frances. Also, that spring Mrs. Crawford died. Betty was with her, and Betty made all the arrangements, handled the estate and divided her belongings. Her mother's death depressed Frances further. In addition, the war in Vietnam was becoming more intense and we were strongly opposed to it. The death of President Kennedy had not helped either. As a result, Frances was talking of returning to California while I thought we should stay in Paris.

The Bank decided to ask UNESCO to conduct preliminary missions prior to Bank selection, review and investment. This removed one of the principal raison-d'être for the Institute. The Bank shifted positions in an effort to appease other UN agencies and so as to establish closer links within the UN family. Someone in New York or Washington figured out that if the Bank decided to invest in other social sectors such as health, other similar institutes would be called for. New international institutes would be costly, and add to the proliferation of UN institutions. There was, of course, no question of backing down on our Institute. The UN bureaucracies, once established, continue to flourish. But it shifted the balance of power on our Board. UNESCO was now the dominant controlling agent. Soon the Ford Foundation would drop out and Coombs would have a more difficult time with Monsieur René Maheu.

The IIEP became a training center and it also

—

undertook studies of planning problems and experiences. In the spring of 1964, we organized the first conference of Latin American Educational Planners and brought a large group of Latin Americans to Paris. That conference ended with a vibrant party. Latin Americans know how to have great parties whereas the French lack the spontaneous ability to let go and enjoy the moment. But this can be contagious. This is why Roger Grégoire, a distinguished French civil servant who headed the Marshall Plan productivity effort and whom I had met in 1957 at our Time Life –SRI Conference, danced on top of office desks with our shy, lanky and so-English colleague, Raymond Lyons. In the early part of the summer we had a second conference on research priorities in educational planning; John Vaizey from Oxford joined us in Bellagio on Lake Como where Phil had borrowed the Villa Serbelloni from the Rockefeller Foundation.

Retreat Back To California

Frances also came to Lake Como that summer, staying with the children in a hotel. But she had become convinced we had to find a way to return to the US. She thought Mike needed a special school. I thought Mike was doing fine in St. Cloud, but I deferred to her on matters of education. She had the PhD in Psychology, and I assumed she knew more than I did. But I was loath to abandon the Institute and Paris. Moreover, Frances did not want to return to Washington. We had finally sold the Washington house — the real estate lady had us paint only the front facade and that had done it. She wanted to return to California. She assured me there would be programs for Mike in and around Palo Alto. Yet, she had no real idea what kind of school she would find nor did she make any effort to write and find out. I was not keen to work on education projects at the Bank and anyhow I was no longer

—

on their staff. As for California, I could not see how I would return to SRI nor was it clear that SRI would hire me. I did not know what was driving Frances to hate Paris except that she may not have really felt comfortable in foreign cultures. She had wanted to leave Mexico, she had come to Paris and now all her energy was on returning to California. I spoke to Phil about it, he was not the kind of man who decides his career to please his wife. Helen was not that happy in Paris either, given the fact Phil worked all the time and she knew very few people. Phil was adamant: "Just stay, I need you". He was very annoyed at any talk of my leaving.

In February 1964, Paul Hanna, a professor at Stanford University, visited the Institute. Paul was beginning a new program in the Stanford School of Education. They were going to give a PhD. in Education with a specialization in educational planning. He called the new unit SIDEC: Stanford International Development Education Center. I immediately thought that since I could not easily go back to SRI, I might instead, become a Professor at Stanford University. I spoke to Professor Hanna and he pointed out that without a PhD, I did not have the dream of a chance in any American university. But he said, "Why not come to SIDEC and obtain your PhD with us?" I said, "I have three children, a wife…" He answered "We will obtain a fellowship for you and you have the house in Portola Valley, you might need some savings, but you can do it. Come get a PhD and at that point you will become a professor in an American university." I assumed, erroneously, that he meant I would then obtain an appointment at Stanford. I thought he was recruiting a future professor for his program. I did not realize he was only recruiting a student.

I told Frances that I did not see why Mike needed

—

special education. I pointed out that we knew what we were doing when we left Washington. Why the sudden despair about his education at the American School in St. Cloud? As it would turn out, the American School at St. Cloud was a much better school than those we would find in Portola Valley or in Berkeley, but I did not know that and Frances kept arguing that I would not want to jeopardize Mike's future. When I asked to consult someone in Paris, she argued that could only be done in the United States. I very reluctantly gave in and wrote to Paul Hanna.

Yet, we had many friends in Paris. At UNESCO, I had found Sylvain Lourié, my best friend from the Lycée du Parc Imperial in Nice in 1940-42. Sylvain held a high position, spoke fluent English, and Frances liked him. Old friends would appear. As I related earlier we were at the Deux Magots on Bld. St. Germain, when out of nowhere, we saw Betty Bachrach, Guido Tennissen and his young German girl friend. They were delighted to see us and rushed back to Charles Floquet for baths, shave, and dinner. We also had new friends, Ladislav Cerych, who worked at the Atlantic Institute and would soon join us at the IIEP, Raymond Lyons and Charles Berkovich. We also had many visitors from the United States who would look us up, and there was my family. My cousin Colette was in Berkeley that year, but Roger and Monique had returned from Washington, Roland and Geraldine, and Gérard and Lawrence were in Paris. There were my aunts who invited us to dinners or outings. In short, we suffered none of the isolation that afflicted Helen Coombs.

That 1964 summer, five of us in the Simca, first went to Bellagio for the conference at the Villa Serbelloni, then on to Venice. In Venice, we boarded a Yugoslav ferry and went overnight to Dubrovnik. There, we spent a week in the Hotel School with dozens of young servers trying their best. Leaving Venice on board ship to the tune of the ferry's band playing the "Nadrina" march was emotional. Was it that my ancestors had also left Venice on ship to go to Salonika? We also left Dubrovnik on ship, a much smaller ferry, to go to Split. In 1964 the coast highway from Split, did not yet reach Dubrovnik. The Simca was, once again, lowered on deck and we thought we would sit on benches, but very soon the deck was so packed we had to sit in the Simca surrounded by hundreds of happy Croatians going north. It seemed that Croats sang all the time and drank to sing better, so much so, that ship ride was our best concert of folk singing ever. Luckily, the crew drank less. The Simca was hoisted and this time seemed to teeter but made it. From Split, we went north via Trieste and Udine to Vienna, spent time en route and in Vienna; then drove down the Danube to Munich, the Black Forest and eastern France. We had lunch in Provins before arriving in Paris. We were in Udine on 17 August 1964, in Wien for three days and back in Paris on August 23. Phil was out of town. Frances did not want to stay in a deserted Paris. I called John Vaizey at Oxford, and asked if I could come consult him about our report for the Bellagio Conference. On 25 August, the Simca was back on the road; this time north to Calais, another ferry, and a week in England visiting Oxford, Bath, and Canterbury. This is when and where I found spaghetti on toast on the menu. English food can always surprise one. We were back in Paris in September, the five of us.

That fall, Professor Fred Carpenter from the University of California at Berkeley and his wife Betty, and their three children, were on sabbatical in Paris. Betty was a Stanford sorority sister of Frances. They lodged not far from us. Now, Frances had old friends from her college days to spend time with. Fred had an immense capacity for alcohol. He could drink and drink and never show effect.

—

The fall and winter of 1964 were wet and cold. At UNESCO I had commissary privileges where vodka or whiskey could be bought tax-free, for about $1.00 for a good brand. Wine was also available but not at that discount. We had plenty of hard liquor at the apartment and given the cold weather and Frances' depression, we tended to drink more than in the past. Fred and Betty provided other excuses. During one dinner at the apartment, I tried to refill his glass of whiskey each time to see how much he could absorb, and my memory is that he managed an entire bottle of scotch, a one dollar Johnny Walker Black Label.

Stanford admitted me in November 1964, to the new SIDEC course of work in the School of Education. Paul Hanna sought a fellowship for me from the Ford Foundation's Foreign Fellowship Program. It would cover all fees and tuition plus pay about $7000 a year and reimburse for foreign travel at dissertation time. Seven thousand was a long way from $18,000 tax free in Paris, but while I had not decided for sure, I was keeping my options open. I still hoped that Frances would get used to Paris. Frances was happy with the Carpenters and we saw a lot of them, they joined on our picnics and excursions out of Paris.

In December, we spent ten days with them in Wengen, Switzerland where the six children went to skiing classes. The parents enjoyed the sun and light in the mountains and Fred basked in the Swiss hotelier deference to Herr Professor. In January, we were back in the fog and cold rain of Paris. Frances continued to argue for departure; in fact the coming departure of the Carpenters at the end of his sabbatical, added fuel to her desire. Betty spoke of Berkeley, of the California climate, and it was certainly a lure in the cold wet Paris, and the continued

—

series of accidents below our windows. The drinking continued and I realized I was becoming portly. In February, I was notified that I had been awarded a fellowship to attend Stanford. In March 1965, I resigned from the IIEP and UNESCO effective June 20. Phil was angry. He felt I had let him down, and he had some reason to be angry. He had accepted a "minimum" contract of five years, and I was getting out after less than two when the Institute was still in its infancy. I was leaving Paris just like I had left Mexico, with an angry boss, and again I was going to California to try something new, not knowing how I would land.

Frances had fired the Italian au pair. It was not her nakedness below the sweater that bothered her, but she found her unreliable. A very clean, cheery and hard working English girl, the daughter of a school master took her place. She coped with Marc who was enrolled that fall at the Cours Champfleury, a kinder-garden program just one block from 24 Charles Floquet. Marc was mischievous. One fall day he came from the Champs de Mars at full speed, ran right into the apartment and hid under his bed in the back room. The concierge and the Champs de Mars park police came in hot pursuit. Marc had thrown all the metal chairs he could find into the main water basin. The new au pair had her hands full. I spanked him many times, to the point my hand hurt, but Marc was the way he was from the start. He was determined to act out, to be rebellious, to have his own way, and he was, from the start able to cajole, or convince us or the au pair of his good intentions. In restaurants, we had invented a "straight look" he would perform to demonstrate how good he could be. He would sit straight in his chair and not move, looking straight ahead and we would hope it could last.

—

Frances was sure we had to leave when Anne reported that a flasher had shown himself to her in the Champs de Mars. She decided that France was not a good country to bring up children. On one hand the French were far too strict: "ne touche pas" was all one could hear on the sand pile in the Champs de Mars, the children kept immaculate and were not allowed to play as children would. On the other hand, you had these dreadful sexual deviates which obviously indicated some basic national weakness. Frances was increasingly anti-French. The Vietnam War was the result of French inadequacies, but more importantly, the French had such bad taste in such matters as housing and decoration. And they had such bad tempers that all their food and women's clothes could not make up the difference. Yet, we went to see French plays, ate in the best restaurants: La Tour d'Argent where we took the three children, Lapérouse on the quay where we went quite often. Frances ordered a series of dresses in a couture shop on the Faubourg St. Honoré; we bought antiques at the flea market, a large Bahut, a buffet from the South of France. In the spring of 1965, we bought a Volvo Station wagon to take back to the United States. The Carpenters bought a new Citroën — a DS 19 that rose up and down as if it had the intention of leaving ground as soon as it went fast enough. We went on the Loire to Vouvray for weekends, ate venison and Anne became quite a gourmet.

One does not know how it would have turned out if we had stayed. There is little doubt Anne, Michael and Marc would have had a much better education had they stayed in Paris; they would have avoided the worst of the drug scene of the late sixties. I would have had an international civil servant career which suited me. I would have earned much more money over the years. To be sure I would have missed the intellectual opportunities of an academic career. I would not have written books, I would not have taught, but in the last analysis, the one who would have lost out sooner is Frances. She would have continued drinking and she would have gone down much faster than she did in California.

In that spring, the Institute was producing its first publications and we hired a publication officer, a young Englishman named John Hall. He stayed at the Institute and many years later it turned out he was the brother of Peter Hall, now Sir Peter, a colleague for several years at Berkeley. We saw John and his wife in the summer of 1994 when we were in Provence with Peter and Magda Hall. Here he was, a prosperous international civil servant earning nearly three times my Berkeley faculty salary. Maybe I should have stood my ground — I just did not realize that Frances was so poorly informed about schools and Mike's needs. In retrospect I now believe our return may have had something to do with Norway. It was a combination of factors, the Norvegian, the chill of Paris winters when it is overcast day after day (le petit brouillard), the war, the fear of aging, too much drinking to fend off the invading winter cold humidity. Viewed from Paris, California was now the desired land where the sun shone and life was made easier by the automobile, supermarkets, larger houses and gardens.

Once again, we planned our departure. This time the movers were Grospiron, the same movers my mother had used for her own mother during the war. Grospiron packed 14,000 pounds, paid by UNESCO, for shipment to California. The apartment was emptied on my last Friday on the job. That late afternoon, we left Paris to sleep just outside the outskirts in Barbizon. From there, we ate our way into Burgundy, stopping at Paray-Le-Monial where Anne had a never-to-be-forgotten dinner. After that, we went to what was then a three star restaurant Père Bise in

—

Talloires on our way to Italy. We drove down the length of Italy to Bari where we took a ferry to Greece.

The Volvo station wagon came with a rack on which our suitcases were attached. A heavy tarp covered them and held them in place with four locks. Somehow no one in the south of Italy attempted to tear them off. But we took them in at every hotel. We drove from the north of Greece to Athens. I learned that in Greece you hold to the center of the road to the last minute, then elegantly the huge truck bearing on you moves left, you move right and life continues. We saw Delphi, spent a week at a beach resort south of Athens, and went to Piraeus where we boarded the Star line Cruise Ship. We took a cruise in the islands, went to Istanbul and saw the blue mosque, went to Nauplion, swam again and then boarded the Volvo back toward Italy. On the ferry we had a tiny pool and an American model with "exuberant" breasts. We drove to Naples. We had left Paris in mid-June, we were in Greece on 9 July, we were on our cruise at the end of the month and out of Greece on 9 August. We then left Naples about a week later on the SS Rafaëlo — the sister ship of the SS Cristofero Colombo — again first class — to land six days later in New York. We left immediately to drive towards California. We went across in about a week and entered California at the beginning of September 1965. We slept one night at the home of our neighbor Beverly, and the next day the shipment from Paris was delivered at 119 Corte Madera. We slept in our home that night. We had traveled for two and a half months, mostly in the Volvo and here we were, the five of us back in California, back with our furniture including the Bahut from the Paris flea market, right back on Corte Madera Road in Portola Valley.

Anne and Michael spoke a few French sentences. Marc was fluent in French. He had picked it up during his

—

year at the Cours Champfleury. He had also been awarded the "Premier Prix d'Espièglerie" a first prize in pranks, by the "strict" French educators who had come to know him well. As soon as we reached California, Marc announced he would never speak French again. "I do not want to talk that icky language."

But Frances had bad news when she returned. The Norwegian no longer wanted to see her. He had found someone else. The long affair was over. There were many phone calls between Portola Valley and Washington but it was clear. Frances had lost the Norwegian. I do not remember exactly when I met him, I did only once, and it must have been in Washington, at a party. He seemed nice, reserved and thoughtful. This loss depressed Frances further. It did not depress me, but I resented her sadness. The Norwegian was in some complex way the beginning of the end of our marriage. It was obvious to me that Frances blamed me, or the Paris episode for her loss and I resented being blamed.

—

XI

CALIFORNIA FOR GOOD: STANFORD

I was quite unprepared to be a student. In my mind it was a pro-forma arrangement. I did not have a PhD., Stanford was creating a program in educational planning, I was an expert in this new field, surely I would take some courses, but this would be done gracefully and I would rapidly be given the degree and settle in to teach. I expected some red carpet treatment. Of course, nothing of the sort was intended. Paul Hanna had hired an anthropologist, Robert Textor, and a political scientist, Hans Weiler. They had no idea what an education plan might look like, but they were the professors. I discovered I was a student after waiting an hour and a half to register. Monsieur le Directeur with CD plates on his car was to take courses, pass exams and hope to finish the degree.

Frances had found employment. Her mentor in the Psychology Department was re-standardizing the Stanford-Binet Intelligence test. Frances could work while the children went to school. Suddenly Mike's school problem had evaporated. Frances had made a few inquiries and was assured that Mike did not require any special education. In any case, Frances was convinced that the Portola Valley School was excellent and there would be no reason to look further. Marc was placed in the elementary school near our house and Mike and Anne went to the school down on Portola Road in the center of Portola Valley Village.

—

I registered for the fall 1965 semester and discovered that I had to take a number of courses such as the history of education, statistics, philosophy of education, and so on. These courses were required of all students in the Department of Education. They were large lecture hall courses and we were graded by graduate students. Within the Stanford International Development Education program, I had to take courses with Textor, Weiler and Paul Hanna. I went to see an old friend, Irene Blumenthal, who at the time held a research appointment in the Political Science Department to ask her if she knew anyone who might be interesting, and she suggested I take a course with Professor Morris Zelditch, a sociologist.

I knew there was a field of knowledge called Sociology. I had met a number of "Rural Sociologists". These were people who studied how rural people managed to live. But I had no idea Sociologists ventured outside their rural environment. I decided to take a course with Zelditch. He was giving a course in "Sociology Theory". I registered for that course. I had no idea what that might be about.

From the very start I did not do well in the Education Department at Stanford. I could not stand the "Mickey mouse" courses I was required to take with all the new graduate students. In the sixties there were still, in Schools of Education like Stanford, professors who might best be thought of as high school teachers. The men who taught history or philosophy of education were good high school teachers. They simplified every thing to the point that it was not clear what might have been there in the first place. The graduate students were after key phrases they wanted to be sure we had retained. That part of the program was still geared to meet the needs of teachers — it

—

was the kind of course a teacher training college might provide. I found the entire atmosphere distasteful. The courses with Textor, Weiler and Hanna were another problem. They had PhD's but they had very little experience with the topic of the program. Some of the students had traveled and many had served in developing countries with the Peace Corps. Both Textor and Weiler were younger than I; Paul Hanna was older but the best one might say about his contributions was that he was very enterprising. He lived in the only Frank Lloyd Wright house on campus — a house designed for him and his family. He had made his money with school textbooks and was near retirement. He enjoyed traveling abroad, hence his late interest in international education.

Professor Zelditch explained this phenomenon in his course. Either professors did research or wrote books; or if they had nothing to contribute, they did administration and traveled to conferences — preferably abroad. Therefore we should not be surprised by the dire straights of university administration and the dullness of academic conferences and meetings.

My relations with the two younger SIDEC staffers were not made easy by my tendency to speak out in class. I would attempt to politely correct what they said and they made desperate efforts to reassert their intellectual dominance. I may have known some facts, while they were trained in an academic discipline I wanted to learn. Meanwhile, in the Zelditch course, I found myself with sociology graduate students trying to understand theory — we were reading about peasant revolts and trying to explain why they occur. Here, I was discovering how little I knew and spent all my time trying to catch up on my sociological ignorance. I was fascinated by the classics that I was discovering for the first time: Max Weber, George Simmel,

—

and Durkheim; and also anthropologists such as Marcel Mauss, Malinowski, and Edmund Leach.

The idea that one could explain behavior by focusing on social conditions instead of paying attention to individual traits pleased me. Maybe this had to do with my relationship with Frances. She was the psychologist and I had learned to defer to her views because I somehow thought that psychology gave her an insight into why people did what they did. This was greatly reinforced by her sister Betty, who was a psychiatric social worker, and who had recently remarried a psychiatrist. They now lived in San Francisco and we saw them often. With them and Frances the conversations tended to explain events in a terminology I never understood adequately. For the first time I was discovering with Zelditch that social power and norms were probably as good, if not a better way to look at problems; at least a quicker way to understand why and who was doing what to whom.

Since SIDEC did not have much, if anything to offer me, I decided that I should learn sociology. I had to find a way to get out of SIDEC. I approached Paul Hanna to see what he thought. I pointed out that I was a problem for the new SIDEC faculty and that it would be preferable if I were in a different department. Paul informed me, what I should have known all along, that there were little chances of my being appointed at Stanford because universities like Stanford rarely hired their own graduates. One had to go elsewhere, that was the general rule. He also thought Sociology would not take me in. They wanted to prepare future professors of Sociology and unless I wanted to go in that direction, Sociology would not work for me.

There was another alternative. I could create my own committee and work inter-departmentally, that is do both sociology and some education. I would be able to

—

remain in touch with SIDEC, avoid unwanted courses and take as much sociology as I wanted. At first the Dean of the School of Education was against it. He pointed out that if I did an interdepartmental degree between education and sociology, I would want a PhD. in Sociology of Education. But if they gave me such a degree, every student in Education with an interest in Psychology would want the same arrangement. They would want a degree in Psychology of Education instead of the PhD in Education the school provided. I had to think of something else. I then came up with the idea of a PhD in the Sociology of Planning. That did not seem to threaten anyone. I also had to convince the Graduate Division that there existed a legitimate reason to grant me such a degree.

Luckily there existed at that time at Stanford a new Department of Engineering and Systems Analysis. Several faculty members in that unit had an interest in methodologies of planning. Professor William Linvill became interested in my project. I was therefore able to create a committee of faculty from three departments. I was truly interdepartmental. The Graduate Division approved. I was liberated. By then, it was the fall of 1966.

The war in Vietnam had expanded. President Lyndon Johnson had become a war president and the anti-war movement was emerging. Frances was doubly depressed by the war. She saw it as we both did, as destruction in the name of "saving" people. But she also saw it as a disgrace for the American Army. She felt very strongly about the army, having been born an army brat and having lived in many army camps. She had once, as a small child, been rocked on the knees of Captain Dwight Eisenhower. She therefore resumed her political involvement in grass root Democratic politics. In the fall of 1966, there were senatorial and congressional elections

—

and Frances worked for an anti-war candidate. She continued to be depressed, the Norwegian had come once more to the Bay Area and Frances had met with him. It had not worked. He had broken off again.

Meanwhile, I am in school. I am taking classes, passing exams, writing term papers. Stanford in 1966 and 1967 seems peaceful to me, there are some demonstrations, but since I have a house in Portola Valley, I do not fully participate in campus life. I am aware — or we are aware of new attitudes. Travis, Betty's new husband becomes very interested in the flower children in the Haight-Ashbury district of San Francisco. He goes there and interviews some of them — he tells us about drug use but neither Frances nor I knew much about drugs — except for alcohol and tobacco. I have taken to smoking the pipe because I think it suits my new academic persona. One puffs on the pipe while appearing to think — then "well, I would say..." another puff — "that you can turn the problem around and..." Our consumption of alcohol is quite high. We often take one or more cocktails before dinner — then wine — then, often, after dinner drinks. We often visit the Carpenters in Berkeley, where wine and hard liquor are plentiful. We go there at big football events, drink while watching the game on the television, drink at dinner, drink after, sleep at their house and Fred brings Bloody Mary's to our bed in the morning "to help cure the hangover."

The Portola School reports that Anne is involved with drugs, but neither Frances nor I believe them. We think that they are trying to prevent something that has not happened. Travis continues to report on the flower children, he tells us about their sexual freedom, about their poetry, and the drugs but neither Frances nor I are very interested. It seems false to us, the events in the Haight

—

Ashbury do not seem related to real life, to our life. We are in 1967, I have to finish my course work, write a dissertation and find work. I am very concerned about what I am to do when I finish at the university. I am upset to know that Stanford rarely hires its own graduates. Had I known, I could not have dared leave Paris. Where will I go? I am too preoccupied with my own future and finding a job to become too involved with Travis' research or to pay much attention to what is happening around me.

To Mexico City For A Dissertation

In late June 1967 I drive a second hand Volvo I have bought, to Mexico City to conduct the field work on my dissertation. I am to study the Politics of Planning and I have been invited by Licenciado Manuel Bravo Jimenez who is heading a major planning exercise for the Ministry of Education to come and observe him and his staff in action. I had met Licenciado Bravo many years before at the SRI Time-Life International Conference. He had also attended our Latin American seminar at the IIEP in Paris. He was a friend and was willing to have me "observe" him and watch the Mexican planning process. At this time, I have a "theory" of the planning process and I will observe the interaction to see if reality has anything to do with my theory. I will write it up and it will be my dissertation. It is all explained in detail in *Bureaucracy and National Planning: A Sociological Case Study in Mexico* published by Praeger in 1970.

I drive with Frances down via El Paso and Ciudad Juarez, it is summer and we want to stay on the high plateau. She will stay in Mexico City for two weeks and will fly back to Portola Valley as the children return from camp. We then drive to Mexico City and we stay at the María Christina Hotel since the fellowship is paying travel

—

expenses.

My mother is in town but she is kept occupied by her new love affair. Earlier in 1966, she had met an Italian navy man Commandant Franco Rinaldi who lived in La Spezia with his wife and mother. La Spezia is a major Italian Navy port. Lucy had met Franco in Mexico City where he had been sent for a short visit by the Italian Government. In 1967 Commandant Franco Rinaldi had returned to show Mexico to his wife. I had never met Mr. and Mrs. Rinaldi but by chance I did catch sight of them that summer. She was walking ahead of Franco in Sanborns; she had the manners of a Jewish princess although she was in fact a very Catholic princess. She was showing Franco this and that object and spelling in a loud voice her low opinion of what she saw. Madame Rinaldi was from much higher stock than the Commandant and I gather she never failed to remind him she was aristocratic while he was a mere Navy man, married above his station. Madame Rinaldi is probably an explanation for Franco's long love affair with my mother. Franco and his wife would remain in Mexico City during several weeks.

Mexico City had grown since 1954 but in 1967 I still knew my way. We went to Puebla to buy dishes from Uriarte on 4ta Poniente. We visited the new museums, we saw old friends including Betty and Mike Gold. And since Lucy was busy with Franco, we generally had a good time.

During the daytime, I had many dissertation interviews. I attempted to see many people as quickly as possible. I knew that sooner or later there would be rumors about my visits; real or imaginary. I explained that I expected to publish a study of Mexico's interesting experience with planning education under UNESCO auspices. Some of my interviewees knew vaguely about the

—

International Institute for Educational Planning. I knew that as an American inquiring about details of Mexican education, some doors might be closed. I accentuated my French accent in Spanish and I sat in waiting rooms interviewing whoever was waiting with me to see the big director of this or that department. In due time I had done the bulk of the interviews and we spent more time touring around Mexico City. We went to the pyramids and to Tepozlán, to Tula and down to Cuernavaca.

Frances left by plane, taking some of our purchases and leaving me with a car full of dishes and other heavier items. I still had to complete a few interviews, people who had been out of town, or individuals I had to see a second time. I also had to do the library work, obtain reports and data on Mexican education and on other social and economic indicators. I stayed on at the María Cristina, although Lucy wanted me to move to her new apartment on Homero 1025. By then Franco and Madame Rinaldi had finally left town.

I had caught sight of a very handsome Nordic woman in the lobby of the María Cristina, and after Frances' departure, I invited this woman to visit sites with me. The woman was Danish, on a vacation, and we went out together several times. Unfortunately at that same time, I started suffering from what is referred to as "piles." I had trouble sitting down or driving for a long time and worse still, this trouble erased any and all sexual drive. In fact, I had to admit to my Danish friend that I had this problem to explain why I was seeing less of her. As the days went by, my mother was more insistent that I move to Homero, my suffering was increasing and my adventure with Denmark was becoming a nursing arrangement. I never thought of consulting a doctor, nor did the Danish woman seem to know anything about remedies for piles. I decided to try to

—

escape. I would try to drive back to California, I must drive back, and otherwise I will have to move in with my mother or have an operation or something in Mexico.

Thus, I leave. The Volvo is packed, the trunk is full; the back seat is full. I sit on some kind of cushion, trying to remove weight from my rear by holding myself on to the back of my car seat. Goodbye Lucy, goodbye Denmark, goodbye Mexico, I am driving north, past Lechería and Cautitlán; I am hoping to make it that night to Querétaro. Suddenly out of nowhere on the highway there is a billboard: "si ud sufre..." If you suffer from what I suffer, it says "compre suppositorios Anusol." I stop at the farmacia in the next town. They have a suppositorio and relief is on its way. I just did not know. I slept well in Querétaro. The next day, I could already sit normally in the car. I do not know what would have happened without that billboard. I would not have made it to California propped on one side, driving with one hand on the wheel.

The trip back was hot. We were in August by then. There was no air conditioning in most cars. I would leave early in the morning — around 4 o'clock and drive to 8 — stop for breakfast — continue to 12 — stop for lunch and try to find a motel with a pool around 3 in the afternoon. I went through Irapuato, Léon, Zacatecas, Chihuahua back to El Paso, then west through Tucson and Yuma, it was still very hot when I started coming down toward Oceanside, California, I finally stopped looking at the motor heat gage. The Volvo had made it, but just barely: the heat gage would rise real close to the red and hover there, and I kept hoping and praying the motor would not overheat. I had no passengers but that car was loaded: those Puebla dishes were heavy! Suddenly, I reached the top, California was below me, it was cool, and I swam in the Pacific Ocean at Oceanside. From then on, it was easy; the California fog

—

was in action.I was back in Portola Valley but I kept away from the Stanford campus. I wanted everyone to think I was still in Mexico City gathering data. It did not sound right to say that my field research had taken only a month to complete.

Search for Work

Frances' project on re-standardizing the Stanford-Binet test had terminated so we were living on my fellowship, plus savings. The fellowship would end by June 1968 at the latest. It had been renewed three times and it did not look like it would be renewed again. In any case, once I completed the dissertation, passed the University Oral Examination, and was awarded the PhD., that money had to stop. I was therefore concerned about future work. The problem was complicated by Frances' reluctance — I should say strong opposition to any move away from the Bay Area. In fact, she had no intention to move out of 119 Corte Madera. She thought I might go back to the Stanford Research Institute. She did not think she could find full time work, she did not intend to do more than part time work — when and if available. Strictly speaking, there were two alternatives. The first was to go back to Stanford Research full time. The second was to try several simultaneous jobs. There was a junior college down the road and I went twice there to interview. I thought that I might be able to teach at the junior college in the "Soch" department and free lance on the side. I could maybe obtain contracts via SRI while I taught "soch". I did not realize that the teaching loads at community colleges were heavy, and that I would never have the time to do contract work.

I went to SRI on many occasions that fall. I visited with many of my old friends. But SRI had changed and

—

while I was just about to obtain a PhD. it was by no means clear what I could do at SRI. My new field of educational planning was not high on the SRI agenda. I might be able to obtain contracts from the U. S. Aid Agency. But I quickly realized that if I went on that route, I would spend most of my time working abroad or going to Washington to obtain contracts. My new interest and my dissertation on the politics of planning had no particular market value in that milieu.

Paul Hanna thought they might be able to hire me on a temporary basis as a lecturer but he was not very hopeful. I do not think Weiler or Textor wanted me around, and Paul knew this. A temporary position would be just that; it would end. Sooner or later I would face the same problem. The other alternatives were some distance away. The closest was the University of California at Berkeley. Already, in the spring of 1967, Hans Weiler had showed me an announcement that Berkeley was recruiting for a professor of comparative education. I knew little about comparative education. I had called Geraldine Joncich, the professor at Berkeley who was recruiting. Frances was not enthusiastic, but moving to Berkeley was the less of possible evils. We had friends there — Fred Carpenter in Chemistry and Paul Mussen who had taken a master's degree with Frances at Stanford and was a professor in the Psychology Department. Berkeley was close to Stanford and Carmel so that we would not lose friends. At one point Frances thought I could commute to Berkeley but I refused. The commute would be too long and involvement in campus life would be far more difficult.

—

XII

BERKELEY, MARRIAGE AND PAINTING

I had gone to Berkeley for an interview; I had dinner with the faculty from "Social Foundations," the division recruiting a new professor in the Graduate School of Education at the University of California at Berkeley. Nothing much had happened. This was late March and I still had to go to Mexico City for my field work. When I returned in the late summer, I had contacted Berkeley again. I had met the Dean during my first visit and he had been non committal. A Berkeley appointment did not seem in the cards. Paul Mussen knew a professor in the Social Foundations Division named Jack London who reported that there was a sociologist on their faculty who was totally opposed to my being appointed. That was enough to sink what slim hopes I might still have. To my surprise, when I called in the late summer, the Dean suggested I visit him again. I went to Berkeley to meet the non-committal Dean. He was not enthusiastic but nevertheless suggested I meet with a professor from his own division of school administration named Charles Benson. He thought I might teach the Sociology of Organizations to students of school administration. The Dean seemed most concerned not to antagonize anyone. In fact, he seemed more concerned about having problems with his faculty in Social

—

Foundations than about hiring me. I was to find out later that he was an administrator who hated to make decisions and tried to let things take care of themselves.

I met Charles Benson who was an Economist. Charles was clearly interested in my background. He had hoped in 1961 to be appointed in Paris at the Organization for Economic Cooperation and Development (OECD) for a position. Dr. Selma Mushkin, whom I knew in Paris, had obtained it, but Charles was in awe of Paris appointments. So, Charles immediately said that I should be appointed in the School Administration Division. But he also explained that while the Dean had sent me to meet him, the Dean did not like him. In fact, Charles had been appointed at Berkeley against the will of that Dean, I should therefore be cautious. He wanted to support my appointment but thought the Dean had to believe that I was "his" appointment. All this seemed very murky to me. I was still not attuned to the Byzantine nature of university politics. I went back to Portola Valley quite unsure if I would ever be appointed at Berkeley.

Nothing much happened for several weeks. I finally called Geraldine to ask what was going on. She said her Division was not prepared to recommend my appointment. I told her I thought there might be interest in the Administration Division. Geraldine offered to speak to the Dean and see what he might suggest. Again, I did not hear anything and I waited some ten days and then called the Dean again. He sounded somber and asked me how my conversation with Benson had gone. I said I thought it had been okay, so he told me to come back for further discussion. He told me that the Ford Foundation had given a grant to the Berkeley campus to help internationalize the professional schools. A Professor Warren Ilchman in Political Science was in charge of this activity, would I

—

please see him. He thought I might work with Ilchman and as a result be appointed in the Administration Division. All this was tentative. I sensed the Dean was looking for someone to suggest that I be appointed. He did not dare take the responsibility and wanted Faculty from other departments to vouch for me..

Warren Ilchman who taught in Political Science met with me. Warren was delighted to have me work with him since part of the grant was to be used to run an international conference and I had experience. I explained how my Dean was waiting for his go-ahead to begin the process of getting me appointed at Berkeley. Warren asked for the draft of my dissertation and he told me to call Professor Nathan Glazer — a Sociologist from Harvard — who was spending time in the City and Regional Planning Department at Berkeley. He wanted Professor Glazer to read the draft. All this was done. Glazer was very friendly — said he liked the dissertation and he would write a letter to this effect to the Dean. Warren did the same.

The Dean and I spoke again on the phone, and visited him. He was still somber. He wanted me to fill out some forms. My appointment had to be approved, first by the faculty of the School, then by a campus wide committee. It would take time. There was nothing he could do to assure me of anything. I said I wanted tenure — given my age, experience and publications. I had published a book on Africa, several articles, and my dissertation was being considered by two publishers. He promised — after much discussion to appoint me as an Associate Professor with tenure.

Back in Portola Valley weeks went by and again there were no news from Berkeley. I waited. Meanwhile I went two or three times to meet with Warren to begin

—

planning for the conference on the International Role of the Professional School in America. Charles asked me in December to teach one of his classes and I did so. Finally, Paul Mussen called to say that he had a contact in the Budget Committee where campus appointments are reviewed and vetted. He was told "things seem to be moving in the right direction."

I was appointed at Berkeley effective March 1, 1968 at a salary of $12,600, nothing like what I had been paid at UNESCO, but I was given tenure. My PhD was conferred by Stanford University a few weeks later, on my father's birthday, April 5, 1968. I was to start teaching immediately in the spring quarter. Basically, it had taken a full year for the Berkeley decision. I was to begin teaching in a matter of days.

The children would finish the school year in Portola Valley, this would also give Frances and me time to look for a house in Berkeley. We would move in the summer of 1968. Meanwhile, I could commute to Berkeley and if necessary, sleep at the Carpenters when the schedule became too stressful. I had to invent two courses — one was "An Introduction to Educational Planning", and the other on "Organization Theory". Basically, I had to prepare the courses on a day-per-day basis. Berkeley was not Stanford, where new professors were given a quarter free of teaching duties when first appointed. We only taught three hours a week per course and in School Administration, my classes were small seminars where it was quite feasible to come in without any prepared material and still be able to conduct an interesting discussion with a dozen or more students.

During the spring, Frances and I came to Berkeley on several occasions to look for housing. We finally

—

agreed on a house at 263 Hillcrest Road. The house was being sold by a divorcing couple with a small child. Each time we came to visit the house, the wife and child were there. She wore the tightest and smallest shorts, and seemed quite pleasant. The husband was more difficult — he even wanted money for a set of plastic bags he had bought for the outside garbage can He told me he hoped we would be happy there. He had bought the house from a divorcing couple and now he was divorcing. We would find out later that he had a drinking problem. But I had no qualms. We had no intention of divorcing — we were a very strong family. Poor fellow I thought — why should he divorce such an attractive woman?

If I had been totally unprepared for my student life when I arrived at Stanford, I was just as unprepared to become a professor when I began teaching at Berkeley. This was spring term 1968, Frances and the children had remained in Portola Valley until the end of the school term. The Berkeley campus was quite different from Stanford. Stanford was a "managed" university depending on the goodwill of students, and more importantly on continued financial support from alumni. Government funding — or philanthropic foundations mattered, but the university "paid attention." The faculty was well treated because if faculty is well treated, it treats students better and sooner or later students become alumni. When I arrived at Berkeley, nobody cared or moved a finger; no one knew where my office should or might be. Berkeley is part of the University of California system; it is a state university where you fend for yourself. I had to find an office. I found that a graduate student named Glassman was using an office; he gave Hebrew lessons there. I kicked him out and established myself. Sooner or later the office was officially given to me. No one cared much what I would teach or when and how.

—

The Administration Division where I was appointed was in disarray. There was an old guard faculty who had had been administrators in the public schools who still taught by recalling past experiences. And there was a new generation — Charles Benson was an economist, James Guthrie dealt with politics and now me, a sociologist of organizations. The students were mostly tall athletic types who had been coaches and from coaching had gone into administration. Vice principals of schools — or even principals — all of them white males wanting a PhD — or an EdD (a doctorate in education) to further their careers. In general they had no interest in anything theoretical. They were principals who wanted a degree and not much more. That was the world Charles Benson had encountered when he had arrived a few years before Guthrie and I. Charles had been appointed against the will of the Dean because someone in Sacramento in the State Government had wanted to have Charles around. Charles understood about the economics of financing of education and Sacramento increasingly, had to provide funds for the public schools. The Dean hated Charles and I now understood he had hired me in the hope of having an ally in his own unit.

At first the Dean was quite pleasant. I pointed out that one of my past talents was to find money from foundations and the Dean encouraged me to do so. Charles had been in touch with the Ford Foundation as they wanted him to go to Pakistan to advise that government on future spending for education. This meant that Charles would be leaving for Pakistan later during that year leaving Guthrie, who had been appointed in the fall of 1967, and me alone to try to redesign and focus our program.

It occurred to me that we should go to the Ford

—

Foundation and ask them for a three-year grant to help us upgrade our Berkeley capability while we transformed an administrative program based on "experience" into a theory based analytical approach more focused on preparing policy analysts and planners, than line administrators. The Dean was most agreeable and later that spring he provided travel funds so that I could go to New York and consult with the Ford Foundation. I consulted and we were invited to prepare a proposal. The idea was to strengthen Berkeley so that we would be in a better position to assist the Foundation in countries such as Pakistan. I will return to this story soon because it became my immediate experience of academia — but meanwhile let me continue with campus life.

At Stanford, I had had little contact with the campus simply because I was living at home in Portola Valley and knew few students, so I had not been involved in any protest movements regarding the Vietnam War. Frances was depressed by that war. When she finally moved to Berkeley in the summer of 1968, she decided to get involved in local politics. There was going to be an election in the fall of 1968 — a presidential election. Frances volunteered herself and me to do precinct work for the Democratic Party. Lyndon Johnson had decided after the Tet offensive not to run for the presidency. The Democratic Party was in disarray. That summer we had a spectacle on black and white television of the Democratic Convention in Chicago where anti-war activists were being clubbed in and around the Convention Hall. Richard Nixon was back (he had run for the presidency against Kennedy in 1960 and lost). Now he was running again and this was enough to stir all of us into wanting to do something.

As soon as we were settled on Hillcrest Road, Frances and I worked the precinct. By 1970 when we had the mid-term elections, Frances was running all the precinct work for the local Democratic Party. In fact, she was instrumental in getting Congressman Ron Dellums elected. I also joined the Faculty Union. The faculty was not unionized, but there was a small Faculty Union and I thought that the faculty should be able to organize itself. I was quite unimpressed by the salary I had finally been offered and attributed our relatively low salaries to our lack of organization.

I not only joined the faculty union, but I spoke out. I made speeches at Faculty Senate meetings. My speeches tended to be anti-war, pro-feminist and generally pro-student participation in the governance of the campus. I was good at speech making because of my experience in government. I had gone to enough international conferences to know how to make brief but pithy statements. Of course I could no longer enunciate slowly "my government stands by its commitment and declares..." But still in those turbulent times what with demonstrations starting nearly everyday, I made good speeches. Later, I would realize when my promotions were denied, that one might pay a price for talking at Faculty Senate meetings on a campus where most of the senior faculty was, contrary to general perception, quite conservative.

Conflict With A Dean

My early mentor, Professor Warren Ilchman of the Political Science Department, had been clear: you have to publish. Teaching is done in your spare time, but it is impossible to progress if you do not publish. Warren helped. He had a grant from the Ford Foundation to help the professional schools become more international. Some of that money was given to faculty to travel or work on proposals for research abroad. But a good portion was used

—

to organize a conference at Berkeley about the international role of professional schools at universities. This conference was going to yield many papers written by the people we were inviting. Warren and I would edit the volume and presto — I would be the co-editor of a book. In fact, Warren dumped the entire grant in my hands as soon as the conference was over and I did most of the editing. That book, *Agents of Change: Professionals in Developing Countries*, came out with Praeger in 1969 and my dissertation, *Bureaucracy and National Planning*, was also published by Praeger in 1970. So I was busy getting books out and at the same time developing my courses. You just could not go into class and not know what you would be talking about, although that did happen from time to time.

My proposal to the Ford Foundation to strengthen our unit was accepted. At least we heard it would be accepted in early September 1969. But I also heard that the Dean had asked that the grant be made to him, not to Benson and me. In September, I was on my way to Rawalpindi, in Pakistan, where Charles was spending two years. From Pakistan, Charles and I cabled New York and told them to be sure to make the grant for our program and not to the School if that was what they wanted. If the idea was to strengthen our unit, there was no point making the grant to the Dean who might use it for other purposes — including to take trips on his own. The Ford Foundation understood this quite well, and since the grant was intended for us it was written that way; it would go to Charles and me.

When I returned at the end of September, the Dean announced that unless the grant was awarded to him, the School would not accept it. I was dumbfounded. This was beyond my imagination. As far as I was concerned, in

—

terms of my experience in government, at the Bank or at UNESCO, this was unheard of. Sure, Charles and I had beaten the Dean on a small matter — we had made sure he would not use our grant for his personal pleasures. Yes, he had lost and we owed him one since he had used school funds to send me to New York. We would want to have him do some traveling with the grant. But refuse a grant? What kind of nonsense was that? Did he expect us to cave in? Deans and departmental heads have considerable power in academia: ours was both. They send recommendations for promotions forward after consulting the faculty. So our Dean expected us to cave in and tell the Ford Foundation to award him the grant. We did not oblige him. Starting in October through December, and well into the next spring, the Ford Foundation sent emissaries to Berkeley to get a Dean to accept a grant designed to help a unit of his school and improve it.

Since the grant had been awarded, the language of the grant could not be easily changed by the Foundation staff since they would have to resubmit it to their Board of Directors. So the Foundation staff who more than anything else, wanted to avoid trouble and bad publicity. Having a grant rejected is not indicative of careful staff work. They were trying to find an accommodation. But Charles from Pakistan and I in Berkeley saw no need to cave in, we found the behavior of the Dean intolerable. We had at least four or five meetings with the Ford people over that many months and the Dean still refused the grant until pressure was applied by the Foundation on the campus unit that coordinates all grants. Late in the spring the Dean caved in — he accepted the grant.

But I was sore; to me that kind of behavior was corruption. I had taken careful notes after each meeting with the Foundation staff, a practice I had learned from

—

government. You write down the date and time of meetings or conversations and you summarize the pertinent points made. I wrote up my notes, titled them "aide mémoire" — a French term for a document that is supposed to help the reader understand something or recall past events — and sent this document to the Chancellor. At that time — late spring of 1970 — I had inherited Professor Ilchman's grant including the administrative assistant, a Miss Rudy — Miss Rudy had a contact in the Chancellor's Office. The contact first told us that my "aide mémoire" had gone to some Assistant Chancellor, and then several days later she called to say that it had been sent back and was on the desk of the Chancellor! Just before the end of the term, the Dean announced that he was resigning his post so that he could "return to teaching." The "aide mémoire" had convinced the Chancellor. A university like Berkeley cannot tolerate embarrassing a major grant giver like the Ford Foundation. So I had made a major enemy. In the arcane world of academia, vengeance and repayment for slights may take time — but it happens for the pettiest reasons and this was more than a petty matter.

Spanish Interludes

In the summer of 1969, I went to Spain invited by UNESCO to work on a project to assist Ricardo Diez Hochleitner who had left the World Bank and UNESCO to become the Under Minister of Education under Franco. Ricardo's main life plan had always been to become Minister of Education in Spain. He waited for the Franco regime to end and this is why he had joined UNESCO, the World Bank, etc. But Franco kept on living and time was passing. Ricardo decided he could wait no longer. Ricardo was also getting older. He accepted to head a major reform of Spanish education. He thought that while the reform was underway Franco would sooner or later die and that

—

timing would be good for his advancement. These plans did not work out because Generalissimo Franco did not die soon enough, and Ricardo made so many enemies with his reform that he had to resign in 1973.

I arrived in Madrid to work with two other UNESCO experts and draft a broad outline of the proposed reform. We stayed in Madrid but this was the month of August and it became intolerably hot. At that time there still was no air conditioning. The Spanish Government moved us to Santander and it was cooler, but the work took all day and we had no opportunity to go to the beach or bathe. I worked for several weeks in Santander before leaving the other experts to continue drafting the reform as I had to return to my classes. I liked Spain, the art, the lively night life, we would go to a Flamenco night club and I recalled my time with Paco. I was attracted to Spanish women but did not have time for anything more but watching dancers perform and having an excited Equatorian educational planner on our expert panel repeat over and over "imaginate pasar la noche con ella", think what it would be to spend the night with her.

In 1970, I spent a good part of the summer in Europe with Frances, Mike, Anne and Marc. We flew to Amsterdam on July 1, took possession of a red Volvo 164 sedan. We drove to Paris and then to Italy where we spent several weeks with my mother and her Italian friend, Commandant Franco Rinaldi at a resort on the beach called Marina di Massa. At that time my mother was considering returning to Europe. She had chosen to spend time at Marina di Massa because it was not too far from La Spezia where Franco still lived with wife and mother. I got to know Franco better at that time and basically I liked him. He made my mother happy and that was well worth it to me since Lucy was no fun when she was depressed.

—

That trip ended on September 2 when we flew back from Holland and the car was shipped back to California via the Panama Canal. But early in November of 1970, I left again for Spain to continue the work on the Spanish Education Reform. Since I was not on leave, arrangements were made for the teaching of my courses during my several weeks of absence. I went again to Paris for more briefings. UNESCO by now had a permanent staff in Madrid helping Ricardo and experts like me were being sent in to help give an international legitimacy to the plans.

In Paris, I met with an American "expert" from my old employer the Stanford Research Institute. This was a computer soft ware expert who also had ties to American computer manufacturers. He had just arrived in Paris from Madrid where he had sold Ricardo on a scheme to reform the attitude of Spanish teachers by having them watch films of Spanish children interacting with computers. Presumably by watching children become self-motivated to learn with a computer, Spanish teachers who by and large tended to be dogmatic were supposed to change their style of teaching. The SRI expert had shown a gorgeous movie of American children playing with computers with a lovely close up of their faces as they "understood" or "discovered". The Ministry was going for it. The facts were darker. There was money to be made and the Ministry thought the computer would give them prestige and at the same time provide needed funds for the payroll. The foreign experts, except the one from SRI were quite concerned. What were the goals of the reform? Why this craziness with computers? Was this a right-wing plot to flush out liberals in the Ministry? Was it a bonafide reform or just a way to make money? We had a very tense meeting with Ricardo.

—

In 1973, when I returned to Spain with Frances to lecture in Madrid and Zaragossa, we saw Ricardo again; he had just been asked to retire by the Generalissimo. His reform had made too many enemies. But I believe the Ministry of Education obtained the computers. The teachers and pupils probably never saw them.

Turbulence On Campus

On May 15, 1969 the University erected a fence around a property at Haste and Dwight streets in Berkeley where a "People's Park" had been started. This action resulted in what the minutes of the Academic Senate (May 23) called: "a state of armed warfare on the campus and in the neighboring community between roving groups of townspeople and students on the one hand, and police and national guardsmen on the other....this situation has produced as irresponsible a police and military reaction to a civic disturbance as this country has seen in recent times..." The then Governor of the State of California, Ronald Regan, had acted "strongly" using helicopters to gas the campus, the first U. S. campus attacked from the air, and in the process killing a young man named James Rector who was watching from a rooftop. The campus was occupied with troops and tanks for weeks.

On April 30, 1970 President Nixon enlarged the Vietnam War by committing American ground troops into Cambodia resulting in a massive outcry from all centers of American higher education including Berkeley. From the time I arrived at Berkeley, we were in constant upheaval. There was a brief interlude — spring or fall of 1968 when the flower children and woman's liberation dominated the scene. I liked that movement because I had always liked strong women; I was in favor of total equality between genders. I also liked it because this was when young girls

—

no longer wore bras and were proud to do so. Immediately after that it was constant demonstrations and constant use of tear gas to disperse the crowds. The entire family was involved. The children took part in the creation of People's Park; some of them were hiding in the laundry building when James Rector was killed on the roof just above them. I witnessed a number of beatings; the use of police cars to ram the crowds; all sorts of violence that radicalized us against the authorities. I once tried to stop a police car on campus and was nearly run over. I went to our Academic Senate meetings where we passed or attempted to pass resolutions. I stood on the steps in front of Sproul Hall, the administration building, with signs asking for the end of the war. I even wrote a letter to the Washington Post which was published on June 15, 1970: "….Mr. Alsop (a well known columnist who had written on May 27 that Berkeley had been sinking in the "mire of new leftism") would have us spend all our energies in those far away jungles while the best of our youth loses faith in our government. How foolish and shortsighted…the long term security of the United States depends more on the availability of creative and talented people than on what happens in Indochina…"

The demonstrations did not stop, particularly after May 4, 1970 when the National Guard were called on the campus of Kent State University and killed several students. There were major demonstrations on most American campus. And the turmoil did not end until the end of the war in Vietnam at the end of January 1973. This turmoil translated itself into a change of relationships between students and faculty. For many months at the height of these disturbances students exercised far more influence on campus life prodding the faculty into action. Here is a vignette: we were having a School of Education faculty meeting. With a few exceptions, most of the faculty was conservative — at least as far as demonstrations were

—

concerned. Some students were attending the meeting — I suppose as observers. We were arguing about passing a mild resolution "deploring" the events — all this in nice, careful, polite academic language. Among the students there was dissatisfaction with our collective meekness. One of these students, an ex-nun, was quite an activist. She suddenly jumped up went to the front of the room and screamed at the startled academics: "What the fuck do you think you are doing..." and she went on accusing the faculty in the starkest language. The faculty meeting was brought to an abrupt end. As I left, I could see that most of my colleagues were shaken. They had never experienced any such indignity.

Another Affair

As a recent graduate student, I had many contacts with students in the School. I often went to graduate student parties where we would dance, drink wine and pass marijuana joints. I did not like the weed, not so much for its taste or effect, but its impact on social gatherings. I thought that parties became silent, people retreated into themselves and just waited. At these parties I had joined a group of students in the program of Early Childhood Education — therefore not students from my unit in the School. We would organize parties including members of the staff and participate in the demonstrations together. This is how I met Bertha in 1969. She was in her late twenties, married to a student in Engineering who never came to the parties. She was living in Albany Village where married graduate students shared old World War II temporary housing. I think it fair to say that she was bored with her husband. In fact, they were to divorce shortly. We had an affair — it was nearly expected in that atmosphere of revolt. The male faculty who were "engaged" in the opposition against the war tended to

—

attract a following including many young women. It was a time when the AIDS epidemic was unknown — when birth control was at hand and when free love was part of the revolt: "the more I make revolution, the more I want to make love..." I was not a campus faculty leader but my affair with Bertha took place in that context. We would leave early in the morning after her husband had gone to school, drive to Carmel, make love, drive back and she would be home before he returned. All this required a lot of careful planning — but we somehow managed.

My thought was that after Bertha divorced, she should live with us. The idea fitted with many of the current ideologies of the time. People living in communes — living in expanded families. But I did not want her to know all this because I did not feel right at being a cause of her divorce. I repeated the pattern followed at the time of Frances' divorce: we stopped seeing each other until Bertha decided what she wanted to do. She divorced, and we started seeing each other again. Frances had lunch with her. Bertha did not move in with us. She took instead a room close to campus and for several months, we had an arrangement with Frances. I contributed one third of the rent and spent every Tuesday night with Bertha. Thus, I had a fairly typical French or Mexican arrangement: the "casa chica".

This continued for a while but it was not what Bertha wanted, and there was opposition at home. Not only from Frances who quite correctly pointed out that this kind of permanent arrangement was totally outside our agreement, but also from the children who like all children want their parents and no intruder. I was in considerable doubt as to what I should do. I was attracted to Bertha. She was young — Frances was about to enter her fifties. I loved the chance of being with young people. I had

—

reached that age, my early forties, when you begin to realize that time has passed. Frances did not help; she had aged considerably, the drinking did not help and she was far more depressed by the events than I was. In April of 1971, Marc was apprehended by the Berkeley police in a theft charge of a bicycle from Velo Sport. The case moved to Juvenile Court and a social worker was assigned to the case. The report to the court described the father as young looking, while the mother was reported to appear much older. Our lawyer had suggested that Marc's actions be explained to the court in terms of the father having had an affair; and the social worker had been told as much. But my reading of that report had a very strong impact on me. I had not thought of Frances' aging. I was realizing for the first time that Frances and I were aging differently. I saw myself as young — or living with the young and Frances was separating herself from that life. She was drinking more and more, others saw it also. The court report made it clear.

But Bertha did not wait for me. She suddenly moved out and went to live with an African American student, one of the new affirmative action young school administrators we were training in our own program. She told me she had been madly in love with me but now she was madly in love with this young, tall, and good looking man. I was relieved by this sudden change of fortune; at least I had no decision to make. We were now in the early months of 1972, the year that was to bring us the re-election of President Nixon and soon after that, the scandal of Watergate, Nixon's forced resignation and the brief presidency of Gerald Ford.

Bertha's love story with a black student did not last long. By the next summer he had left her and she was now alone and in some despair. I saw her and drove with her

—

mother to Big Sur to have dinner at Nepenthe Restaurant. Both her mother and I, now in the role of substitute father, attempted to comfort her. She was in great despair that night as we drove back from Nepenthe. Her mother lived in Pacific Grove, and I stayed in the Carmel house. But our relationship was finished. Shortly after that dinner, Bertha left Berkeley, never finishing her dissertation and I do not know where she went, I never heard from her again.

Illness And Drugs

Frances never recovered from those early years at Berkeley. Our direct opposition to the government and the laws of the country because of the Vietnam War incited us to oppose the government and its authority in more general terms. It resulted in our tending to distrust not only the State Department or the Pentagon, but all the institutions of authority — the local police to start with, the state police, the judges, and the administrators of the University among others. As a result, we did not pay attention to warnings about the use of drugs in the public schools. In fact both Frances and I thought that smoking marijuana was totally normal, and that marijuana should be legalized. We did not see any connection between using marijuana and the use of stronger drugs. We remained totally naïve about the drug scene in Berkeley or what was happening to our children. Frances began a drinking habit. Frances' father had had a drinking habit, as mentioned before; Major Crawford had to take early retirement from the U. S. Army when he had slapped a Colonel while under the influence. We did not know in the early seventies that substance abuse might have a genetic explanation. Had we known we might have thought twice about taking drinks or few puffs of marijuana? We drank the way our friends drank; we had drinks before dinner; martinis, and wine with dinner. We did not drink excessively but there always was some

—

alcohol in the house.

Beginning in 1971 or '72, Frances began to drink on her own when I was not home. I did not notice for a while until it became obvious when I returned home that Frances was already quite high, having had several drinks during the afternoon. I thought this was a passing problem. Frances had an operation on her kidney and stopped drinking for a while. I did not worry but when she started again, I tried to control alcohol consumption by rationing the supply. Bottles were marked to make sure they were not over used, as if this would make a difference. I was astonished to discover one day a bottle of hard liquor underneath our bed. I had never thought Frances might buy a bottle or bottles and hide them and I did not know what to do. In my family drugs were unknown. My father even had an allergic reaction to alcohol. His face would turn a reddish purple with one glass of whiskey and he would try to sip just a little bit at business receptions, but no more. There was no wine when I was a child in Paris or later in Mexico City. Frances' drinking was something totally incomprehensible to me. It made no sense and I recoiled from it. This was the moment I began thinking of divorce. I just could not deal with her drinking and with her transformation into an alcoholic. I hated finding her at home slurring her speech. I hated the drinking person she had become and to some extent, I began to want to take some distance from her. I suggested seeking outside help but Frances would hear none of it: "It was the war, not her."

Meanwhile Marc, who had always had a very independent streak was at age 12 economically independent. He had joined a small group of children who had access to drugs and made money. This mini-mob as they called themselves fitted well in the permissive, anti-

—

authoritarian environment of Berkeley and neither Frances nor I were aware of what they were doing. Anne had met a Jewish man from Chicago named Jim Becker and had moved away from our house. She was independent and very soon became a very young mother. Her daughter Tania was born in January 1972. We helped at the beginning but they moved to San Francisco, joined a commune and we practically lost contact. Marc left the house and was gone to Colombia. Frances' drinking had limited her ability to deal with problems. I had little time to handle the collapse of the family. At one point earlier, we had tried, the five of us, to see a family counselor, but the dynamics of our lives were already set. Frances was drinking, Marc and Anne were leaving, and Mike was remaining alone. I hated Frances' drinking and wanted to leave. The counselor saw us three or four times but it was too late.

In 1970 after our Dean resigned, we began searching for a new Dean. Interim deans from the ranks of the faculty were appointed while the search went on. A search committee was appointed in the fall. Candidates were interviewed and sometime in 1973, a new Dean was finally appointed. Early in the fall of that same year the new Dean organized a "retreat" of faculty, staff and selected students at Camp Cazadero, a City of Berkeley music camp facility north of San Francisco. We were to spend three or four days reorganizing the School, changing the curriculum and getting to know each other. I drove to Camp Cazadero with Alice Ilchman, the wife of Professor Ilchman from Political Science who was then working with us on our Ford Foundation grant. We were housed in cabins and I shared a room with another male faculty. During the retreat, we split into work groups, discussed many issues, agreed on very little if anything. We had plenary sessions where more was said and little done and a

—

fair amount of social gatherings.

One afternoon, we had had lunch with wine and there was a free period. I had managed to keep a bottle with me. The faculty, staff and students were finishing their drinks and food in small groups and I had walked by the bank of the small river that goes through the camp. Several small groups were sitting on the grass by the river. I came upon a graduate student with two faculty members from the Educational Psychology Division I knew and liked.

Since I had a wine bottle and they had glasses, I offered some. Professor Harriett Amster introduced me to the graduate student. She was a tall blond woman named Karen Nelson. Alice Ilchman and other colleagues were ahead on the bank waiting for the wine, I said hello, goodbye and rejoined my group.

Conflict Again: Promotion Denied

My dissertation had been published by Praeger in 1970 and now I was writing book after book. My mentor Ilchman had made it clear that publish or perish was the rule of the land. Writing books took a considerable amount of time. I had the good fortune to write theory books based on general information. I did not conduct experiments or field research the way many of my colleagues did. I relied on my own professional experience or published articles and books to illuminate my arguments. I developed my own theories about the process of planning and bureaucratic life. Much of my work took place in my mind at any time or place — and of course sitting at a desk — usually in my office with pen and paper. I had to read and keep up with a large volume of literature. In general, I did not use graduate students to do the ground work for my books. I was spare with data, graphs and the like and

—

tended to write more like a European writer, pursuing ideas — many my own and many, of course, borrowed and credited to others.

This writing took a lot of time and I was under pressure because the promotion review process for an Associate Professor was every two years and books or articles had to be available for the tedious review process. Later, when I became a full professor, the timing shifted to every three years. But it still forced one to package one's production in discrete units. This explains in great part the huge explosion of academic writing — at least in the social sciences — explosion in quantity but not necessarily in quality. I was also fortunate to find a publisher called the Glendessary Press, a small venture started by a colleague in the School of Education, Professor Donald Hansen and his partner, who was a professional publisher. They were efficient, they were able to edit rapidly. They took my manuscripts, printed them quickly, which is what academics want, and managed to sell quite a few copies. For the first edition of *The Politics of Expertise,* I drew the cover. Without the burden of running experiments or conducting field research, I still had to write and writing ten handwritten pages per day was my goal. Ten such pages translate into four or five printed pages which means that a 300-page book takes some 100 days to write but one cannot write everyday and after writing there is editing, publishing, revising proofs and so on. Each book took me around two years to write, and with the research, it more often came to three years.

In addition, I ran programs. Publish or perish was the first rule. The second rule was to bring money to the campus. We had to scramble for government or foundation money, to enhance our visibility, to provide professional experiences and remuneration to our graduate students, to

—

employ worthwhile colleagues and last but not least, provide a percentage of the contract or grant in the form of an overhead to the campus. At first I had managed Ilchman's grant to provide an international dimension to our professional schools. After that we obtained the Ford Foundation grant that resulted in my fight with the Dean and his forced resignation. Then in 1972, Charles Benson and I went to Washington and applied to the US Aid Agency for a major one million-dollar grant to create an international research resource on the financing of education — in other words a think tank on the policies for financing education with a specific reference to newly developing countries. In February 1973, we obtained this grant and I also ran it, which meant developing a program of activities, hiring people, undertaking studies, seeing they are published, and endlessly filling out forms for the U. S. Aid Agency, our sponsor.

Amusingly or sadly, this was a period when program budgeting came in vogue. I had promised that if we obtained the grant, we would hire the best people and try to answer some of the questions being asked in the field: how much to spend on education — how might systems of education be reformed — what were crucial avenues to pursue if one wanted to reform a system and so on. But the U. S. Aid Agency insisted on program budgets. They would send their minions to Berkeley to instruct us how to submit our reports and our applications for the annual renewal of the grant (it lasted six years). We had to select major goals — then specify specific targets and tie money requests and expenditures to the pursuit of these specific targets. It was the most artificial and contrived performance and it took huge amounts of time. First you hired someone, agreed more or less what they might work on — then concocted a long detailed program budget to justify what they were doing using an obscure language of

—

major goals, targets, measures — breaking down activities that never neatly fit in the straight jacket of the administrative scheme.

In 1973, with my *The Politics of Expertise* published in 1972 I applied to be promoted to full professor. I had been hired in 1968, received a step increase to Associate Step II in 1970, and had delayed one year as I waited for the book to come out. I thought that with three books (dissertation, the book on professionals and politics) plus all the grants, I should be promoted to full professor. I thought that *The Politics of Expertise* was a major work and the reviews of the book were excellent. The book demonstrated that planning was not only a technical or "scientific" exercise, but also political. It detailed how planners could identify the principal relevant political actors and stake holders, how they could create coalitions of supporters and how they could design plans to facilitate this process. In 1972, there were not too many books saying that, even if later on many said it. The book also justified how successful planners were able to use the political process to implement plans. The review process within the School was favorable and the promotion went forward to the campus. It was then reviewed by a secret committee including someone from the City and Regional Planning Department. The promotion was denied.

I found out later that my writings were considered subversive by some faculty members in the City and Regional Planning Department. They preached a "professional" approach to planning — an ethical stance whereby the planner would provide the "good" or the "desirable" solution to planning issues — in contrast to my more realistic admission of the relative weakness of the technocrat in the face of power. In those quarters, consideration of politics in planning exercises was not

—

considered desirable. I argued it was better to find partial political solutions than producing utopian plans that died on shelves. I showed how the planner could move the "political" solution closer to the utopian design.

In 1973, we obtained another grant from the European Foundation — courtesy of Ladislav Cerych, my old friend from UNESCO days. We were to undertake a study of California education for possible use by European planners. The levels of enrollment in higher education in California in 1973 were the highest in the world — therefore the California model might provide insights to Europeans as their higher education expanded. Charles Benson produced some chapters and I the rest. The unpublished manuscript was available in 1974 when I resubmitted for promotion to full professor. Meanwhile, since February 1973, I was working full time on the large U. S. Aid project, getting it underway. I was rather surprised when this second promotion was denied. Here I was in 1974, with *The Politics of Expertise* receiving important reviews, a manuscript for a study of California's education while directing a major research project — being told that my work did not meet the standard for promotion to full professor.

There is not much one can do about the review process in universities such as Berkeley. There is no way to argue that what is considered inadequate by the reviewers might be considered adequate by other reviewers. Unknown peers read your work and pass judgment. There is little that can be argued against these judgments. The only remedy is procedural: something was done in the review process that somehow is unfair or incomplete and the reviewers may be reversed.

I appealed the decision to a committee called

—

"privilege and tenure." I pointed out that I had submitted practically the same materials in 1973 and 1974. That in 1973, I had been told my work was excellent but did not justify acceleration. How could the same work now be labeled as lacking academic qualities needed for promotion? The language in 1973 had been inviting, suggesting I reapply for promotion to full professor in one year, never indicating that my work did not meet some standard. At the time I had asked whether I should head the U. S. Aid grant since that work would delay my publications. What had happened was procedurally incorrect. The Chair of Privilege and Tenure was friendly, he looked into the case. He came back to me and informed me that the secret committee that reviewed my work had, in fact, recommended I be promoted — one faculty voting no — the majority voting yes. It was the overall Budget Committee of the Academic Senate that had voted negatively — a not uncommon occurrence — namely that on promotions the Budget Committee tended to pay close attention to voices of dissent. At the time, I assumed that a friend of the Dean, who had retired as a result of my "aide memoire" to the Chancellor, was paying me back. But as mentioned above my work was not liked by a faculty member who did not see the merit of my arguments since it seemed to undermine the very existence of the policy and planning schools: if it was politics, why bother training analysts or planners?

Knowing how these votes had turned out provided me with a better argument. I started my new memo by assuming that the secret committees had voted positively both years. In that case was it not arbitrary for the Budget Committee to encourage me in 1973 and deny in 1974? It was an arcane argument but it worked in academia. It was logical, it pointed to a procedural defect. I had them somehow cornered. A negotiation took place. I was told to

—

resubmit the promotion early in 1975 and that "it would be approved," I did and I finally became a full professor. All this took time and effort. I recount it here in a few pages. There were meetings — with our new Dean, who was most cautious — with the Chair of Privilege and Tenure, — with the Provost, and the effort, while successful, required endless elaboration of carefully worded messages that ultimately resulted in the discrete capitulation of the reviewers.

In the fall of 1973, after the Cazadero encampment, I met Karen Nelson again. I was walking along the little creek just above Tolman Hall. She came across the bridge with a group of visiting scholars. She was showing them the campus. We said a few words; I remembered meeting her at Cazadero and went on my way.

In September, I went to Singapore on a very brief trip to deliver a paper at an international conference. I stopped briefly in Kuala Lumpur in Malaysia to stay with Professor Allen Wilson of our department, who was spending two years under the auspices of the Ford Foundation helping the Ministry of Education elaborate new policies for education. He was doing the statistical work for them. He encountered plenty of problems since the Malays who controlled the government were loathing disclosing data showing discrimination against the Chinese or Indian minorities. Otherwise, I liked the visit. In the morning when I was still in bed in the Ford Foundation villa provided to the Wilsons, I could hear the gardener sweeping the leaves below my window. I found that sound very soothing — I still recommend it for frayed nerves.

In the fall of 1972 we had witnessed the reelection of President Nixon and Vice President Gerald Ford, who had replaced the very doubtful Spiro Agnew of the first

—

Nixon administration. The Watergate scandal had not yet deterred Nixon. Frances and I were both depressed by his re-election. During the summer of 1973, before going to Singapore, I attempted to break Frances' dependency on alcohol by taking a trip with her to Spain.

I was invited to give lectures both in Madrid and in Zaragossa. I was hoping that travel would help. But luck was not on my or on Frances' side. The second day in Madrid, she slipped on the pavement and twisted her ankle. After that, she had considerable trouble moving and as a result, spent more time sitting than walking; more time drinking than visiting sites and museums. In addition, we had left Marc and Mike at home with my friend from Stanford, Dr. Irene Blumenthal. Now she was working with me on the new U. S. Aid Agency project, and, in our absence had moved to house sit in our absence. In fact it was more than house sitting. She was to keep watch over Marc and Mike. As soon as we left, Marc announced to her that I had agreed to lend our 1970 Volvo to a friend of his. Irene expressed surprise — but Marc was able to convince her that the matter had been settled; the friend had a driver's license and was to drive them out of town for the weekend. In fact Marc drove the Volvo alone and managed to hit another car — Telegrams and letters were exchanged between California and Spain, our insurance agent handled matters, postponing everything until our return. We then had quick negotiations, paid for the repairs on both cars. Between the sprained ankle, the telegrams and letters and the negotiations upon our return — we were exhausted.

In December 1973 just before Christmas, Frances started to nose bleed while carving a chicken at a dinner for friends. The bleeding would not stop. We went to emergency at Kaiser Hospital where attempts were made to stop the bleeding with a painful procedure. The net result

—

was that Frances was more depressed than ever and kept drinking more and more.

Love Returns : A New Life

In the first week of January 1974, I was standing in line at Peet's Coffee Shop on Vine Street in Berkeley when I noticed Karen Nelson at the front counter with several friends. She saw me, came to me saying "I know someone here" and told me how she had had to leave Berkeley with her daughter Margaret and was living in Carmel Valley. She was back in Berkeley on a short visit. I mentioned I owned a house in Carmel and often visited it. I suggested she give me her phone number so I might look her up when there. She did and we parted.

Late in January of 1974, I went to Carmel. I called Karen Nelson; she lived with her daughter on Calle Quien Sabe in Carmel Valley. I had already eaten my dinner when I reached her. She suggested a movie, we went to the movie, we came back to my Carmel house, we went to her house. Our love began as an "Amour Fou". We spent the weekend together before I returned to Berkeley. For the third time in my life, I was in love. I had loved Frances, Rose and now I loved Karen.

During the next three months, I made numerous trips over weekends to visit Karen on Calle Quien Sabe. This was the spring of gasoline shortages — it was not always easy to find gas. There were long queues that made driving from Berkeley to Carmel Valley and back, slightly dicey. One was never sure not to be stranded and I had to return for classes or meetings. But there was a beautiful peaceful view out of her bed room window, Karen kept a groaning refrigerator, the weather in Carmel Valley was warm and sunny. I was back in love and as importantly she

—

was telling me she loved me. I discovered Karen was from Missouri, she had spent many years in Saint Louis, her parents still lived there and I remembered the strawberries with cream I had had in the 40's with Jim Sevin.

Frances was unhappy with me, not so much about my new love, this had happened before, but she did not think I had the right to forbid her drinking. She explained her drinking as a necessity caused by the stress of external events such as the war or the election. She resented my looking for and confiscating bottles. She said that if I did not like her drinking I should move out, we should live separately. Sometime in February, I actively began to look for housing for me in Berkeley. Meanwhile I was coming to the conclusion we had to separate; I could not stand the drinking. From my vantage point, Frances had opted for death. I had not.

The words: "IE HE CE QUE MORD" appears on the back of a presumed portrait done around the 1440's by Rogier Van der Weyden of the French bishop Guillaume Fillastre (1348-1428); I had seen it in the Courtauld in London. From old French it translates: "I hate what is death." I wanted to live and not drink into stupor. Early in April we agreed to a separation.

When Karen came to Berkeley on visits she would join me in the house search. In due time, we found a suitable house. At first, Karen was not convinced she liked the house at150 Montrose Road. A thick white carpet covered the entire house. On the windows double layer curtains hid the light on the walls, endless mirrors and chinoiseries. Effie, the maid would open the front door. A tiny white dog, nearly hidden in the carpet would bark. Mrs. Moore, for whom the house was built, was bed-ridden in the front room. I kept telling Karen to pay attention to

—

the room proportions and not to the mirrors. I bought it in May and two months later the real estate market had risen, so much so that our real estate agent came to ask if Karen still had her doubts about living there. She could sell it easily, she said for $20,000 more than I had paid — that was good money in two months, but we stayed.

At first Frances was happy with my moving out. She called our lawyer and we worked out a separation agreement that split our assets in half. For a brief period I thought I might be able to remain on good terms with her. She visited us on one or two occasions at 150 Montrose and so did her sister, Betty. But her lawyer gradually turned her against me. I kept insisting that we should divorce the way we had separated using the same single lawyer and thus avoiding litigation. But the lawyer kept insisting he did not want to represent both of us at the divorce; he would only represent her. I would have to hire my own. We had split all our joint assets in half. She was also keeping her separate pre- marriage property. At separation she was left with a higher income than mine. I did not see the need for litigation. Unfortunately Frances listened to that lawyer, he just made our separation and divorce that much more bitter while only marginally changing our separation agreement. As a result his law firm and my lawyer collected their fees. Lawyers, who suggest you litigate, are also thinking of their own purse.

In the summer of 1974, I went with Karen and her daughter Margaret to Denmark where we met her parents who had flown in from Saint Louis. We traveled with them to Sweden and then to France where we drove from Paris to Cannes so that her parents could meet my mother who had recently acquired an apartment at 83, Ave du Maréchal Juin, while still keeping her house in Mexico City. We left on June 10, went to France on the 19th and were back in

—

the U. S. on July 8th. In September, I was invited to consult with the U. S. Aid Agency in Colombia. We flew together to Mexico City to visit my mother who had returned there. Karen went back to Berkeley while I continued to Colombia where I hoped to be able to find and speak to Marc. I visited Emily Vargas Baron a "half Colombian" I had known and liked when she worked for UNESCO in Paris. I also saw other friends, ex-graduate students from Berkeley. I met with various embassy people to attempt to locate Marc and alert them to notify me in the event the Colombian police arrested him. I returned to Berkeley at the end of September, where I plunged into my personal conflict with the University — conflict that was finally resolved in the spring of 1975.

Abolishing The Education School

An English don had come to America courtesy of the Ford Foundation and written a blistering report about American Schools of Education in the leading research universities. Schools of education had no prestige and therefore their research had little impact. The English report did not specify what should be done. It suggested radical surgery was needed. Sometime in the mid seventies our School had been routinely reviewed by an outside committee; meaning faculty from other departments at Berkeley. The review was thumb downs. The School needed to improve. Campus leaders looked into the matter. Early in 1980 two leaders of the Academic Senate came up with a novel idea: Since schools of education had no prestige, why not move all their activities into the relevant academic departments? In other words why not ask, say the English Department, to train and do research on the teaching of English? And do the same with other activities of schools of education.

—

Since these were two influential faculty leaders, their ideas were soon discussed in the appropriate campus committees. Berkeley would innovate. It would lead the way and transform the training of educators. This was important and this new idea of abolishing the Graduate School of Education had much appeal. Campus wide, it was seen as a new way to improve all of American education, no small matter.

The non-tenured staff in our School could be dispensed with and the entire tenured faculty would be moved into other departments. In our case, Charles Benson, James Guthrie and I would go to the City and Regional Planning Department in the School of Environmental Design where we would mount a sub specialty in Educational Planning. Personally I liked this alternative since I had very close friends in that Department: Peter Hall, a well known English geographer turned planner, now Sir Peter, and Manuel Castells a Spaniard who had taught sociology in France and was well known for his many books. At the time I was unaware I had detractors in the Department. Yet when I met with the Dean of the School of Environmental Design, he said he would be quite happy to welcome us but he pointed out he had no spare office space to give us. This clear indication that all was not well with these transfers was probably experienced by other members of our School. In fact it was soon clear that none of the units from Education would be easily absorbed in other departments. In any case, many of our experimental teaching programs were conducted by non-tenured staff, and while ending these sounded fine to academic ears; it would have repercussions in Sacramento.

The plan hit a major snag. At first the campus departments were in favor of these personnel transfers since this meant more budgets and faculty slots coming their

—

way. But they were not interested in our faculty. In each department there were factions. For example in English you might have linguists and also people who write and publish novels or poetry. In City and Regional Planning there were two main camps: those who came from a tradition of design, say with a background in architecture or geography and those who came from the social sciences, say economists or sociologists. There was a balance between these two camps. Bringing three social scientists from Education would upset the balance. The same problem arose elsewhere. The Plan was flawed and would ultimately collapse but not before a long agony lasting more than a year of internal debate. During that time alternatives were proposed where we would be appointed with no voting rights in other units.

I had already concluded that the main purpose of the exercise was to grab our rather attractive office and laboratory space in Tolman Hall. In 1981 an outsider to the campus was appointed Dean to head the School of Education and institute the Plan. By then I was opposed to the Plan and I was not alone. The entire staff and faculty of the School of Education was opposed and fighting for survival. At that point I was elected to become the Chair of the Education Faculty. The Chair of the Faculty represents the faculty vis-à-vis the Administration. It was my task to represent our faculty vis-à-vis this unknown outside Dean and also vis-à-vis the rest of the campus community.

It took a huge quantity of memos. We counter-attacked by sending notices to contacts in the relevant parts of the California legislature in Sacramento. We mobilized our alumni including some wealthy donors to the University. But most importantly we used humor and tried to make the entire Plan seem foolish. The academy is somewhat pedantic, particularly when skating on thin ice.

—

Academicians do not easily joke about their enterprises. Humor plays well in those fights. We even asked the Faculty Committee for the Protection of Human Subjects to intervene and protect us. We pointed out that the University was initiating an experiment and we were the guinea pigs. Between pressure from Sacramento and rich alumni, misgivings in the affected Departments and our humor, we sent the Plan down the drain. Meanwhile Stanford had announced a new major effort to upgrade their own School of Education. Chancellor I. Michael Heyman and other campus leaders decided the scheme would not work. They gave the Graduate School of Education a second lease on life. As a result I had many more friends within my Department but it is not clear to me how many enemies I had made on the campus. Later when I was denied another promotion I thought about that episode and the animosity it created.

Love And Duty

We are coming to the end of this tale. Maybe there is less to say as there is less action, fewer moves, no more inappropriate sex, happiness is less interesting to recount. When I began living with Karen in 1974 I became monogamous which simplified life considerably. Karen had always been monogamous during her two previous marriages. It should also be said that there had been long periods between those when she had not been waiting alone. We both came together with considerable experience and did not need further experimentation.

We were married two years later on March 25 , 1976 in Ashcroft, Colorado a small abandoned mining town just above Aspen where we were spending a winter vacation. We were married by a local Protestant Minister who happened to also serve as cantor for the Aspen Jewish congregation. There were a few family members: Karen's father Carroll Nelson, her brother Ivar, two of her cousins and one or more friends. The ceremony took place in the open, on the side of the snow covered road leading to Ashcroft. At one point the Minister/Cantor took a step sideways and suddenly sank to his hips, deep in the snow. We helped him up and continued the ceremony. It all ended in a French restaurant in Aspen where the wedding cake was a magnificent construct, a croquenbouche of profiterole cream puffs. Later, in San Francisco, the wedding was certified at the French Consulate in my own "Livret de Famille" the French document that lists all births, marriages and deaths. With this documentation Karen may, at a future date, decide to seek French nationality. But the Consul reminded us that she would still have to take a small examination conducted in French.

I taught courses, I organized an inter-professional school administrative training service — since there was no school of government at Berkeley. I wrote papers published in other academic books or in journals and I wrote my own books. I was promoted to Professor Step II in 1978, Step III in 1982, Step IV in 1985 and Step V in 1988. Meanwhile, I published *Bureaucracy* in 1977; *Regulation and Planning: The Case of Environmental Politics* in 1981; *Professionalizing the Organization* in 1987; *Mastering the Politics of Planning* in 1989; and *Twenty-first Century Organization* in 1994. There were also second editions of *Politics of Expertise* in 1977 and *Bureaucracy* in 1983. I came up for promotion to Step VI in 1991 — the promotion was denied. My work was considered by academic reviewers to be "written for the layman."

I can only assume that I had once again obtained reviewers from the professional schools involved in policy

—

analysis and planning. And once again they had objected to an analysis stressing the inevitable political nature of any planning or policy research that is implemented. They wanted to stress the analysis, to do research on ways to analyze problems so as to be able to talk "truth to power" as if, in much of social life, there were societal truths independent of social power. This time there was no remedy. I was quite incensed since *Mastering the Politics of Planning* was well reviewed at that time. Later, after the denial of the promotion, it was the principal focus of eight articles in the summer 1993 issue of *Planning Theory*, an international journal of planning. In 1992 the University was offering a "golden handshake" to encourage more retirements — calculating retirement pay with five more years of service. I retired on January 1, 1993 although I still taught courses in the summer of that year. After that, I essentially departed from the University and had very little contact with my ex-colleagues.

Karen and I traveled. Most of our trips to Europe included visits with my mother. Family always played an important role in my life including travel. I was a dutiful son. We went to Nice in July 1975 — then to London, to Mexico in November 1978 to recover Lucy's belongings as she had settled in Cannes. She had bought an apartment in a huge new building built right in front of Picasso's villa called "La Californie". The building was at 81, Avenue du Maréchal Juin. As a result Picasso had moved out of his villa. Lucy was not guilty but the building contractor was. But let me not digress and come back to our travels. Both these trips were about my mother. We went to Sweden in 1979 and bought a Volvo — we drove to France and went to Paris to pick up my mother. We then went with her to Roscoff in Brittany in late August. We left my mother in Roscoff with friends of hers on September 21, drove to Pont Aven, Karen fell ill and we spent several days

—

recovering in the Sologne until early October when we drove back to Sweden and flew from there. By then the days were very short in Sweden, the sun would set in the afternoon.

I went to Spain on a mission in 1980 and stopped with Anne and Tania, Anne's first daughter, to visit my mother in Cannes on my way to Sevilla. I returned with Anne and Tania whom I met again in the London airport on 12 July and flew back with them to San Francisco. Karen and I flew to Nice and Cannes in June 1981 — saw Lucy — then went to London for ten days. We flew to Paris, went to Cannes the end of June 1983, returning in August. We flew to Paris in May 1985 — went to Cannes returning the end of May. We saw Lucy in 1987, then went to Greece with my cousin Colette, staying on Lesbos at Molivos. We were in the UK in June 1989, then on to Nice and Cannes on 18 June and back to the U. S. on 25 June. We were in the UK on 18 May 1991, then in Cannes returning on June 14, 1991. I give you all these dates, to illustrate beyond any doubt that I kept in touch with my mother during all those years and as mentioned earlier, dutifully telephoned her once a week month after month.

In 1993 Lucy died. She had an ovarian cancer. I will tell you more about her death later. But her death also changed our travel pattern. I went to Cannes before she died and just after, Karen and I went to Geneva to transfer her account at the Crédit Suisse, then to Barcelona where I gave several conferences. Finally we were in Cannes to sell Lucy's apartment; toward the end of June 1993. We also went to St. Louis to visit Karen's parents, often spending time at the cabins in Henley, Missouri on the Osage River with the vast Nelson clan of brothers, cousins, and their families. One year Stephanie, Karen's older daughter, her husband Herman and their daughters Kristina and Katie

—

joined us to swim and enjoy canoe trips down the Osage River. In short, after my mother's death what little travel we did together was no longer tied to my filial duties but to Karen's. Later when I was diagnosed with cancer I would stop traveling.

My point is that we were a generation of dutiful children. We did what our parents told us to do. When we did not, Karen eloped at 17 with the man who was to be her first husband, I started living with Frances at 21, and these brief acts of independence resulted in major family upheavals. Our parents expected the homage due to the older generation and they obtained it. In return, they provided help at crucial times. My parents helped me through the years but never to take trips or facilitate day-to-day living. They were only willing to transfer money to me if this money was invested. In fact, most of their help went into buying houses. When my father died in 1962, my mother, according to French law, gave me her estimate of one-fourth the value of his estate. That money was used, when we returned to Portola Valley, to build a small house next to ours where Mike moved; the rest was invested in stocks. In the 1970's my father's business was doing very well at the time and Lucy gave money to be invested to Mike and Anne. I had to assure her that those investments were safe. She did not want to give to Marc since he was gone and living in Colombia. Later, as my father's business increasingly faltered, due to competition from the Far East, Lucy was very reluctant to give any large sums as she had done earlier. I did obtain some money for Marc when he moved back to California. He convinced me he would straighten out if he could acquire a property he wanted around Ben Lomond. Lucy was very reluctant but since it was an investment in land and a farmhouse, she thought the money safe. Later when Marc lost his investment by defaulting on his loan, Lucy was furious.

—

She was even more furious when some of our silver disappeared and Marc was thought to be responsible. For her generation this behavior was simply inadmissible. She expected her grandchildren to behave and when Marc did not, she simply wanted to have nothing to do with him. In fact, she wanted me to remove him from my will. I argued with her that Marc might straighten out someday and that there was no reason to remove him. But she was frantic that her money would be dissipated, that Marc might inherit through me and then lose his inheritance, lose her money. We had many arguments about this topic and as she grew older and the business in Mexico collapsed, she became more adamant.

Karen and I had a difficult time with my mother. She could be charming and great fun when she was in a good mood — usually when she went out to restaurants with some of her friends. But when she was depressed which happened often enough, it became painful to deal with her. Lucy had never liked Frances and Frances always avoided her. But Lucy had been inclined to like Karen, especially since she did not like Frances. But Karen wanted to like Lucy and Lucy was not prepared to have someone wanting to like her. She would like Karen but if Karen seemed to like her, she did not. Matters became more difficult later. Lucy had her Italian lover, Commandant Franco Rinaldi. As recounted above, she had met Franco in Mexico after my father's death. Franco was married and lived in La Spezia where the Italian navy had installations. Lucy spent her summers in Lerici — a small resort just below La Spezia. This way the Commandant could easily visit with her. Lucy had a taxi from La Spezia come fetch her in Cannes and take her to her hotel in Lerici. One year, in Cannes she suggested we spend a week with her and Franco; we could easily go, the three of us in the taxi to Lerici and stay at her hotel. I had already met Franco and liked him. In fact, I had encouraged Lucy to marry him at a time when he assured her that he would divorce his wife as soon as his mother died. By the time the mother died, Lucy was no longer sure she wanted to marry and in any case Franco never divorced. We went to Lerici and Karen met Franco, and Franco was very gallant. To make matters worse, Karen wore to swim one of those tiny bikinis I had bought for her. It dawned on me that we were in trouble. Franco remained the most charming, polite, kind lover of Lucy — but Lucy was angry with Karen. Nevertheless, we were dutiful children, we went to visit her at least every other year, and I called her every Sunday at precisely 9:30 in the morning our time. She expected the call and she was always resentful if I was late calling.

The next generation, our children, do not have this relationship. I had suffered too much from my mother's expectations and never insisted on receiving similar attention from my own children; also, the times had changed. Now children spent some time blaming their parents for their upbringing. Our generation remained stuck in the middle — with our parents breathing hard on us — and in contrast, our own children at times blaming us for their own difficulties. We never imagined blaming our parents. We are the "blame sandwich generation". There is another difference. With my generation parents usually kept up with everyday life. They had age and experience, therefore we listened to them. Today many of us elders hardly keep up with technological changes. We need children to explain how the latest electronic gadget works. They know and we are obliged to ask for help. They listen less well to us.

Painting

I started painting my last year at Harvard in 1950.

—

There were periods when I painted more — periods when there was far less production. I had several shows in the 50's one at the Lucien Labaudt Gallery in San Francisco which was reviewed in the newspaper at the time. But in 1984, I started painting more intensively. At the time we knew Inez Storer and Andrew Romanoff both painters from Inverness, whom we saw at Tassajara at the Zen Buddhist summer camp where we went for many years. They introduced us to Marian Winterstein who was running the San Francisco Museum of Modern Art Artist Gallery at Fort Mason. Marian took my paintings into her gallery, and later gave me a show. I also had several shows in a Berkeley gallery, a San Francisco restaurant and an Oakland café.

After my retirement in 1993, painting took the place of writing books. Painting gives the same high, but I usually complete a painting in less than two weeks, whereas it used to take me some two years to finish a book. My books were published, and had visibility in academia and to some limited extent, in management and planning circles. *Mastering the Politics of Planning* was translated in Russian and *Twenty First Century Organization* in Chinese. This provides minor rewards. People come up at conferences and say how they liked my work — or how they have found it useful. With painting, there is less of that since I am not as well known. But there exist enthusiastic viewers and collectors. That is pleasing but I had no interest in doing all the tedious work of promoting my art. The gallery sold a few works a year. I sold or gave away others to avoid an increasing accumulation both in Berkeley and Carmel.

I never studied painting. In 1950, I bought a book by Salvador Dali on painting technique but I could not understand what he was doing or how he was doing it. I

—

simply went on my way, with a very primitive technique applying the paint as it came out of the tube, sometimes adding linseed oil but nothing else — no turpentine, or varnishes and mixing as I needed. At first, I was unable to work on a painting over time. I found I had to finish it in just one sitting. I did not understand or did not feel right retouching a painting. In most cases I painted in one or two days going from one end to the other and finishing it with only a single layer of color. Since I did not use turpentine every surface tended to be solid and opaque. I never understood the language of painters such as tonalities or warm and cold colors. But I assume, I practiced what I did not know. In due time, I found ways to cope. Perhaps the only innovation was the very simple expedient of letting a painting dry before attempting to modify it. But I did not do this until the end of the eighties. By then I had more experience, I was teaching myself. I came to realize that the painter never or rarely controls the painting; the painter looks for the painting and does what he can to find it. One may want to achieve a given pictorial effect but after one starts painting, the painting takes control. What I paint is what I am able to paint not what I thought I wanted to paint. That is not true if you copy or do very derivative work. You can control that kind of painting. This is why learning to paint from mediocre painters is so dangerous. They teach you to control the painting: you paint the tree this way; you put a little shading here to suggest a setting sun. You learn to paint mediocre paintings. I was fortunate not to be trained.

In Carmel there exist many art galleries selling paintings. In fact, Carmel is a leading center of the American art market. Unfortunately it is a peculiar segment of that market. What is sold, by and large, is the kind of safe, derivative art that often decorates business premises or the homes of the good citizens. Today much of those

—

paintings are produced in "factories", often in China or elsewhere in the Far East. There are painters in the Monterey Bay Area. I mean real painters as contrasted to the authors of the mass-produced art. In 1991, I began to have lunch at Fifi's Café, on Tuesdays in Pacific Grove with a group that included Gerald Wasserman, Steve Brown and Dick Crispo. At one point I applied to join the Carmel Art Association (both Wasserman and Crispo were members) but they did not take me in which was just as well as the Art Association is a cooperative requiring participation of its members. Since we live in Berkeley, coming to Carmel from time to time, would have made my participation difficult. Even a few artists at the Art Association respond somewhat to the demands of the market. As elsewhere in Carmel it is the safe art that sells, the paintings that can be understood without offense — the sea wave, the vague imitation of 1910 impressionist scenes of Paris life with horse drawn carriage, the quaint cottage with flower beds, the little vase with a nice rose bouquet.

Some friends criticize my paintings, Nigel Young, an Englishman recently chided: "there are too many nipples". Well not quite, he said "Have you ever counted the number of nipples in this house?" We were in Berkeley and he was referring to their representations on the walls, many by other painters we collected. But yes, I have painted many women although I have painted other subjects — children, landscapes and sometimes my women have company — men, animals including tigers and polar bears to give examples. I do not know why. When I was younger — when I was in college — I was fascinated by pictures of women. I collected Petty and Vargas girls from magazines; these were slightly erotic drawings and paintings which college students used to adorn their walls. My first paintings were not of women, nor did I attempt to do nudes for a long time. The only time I ever used a nude

—

model, Betty Bachrach posed for me in Mexico City in the 1950's, the painting was a total failure and I painted a double portrait of her over it, but a clothed portrait. Yet I have found that images of women please me. Most wear clothes and I rarely paint nudes as it is more difficult. Clothes transmit messages quicker than nudity and painting has to do with messages. I usually take photographs from magazines such as Vogue or Elle and combine several photographs with invented scenarios as suggestions for paintings. But I cannot copy the photograph if I do, the painting seems dead. I have to move the legs or arms change very slightly the angles or volumes to give my people pictorial presence. I have also used old master's nudes as models, for example nudes of Rubens. In those cases I have to change everything. Our sensibility is so different.. Quite often my most successful paintings are accidents. I always have good intentions when I start, but never know why some fail. Most of my nudes fail, probably because I want them to succeed. The accidents that succeed probably result from my caring less, not being preoccupied with the result. Over time, my success rate has gone up. Success means that I like the painting, there is nothing blatantly wrong with it. Most of those paintings improve with age, at least to my eye. After a short period paintings escape me. I cannot do that painting again, I have changed. If I try to do a similar one, it fails; it is in no way similar. There is a gradual evolution taking place, a life of the paintings. The paintings are in charge and they proceed as they see fit.

Zen Again

We went to Tassajara on the last day of August 1982 for a one day visit. We had heard about it and were curious to go look see. Tassajara Zen center in the Los Padres National Forest is about an hour and a half drive

—

into the rugged Ventana area south west of Carmel. The last stretch of road is a narrow fire trail that goes up and down requiring a stick shift to avoid burning the brakes of the car. The Zen training monastery is built along a small stream at the site of a hot spring. There is no electricity except a generator to run basic equipment in the kitchen. There are cabins and yurts to sleep in, a pool and down stream a natural plunge called the narrows where nude bathing is de rigueur. There are hot baths and saunas at the hot spring. They border the stream, one sweats in the sauna and plunges in the cold stream. There is also a plunge, a large communal warm bath. The food is vegetarian; the weather much warmer than on the coast, there is a large staff of aspiring novices and seasoned Zen practitioners on hand during the short guest season. In 1983 we began to spend a week to ten days there each August and returned for a decade or more.

Tassajara was the easiest way to leave the United States. The Zen monastery and the facilities in San Francisco and Marin County were brought about by Suzuki Roshi, a Japanese Zen master in the Soto tradition, who came to the United States in the late fifties and was able to establish a self sustaining Buddhist movement in the Bay area. He found American disciples and he and his followers were able to recruit generations of men and women interested in Buddhism. They acquired a reputation among the pleasure seekers for the food, the calm and also the teachings and initiation to Budhism. There were no radios or televisions. One had the opportunity; to attend their services in the Zendo, the baths, to view the rugged scenery and to talk to the friend's one met or made. Around 5:30 am, a discrete bell carried by a runner, alerted those who wanted to attend to go to the service in the Zendo. I did not attend the service but would walk up the path to the hot baths later, before breakfast and pass the Zendo. I would try

—

to arrive there at the moment the monks and guests were chanting. I would be alone on the path. On my right, I had the Zendo with the repetitious deep chants. On my left I could hear the murmur of the stream; a bit ahead I would hear the kitchen staff getting ready. I would walk in a hush to the hot bath, the plunge where, until breakfast, men and women were allowed together. The day was starting.

Both Karen and I had always been attracted to Buddhist thought. I had read *Zen in the Art of Archery* during my Harvard days. We attended service in the Zendo only once and did not return. We could not sit still that long and I did not like the authoritarian discipline. But we would attend the evening talks and read a few Buddhist introductory texts. This is when I began to be aware of the present, the here and now, of the simple happiness of existence. This was a great help to me in later years.

Cancer

My mother died in January 1993. She died of ovarian cancer on the 27th. She always thought 7 was her lucky number. She had been hospitalized in a British clinic in Cannes where cheery British nurses took care of her. I visited her several times when she was still alive at the clinic. She had me remove the few paintings she had in her apartment as she feared the French would tax her small estate. She told me not to weep for her; she had had a good life she assured me. She did not regret anything, she told me simply: "there is no reason to cry". While I was back in Berkeley, she died one night, unexpectedly, when her tumor reached an important blood vessel. I flew again to Cannes to finalize her cremation and take necessary legal steps. She had asked to be cremated "with no remains". This is permitted in France. As soon as she died, her remains were cremated and I only had to obtain the

—

certificate of death to initiate the legal proceedings. She had willed her apartment to me and this meant visits to the "notaire" and also packing and sending some of her furniture to California.

Right before my scheduled departure for California where I was still teaching a course, I was told to go to the "Mairie" the City Hall to record her death in the family French document called the "Livret de Famille", a document that records all births, marriages and deaths in households. At the Mairie I stood in line and noticed several young mothers with babies. I was waiting at the registry of births and deaths. When my turn came, the lady said she was so sorry but this was a "birth" day. I should return the next day. They alternated births and deaths to avoid mixing joyous and sad people. I was to leave at dawn the next morning. I explained my predicament. French bureaucracy these days is far more flexible than ours. They stamped the "Livret de Famille".

In 2001 I was told I had cancer of the prostate. It was an active tumor. Removal of the prostate was not recommended as it was too large. I had been told by the first cancer doctor I saw to undertake radiation. Our doctor, Edward Kersh, who happens to also be a cardiologist, thought I might look into diet and the work of a friend of his, Dr. Dean Ornish. He called him and put me in contact with his staff. Dr. Ornish was a cardiologist who had worked with diet and heart patients and had been successful in using diet to reverse heart disease. At that time, he was just starting a research project to see if a diet might also work for prostate cancer patients. I spoke with some on his staff and while I could not join the research project, I obtained enough information to be able to adopt the diet.

When you are told you have cancer, you panic. You

—

want to do something: you want to get rid of it. Cancer and prostate cancer can be treated in different ways. In general each doctor you meet prefers a given approach. Surgeons will tend to want to operate. Radiologists will prescribe a radiation treatment. But, in any case, while the profession is well aware that watchful waiting is an option, it was not inclined at that time to believe in diet. I was fortunate to be able to see Dr. Peter Carroll at the University of California in San Francisco who had successfully operated Manuel Castells, a good friend of mine. He did not want to operate since, as mentioned above, my prostate was too large. He had me meet with a radiation specialist. Meanwhile, I was reading what I could on the subject. I had found a paper by a Stanford doctor which demonstrated that, all things being equal, patients with prostate cancer who did radiation died at about the same rate as patients who simply waited. The radiation slowed or cured the cancer but they died faster from other causes as their immune system was weakened. Some of them probably responded less well to other possible later interventions such as hormonal treatment. When I met with the radiation specialist, I mentioned the paper. " Oh yes, he said, I went skying last winter with him (the author of the paper) and he has changed his mind somewhat since writing it". I pointed out that if he had changed his mind, he had not yet published anything about it.

I did a simple calculation: If you die at the same time having a radiation treatment or choosing watchful waiting, I would opt for to wait and do a diet since I would be doing something more than waiting. As a result, I opted for "watchful waiting". Dr Carroll agreed to this course of action as he knew of the work and was collaborating with Dr. Ornish. He encouraged me and I went on a severe diet to which I added elements of Japanese macrobiotic and Chinese medicine. Although the

—

cancer was an active Gleason scale 7 (6 is normal, 8 and 9 bad) I did well for 8 years. During that period I stopped traveling as I could not hope to follow my low fat modified Ornish diet in French restaurants. Every day for lunch I also prepared a special soup with Japanese sea weed, tomatoes, garlic, tofu, ginger and Japanese maitake mushrooms.

Aware that my cancer would some day metastasize, I decided to ask Dr. Carroll in San Francisco to arrange for me to be treated in Berkeley. I did not think I could handle the commute across the Bay Bridge that links Berkeley to San Francisco. Dr Carroll referred me to a good friend of his Dr. Patrick Swift who worked in Berkeley. Sure enough, in 2009 my blood test tumor marker (PSA) suddenly more than doubled in a year, from 20 to 47. A "CT" scan revealed a new tumor in my lung. Was it lung or metastasized prostate cancer? Dr. Swift had me begin hormonal treatment. Two months later a PET scan revealed it to be metastasized prostate cancer and responding to treatment.

Meanwhile I had discovered David Servan Schreiber's book called *Anti Cancer – A New Way of Life*. It gave new information on the diet which I readily adopted. Leeks, brussels sprouts and turmeric were added to the daily soup. The hormonal treatment worked and the PSA sank to 0.5. I continued not to travel. This is very relaxing. The diet provides an explanation for refusing to visit Europe, New York or Missouri. I remain in California. I have always been nervous about air planes. Knowing I no longer have to board a plane pleases me. No more dust storms in Afghanistan, no more lost luggage, cramped seats in tourist class, standing in line at security. I travel but only between Berkeley and Carmel, a two hour and fifteen minute trip by car.

—

Aging

I have not said much about my life with Karen because as I mentioned above, the simple joy of living does not lend to fascinating literature. Suffice it to say that we are both very happy, that we are aging well together. She is the optimist and I the cautious one. We form a good team. I have not said much about the life of our children or about our grandchildren and one great grandchild. Again, it is for them to write those accounts when they grow older. Let me list them here, for the record: Michael; Stephanie, Herman, Katie, Kristina and Scott; Anne, Elizabeth, Tania and Brian and Sophie; Margaret , Francisco and Daizee; and last but by no means least, Marc.

I have purposely said very little about our friends or my friends, about social life in Berkeley or in Carmel, about dinners, about restaurants and theaters and movies and other vacations in Europe, on the East Coast or at the Henley cabins in Missouri, I have not mentioned many students who became friends and what happened to them.
I have not said much about those I knew who became sick and increasingly about those I knew who died. For example, Sylvain Lourié with whom I used to play and ride our bicycles back and forth to the Lycée du Parc Imperial in Nice in 1940/42. Sylvain turned up at UNESCO when I was there in 1963-65 and I saw him at that time and later during visits. He became the Deputy Director of UNESCO in the 1980's then had serious health problems. Karen, my cousin Sylvette Jehiel-Saurel and I visited him in 1996 in a fantastic apartment he had rented at the very end of the Ile de la Cité with a view of the river, the Louvre in the distance, the roofs of Paris. He said he would leave that apartment feet-first. He told us how, when a child, he had come to that same building with his father and told his

—

father he wanted to live there. Sylvain left the apartment as he predicted, during the summer of 1998.

Death becomes more prevalent as time passes. The family had its share of strange or tragic deaths. My grandfather de Botton committed suicide but my grandmother kept it a secret. In contrast, Elizabeth, Frances' sister was strangely murdered in 1977 by a young boy who was working at her house. Elizabeth had found out he had stolen something; the boy panicked, grabbed a brick and killed her. Frances died one year before my mother, so my children lost their mother one year before mine. There was the death of Karen's parents, her father in 1986 and her mother in1995. There was the suicide death of her first husband who had remarried. My Harvard friend James A. Sevin had died shortly after graduating in an air plane crash. He was training to be a pilot. There was also the strange death of Rose Van Vliet who died shortly after I called her in Paris in 1969. There were the deaths of so many relatives deported by the Germans in 1942-44. Now , as we grow older, friends die, too many go before we are willing to let them go. And it is not death alone that saddens us, illness prevails also. Many around us remain sick as we age, we are sick and we suffer when our children become sick.

But, in a strange way, illness and death also make life more worthwhile. As one's own life span seems to grow shorter one appreciates it more and one is less anxious about achieving or not achieving or about success or vanity. The thought of death has a calming influence. Problems are seen in clearer light. But it does not mean that the transition into aging is easy and not without bumps or dreary anxieties. We know we have to perform and we know that the historical empirical evidence is clear: there is something inevitable about it. The only lingering fear is

—

illness, severe pain and a highly diminished life. I once saw a rest home filled with old women and men. We were walking down the corridor to visit Karen's mother who had gone there briefly at the time of Karen's father's funeral. All the doors were open and in each room you could see the patients on their beds staring ahead, some with tubes connecting them to machines, none moving much. It was as if time had stopped. They just stared ahead, no expression, no hope just plain waiting.

Life, in contrast to death, is revealed by children, works accomplished, and memories. It is the morning that is repeated, our child's smile, the friends that visit or write, the meals enjoyed, projects initiated, and paintings, books, or poems seen, read or completed. It is in finding the small sea horse on the beach, hearing the wind swept leaves on the trees or the moving waves of the sea seen through the pines. Life is simple, one has to accept it.

Way back I cared about peace of mind. I liked Zen thought but I never knew if I had found peace. A Zen teacher once told me that I never really tried. That I did not make the effort. It is true. I did not find solace in the Zen discipline. I tried on my own but I did not reach the goal, I did not know. In contrast, time passes and times passed serves to teach. One slips into peace of mind without notice. Peace of mind is having the Proust Madeleine in the vivid present while the expected future raises no doubts. One just slips into calmer waters.

It is life we pursue when old. Our children are life continued but even if we have no children of our own, we see life all around and we keep looking at it for as long as we can.

—

MINI INDEX

—

ABOUT THIS BOOK

Most of this text was first written in the early nineties. It was handwritten as a straight narrative, without any corrections. I only intended it for my family. One day a secretary asked me if I had any outside, non university work, as she was short of money. I gave her the text and she typed it. She gave me a floppy disk. I had no computer at the time so I placed the disk in a file and forgot all about it. In 2009, my friend Hank Massie told me of writing a biography of his mother. I mentioned I had written about my own experiences, nearly two decades earlier. He asked to see it.

I dug up the floppy disk. I was unable to insert it in my computer, but in due time with the help of experts the problem was solved. I spent several months on the revisions.

I decided to keep the simple narrative. I did not attempt to alter the historical sequencing. I decided against using any photographs. If there is any lesson to be learned here, it is in the text, in the story not in photographs. The reader can imagine better, without prompting, and need not be distracted by the smaller reality captured on film.

I ventured in the world of self publishing and was happy to see *From Paris to Berkeley* first appear in print in the summer of 2010 . My experience with self publishing and print on demand was flawless, I recommend it.

—

LaVergne, TN USA
21 October 2010
201616LV00012B/16/P